COLLATERAL DAMAGE

COLLATERAL DAMAGE

Women Write about War

Edited by Bárbara Mujica

University of Virginia Press • *Charlottesville and London*

University of Virginia Press
© 2021 by the Rector and Visitors of the University of Virginia
All rights reserved
Printed in the United States of America on acid-free paper

First published 2021

9 8 7 6 5 4 3 2 1

Library of Congress Cataloging-in-Publication Data
Names: Mujica, Bárbara Louise, editor.
Title: Collateral damage : women write about war / edited by Bárbara Mujica.
Description: Charlottesville : University of Virginia Press, 2021. | Includes
  bibliographical references.
Identifiers: LCCN 2020039749 (print) | LCCN 2020039750 (ebook) | ISBN 9780813945729
  (hardcover ; acid-free paper) | ISBN 9780813945736 (paperback ; acid-free paper) |
  ISBN 9780813945743 (ebook)
Subjects: LCHS: War—Literary collections. | War and society. | Literature—Women
  authors. | Literature, Modern—20th century.
Classification: LCC PN6071.W35 C65 2021 (print) | LCC PN6071. W35 (ebook) |
  DDC 808.8/03581082—dc23
LC record available at https://lccn.loc.gov/2020039749
LC ebook record available at https://lccn.loc.gov/2020039750

Cover art: *Die Mütter* (The Mothers), from *Krieg* (War), Käthe Kollwitz, 1921–22,
published 1923. (Gift of the Arnhold family in memory of Sigrid Edwards; digital image
© The Museum of Modern Art/Licensed by SCALA/Art Resource, NY)

CONTENTS

PREFACE

The idea for this book originated in a symposium I organized in October 2016, at Georgetown University, called "Women Who Write about War." At the time, I was faculty adviser of the Georgetown University Student Veterans Association and co-chair of the Veterans Support Team, a coalition of administrators, faculty, and students working to make Georgetown a more veteran-friendly campus. The veterans I worked with often told me stories, and I had begun writing fiction based on their testimonials. I noticed that many of my women friends who were authors also wrote about war, and I was interested in knowing why war was such a persistent topic in their writing.

With the help of LeNaya Hezel, director of our Veterans Office, I organized a panel of five authors from different countries: Marjorie Agosín (Chile), Christine Evans (Australia), Aminatta Forna (Sierra Leone), Domnica Radulescu (Romania), and myself (USA). The symposium was sponsored by seven university organizations. It was so well attended that we could hardly fit all the attendees into the room. The animated discussion that followed focused on the need to validate women's war experience and the value of women's war writing. Afterward, many in the audience encouraged me to compile an anthology of works by women who write about war. *Collateral Damage* is the outcome.

I would like to thank the following friends who suggested readings to help me prepare this book: Beth Simon, Billie Wilson, Susan Stern, Barbara Rappaport, Sami Al-Bani, Waleed Al-Ravi, Marty Thompson, Helmut Strey.

INTRODUCTION

Whenever I tell people I am compiling an anthology of women's war writing, they always, without exception, answer in the same way: "What? Do women write about war?"

They must be forgiven for their mistake. Although the situation is changing, traditionally, men have fought wars, and men have produced our greatest war literature, highlighting the heroism, exhilaration, and pain of battle. Tolstoy's *War and Peace* has been considered a manual of military art for its masterful depiction of combat. Novels by Hemingway, such as *The Sun Also Rises* and *A Farewell to Arms,* decry war as a destructive, senseless endeavor yet celebrate the battlefield as a proving ground for manhood. Even indisputably antiwar novels such as *All Quiet on the Western Front,* by Erich Maria Remarque, depict moments of beauty amid the violence: rays of moonlight shining on the manes of galloping warhorses, a meal shared with comrades amid bursting bombs. In literature as in life, war is seen as a rite of passage, a bond among men. It is not surprising, then, that people should think that only men write about war.

However, women and children have always suffered disproportionately the consequences of war: famine; disease; sexual abuse; and emotional trauma caused by the loss of loved ones, property, and means of subsistence. According to the International Peace Research Institute in Oslo, although "men die more frequently than women in direct armed conflicts, more women than men die in post-conflict situations" caused indirectly by war.

History does offer some notable examples of warrior women—Semiramis, Zenobia, the Adelitas of the Mexican Revolution—but these are a minority. Of course, now that more women are moving into combat roles, increasing numbers are writing about their experience.

Collateral Damage tells the stories of those who struggle on the margins of armed conflict or who attempt to rebuild their lives after a war. It gives voice to the experiences of the mothers, sisters, friends, children, and victims of those who fight, as well as to a new type of war writer: the female combatant. It seeks to validate the experiences of women affected by war in different ways by bringing their reality to light and showing the actual consequences of war for millions of people whose voices are rarely heard.

Precedents: Women Writers of the Great Wars

Ancient examples of women's laments for sons or husbands departing for battle do exist, but war writing by women really began to blossom in the early twentieth century. Most early female-authored texts depicted women as bystanders, emotional and material casualties of wars fought by male loved ones. Who can forget, for example, the classic American novel *Little Women,* by Louisa May Alcott, which portrays the trials of the March sisters and their mother struggling to cope alone while their father is away during the Civil War?

The first real surge in women's war writing was inspired by World War I, which produced several outstanding women writers from a wide variety of countries. One of the most celebrated was the British novelist Rose Macaulay, whose witty, perceptive *Non-Combatants and Others* (1929) depicts a young woman, Alix, who becomes a pacifist after her brother dies at the front. In *Missing,* published in 1917, the British novelist Mary Augusta Ward chronicles the anguish of women who struggle to locate their husbands and sons reported missing during the war. In her memoir, *The Home Front: A Mirror of Life in England during the World War,* the British author Estelle Sylvia Pankhurst, a fiery suffragette and devoted Communist, recounts the struggles of working-class families in East London at a time when their menfolk were away at the front. Although Virginia Woolf did not write what might be properly labeled "war novels," war is a significant theme in *Mrs. Dalloway* (1925), in which one of the characters, Septimus Warren Smith, is a veteran suffering from the illness we now call post-traumatic stress. Through this character, who grows estranged from his wife, hallucinates, and eventually commits suicide, Woolf examines the effects of war on soldiers and their loved ones.

The Great War also produced a number of poets and playwrights. Chicago-born Mary Borden moved to England with her Scottish husband in 1913. When war erupted, she used her fortune to set up a field hospital for French soldiers, where she herself served as a nurse. Her collection of short stories and poems, *The Forbidden Zone* (1929), reflects her first-hand experience at the front and was so graphic that many contemporary readers found it shocking. The Japanese poet Akiko Yosana began her career before World War I, during the Russo-Japanese War (1904–5). Her collection *River of Stars* contains her best-known poem, "Thou Shalt Not Die," which was dedicated to her brother, who fought in that war. The poem was later set to music and became a protest song. In 1918, Yosana wrote an article attacking the Japanese military class and militarism in general, a risky position to take in wartime Japan. She is one of the few early twentieth-century Japanese women poets to receive considerable recognition in the West, and several of her poetry collections have been published in English.

One of the significant women dramatists to emerge during World War I was Bosworth Crocker (pseudonym of Mary Arnold Crocker), who was born in England but raised in the United States. Crocker is best known for her play *Pawns of War,* which depicts the invasion of Belgium by Germany in 1914. Crocker shows compassion for both sides in her play, in which she suggests that the invaders as well as the invaded are "pawns of war."

World War II produced a new crop of women writers. One of the most significant is the German novelist Anna Seghers, author of the ground-breaking *Das siebte Kreuz* (*The Seventh Cross*). Born into a German Jewish family in 1900, Seghers provided one of the first depictions of a Nazi concentration camp in literature. Published in 1942, the novel traces the hair-raising escape of seven prisoners from Westhofen, a fictional camp, and their attempts to find refuge in a disintegrating and dangerous society.

In the mid-1930s, the British poet and novelist Stevie (Florence Margaret) Smith emerged as a significant voice protesting anti-Semitism. In *Novel on Yellow Paper* (1936), the protagonist, Pompey, visits Germany just as the Nazis are gaining momentum and is horrified by the growing fanaticism. In *Over the Frontier* (1938), Smith ponders the dangers of militarism and the need to fight fascism through her protagonist, Pompey, who returns to Germany and becomes a spy. Smith's third novel, *The Holiday* (1949), deals with postwar reconstruction and the sustainability of the empire rather than themes directly related to World War II.

One of the most prolific of the British World War II novelists was Storm Jameson, whose *Mirror in Darkness* series (*Company Parade, Love in Winter, None Turn Back*) traces the rise of fascism in Europe and the Nazi occupation of France. She continues to examine political issues such as totalitarianism and the rise of nationalism in *Then We Shall Hear Singing* (1942), a kind of science fiction fantasy in which a scientist in Germany devises an invention to subjugate people and make them his slaves.

Irène Némirovsky, a Ukrainian of Jewish origin, was another of the outstanding women novelists of World War II. She settled in France and wrote in French. In spite of having converted to Catholicism, in 1942 she was deported to Auschwitz, where she died in the infirmary. Her *Suite française,* not published until 2004, consists of the first two parts of a planned five-part novel. Part 1 begins with the thunder of Nazi artillery outside Paris and a frenzied flight from the capital to outlying areas. In part 2, Germans have occupied an idyllic village where the French inhabitants are struggling to survive. To the surprise of the villagers, the soldiers who have been billeted in the town behave courteously, and an uneasy tolerance develops between the French and their occupiers. Complications arise when Lucile Angellier, one of the villagers, develops feelings for one of the German officers and is forced to choose between her emotions and her duty to her compatriots.

Pearl Buck, the daughter of American missionary parents who was raised in China, wrote about a different aspect of the war: the Japanese invasion of China. Buck had already established herself as a literary powerhouse by winning the Pulitzer Prize in 1932 for her novel *The Good Earth*, which depicts life in a Chinese village at the beginning of the century. In *Dragon Seed* (1942), Buck describes a community outside of Nanking at the time of the Nanking Massacre, also known as the Rape of Nanking. During the Second Sino-Japanese War (1937–45), which merged into World War II, the Imperial Japanese captured Nanking and subjected the populace to mass murder and rape. Scholars estimate that between forty thousand and three hundred thousand died during the massacre. Buck focuses on the reactions of a fictional peasant family to the violence—their struggle to cope with the loss of their land, the devastation of the surrounding areas, the abuse of their women, and other harsh realities of war.

Like World War I, World War II inspired woman-authored literary works of all genres. *The Diary of Anne Frank* (1952), one of the most beloved classics of the period, was written by a thirteen-year-old Jewish German-born Dutch girl while hiding in an annex of an apartment building during the Nazi occupation of the Netherlands. Her family was arrested in 1944, and Anne died of typhus in the Bergen-Belsen concentration camp the following year. In spite of Anne's constant fear of being discovered, the crowded quarters, and the lack of basic necessities, her account is filled with warmth and even humor.

World War II produced many women poets, not only in Europe and the United States but also in the Soviet Union. Much of their poetry has been inadequately studied, but it is now beginning to attract more critical attention.[1] Among the Europeans and Americans, some the most noteworthy poets are Flora Hendricks, Helen Goldbaum, Babette Deutsch, Josephine Jacobsen, Eve Merriem, Doris Baley, and Josephine Miles. The Soviet Union recruited women to play active combat roles in the war, and

Soviet women excelled in public life as well. Several fine poets emerged, as Katharine Hodgson has shown.[2] One of the most celebrated is Olga Berggolts (Bergholz), who was named the wartime poet laureate of Leningrad.

Around this time, another type of women writer rose to prominence: the war correspondent. In reality, women journalists had been covering wars since the nineteenth century. Margaret Fuller covered the Italian Revolution of 1848, and Jane Swisshelm reported on conditions in Union military hospitals during the Civil War. During World War I, Mary Roberts Rhinehart got closer to the action than did most male correspondents. However, it was during World War II that women really began to excel as war correspondents. Scores of women reported from the front for the most influential publications in America and England. At first, they were unable to obtain press credentials, but after December 7, 1941, when the bombing of Pearl Harbor forced the United States into the war, the situation changed. By the end of the war, 127 accredited female correspondents were reporting from war zones.[3]

Martha Gellhorn, one of the most accomplished, began her career traveling around the United States reporting on the Depression. In 1936, she met her future husband, Ernest Hemingway, in Florida, and they agreed to travel to Spain together to report on the Spanish Civil War, which Gellhorn was covering for *Collier's*. Later, she reported on the rise of Hitler in Germany and on the progress of the war from Finland, Hong Kong, Singapore, and England. In order to witness the Normandy landings, she hid in a ship's bathroom and then snuck ashore by impersonating a stretcher bearer. She was one of the first journalists to write about Dachau concentration camp. After the war, she worked for the *Atlantic Monthly*, reporting on the Vietnam War, the Arab-Israeli conflict, and the wars in Central America.

Lee Miller, also American, was a fashion model and then a photographer before she became a journalist. She was living in England when World War II broke out, and the Germans bombed London. Rather than returning to the United States, Miller became a photojournalist for *Vogue*, chronicling the atrocities of the war in both images and articles.

Ruth Cowen was the first accredited war correspondent for the U.S. Army. During World War II, she reported for the Associated Press from Africa and Europe, often attached to the Women's Army Corps. During the Normandy invasion, she filed her reports from hospital ships. After the war, she interviewed many important military men, including Dwight D. Eisenhower and George Patton.

The legendary Margaret Bourke-White is credited with being the first American female war correspondent, and her career was filled with "firsts." A photojournalist as well as a print reporter, she was the first foreign photographer to receive permission to take photos of Soviet industry in the five-year plan. She became the first woman photojournalist for *Life*, for which she covered World War II, and was the only foreign photographer in Moscow during the German invasion. Later, she was attached to the U.S. Army Air Force in North Africa, and then to the U.S. Army in Italy, where she reported from extremely dangerous areas. After World War II, she reported from Korea and then from India and Pakistan.

The British journalist Clare Hollingworth was another star correspondent—the first, in fact, to report the eruption of World War II in 1939, for the *Daily Telegraph*. She had spotted the accumulation of German troops at the Polish border as she traveled from Poland to Germany and reported on the imminent invasion of Poland—a story called the "scoop of the century." In spite of this success, as a woman, she was unable to get accreditation as a war correspondent. Nevertheless, she continued to work, filing reports from Cairo, Turkey, and Greece. After the war, she began working for the *Economist*, the *Observer*, and the *Guardian*, covering conflicts in the Middle East, North Africa, and Vietnam.

These women were pioneers of the profession. Since World War II, thousands of female war correspondents from myriad countries have covered wars around the world. In fact, the American Dicky Chapelle (Georgette Louise Meyer), who began her career during World War II, was killed in Vietnam—the first female war correspondent to lose her life in the conflict. Sheila Gibbons writes that women are changing the nature of the profession: "As the number of women war correspondents approaches critical mass, they appear to be focusing more clearly on the toll that today's wars take on the civilian population—the women and children—who have little or no say in the decisions that lead to mass killing and wounding."[4] This trend is clear in the work of the German war correspondent Carolin Emcke, who is featured in this anthology.

Women's War Writing Today: The New World War II Novel

One remarkable aspect of today's war writing by women is the renewed interest in World War II. Every year scores of new World War II novels appear in bookstores. Unlike their predecessors, the authors of these novels were born after or, as in the case of Rhys Bowen, during the war.

Although most of these authors did not experience World War II first-hand, they found in the cataclysmic intensity of the conflict a vehicle through which to examine the bravery, determination, and astuteness of women in threatening circumstances.

Some of these novels could be described as witness literature. For example, although *The Lilac Girls*, by Martha Hall Kelly, is largely fiction, it draws on testimony from actual concentration camp victims. The novel recounts the efforts of the real-life Caroline Ferriday, a rich New York society woman, to rescue and heal Polish victims of the Nazis' cruel medical experiments and to bring their tormentors to justice. Kasia, one of the beneficiaries of Ferriday's labors, was a prisoner at Ravensbrück, where Herta Operhauser, an SS doctor, performed painful and debilitating surgery on her leg. Many of Kasia's fellow prisoners die, but Kasia survives, although she is left severely crippled. The novel depicts in agonizing detail the workings of Ravensbrück, where inmates are called "rabbits" because they are treated like laboratory animals.

Like *The Lilac Girls*, *A Thread of Grace*, by Mary Doria Russell, does not draw on the author's lived experience, but on interviews she conducted with survivors of Nazi atrocities. The novel takes place during the final years of World War II, after Mussolini has already made peace with the Allies. Thousands of Jews who find themselves in Nazi-occupied territories now cross the Alps into Italy seeking peace, only to find that the country has become a battleground between the Nazis and their resisters. The real heroes of this novel are the ordinary Italian citizens, including priests and nuns, who hide and care for fleeing Jews, managing to save the lives of forty-three thousand of them.

Not all the perpetrators of evil in these novels are Nazis. *The Piano Teacher*, by Janice Y. K. Lee, portrays the struggles of the residents of Hong Kong to survive during the Japanese occupation. Here the camps are run by Japanese Imperialist officers, who are just as heartless as Nazi prison guards. The interred foreign residents of Hong Kong are deprived of food, basic sanitary facilities, and all privacy. Sometimes they are subjected to harsh physical abuse. Yet many find ways to outmaneuver the system and maintain a modicum of dignity. One of the characters, a wily Eurasian woman, tries to use her charms to win over a Japanese officer, help the prisoners, and survive the occupation, but in this war, there are no winners.

Although few of these novels depict actual combat, several describe extraordinary feats of heroism by women. In *The Nightingale*, by Kristin Hannah, Vianne and Isabelle Rossignol are sisters who defy in different ways the Nazis who are occupying their small French village. Vianne, a schoolteacher, hides Jewish children in a nearby monastery. Isabelle, the more intrepid of the two, joins the resistance, at first distributing anti-Nazi propaganda and later escorting downed British and American pilots across the Pyrenees under hair-raising conditions so they can return to their native countries.

In *Hearts of Resistance*, Soraya M. Lane also depicts courageous fighting women. Her protagonists—one British, one French, and one German—join the French resistance for different reasons and work together to intercept messages, deliver munitions, and lay bombs.

Another novel by Lane, *The Spitfire Girls*, depicts the essential tasks carried out by women pilots during the war. Although the characters are stereotypical—the American is brash and self-seeking, whereas the Englishwoman is stalwart, composed, and supportive of her team—the book provides valuable insight into the terrible conditions under which women pilots had to work. These pilots' primary job was to retrieve damaged aircraft from outlying areas, fly them to a home base in England, and return repaired planes to the fighting men who needed them. Unlike men, they flew without instruments or co-pilots. Furthermore, they received lower pay than male pilots and had to put up with the abuses of male military doctors. In contrast, Soviet women pilots, such as the protagonist of *The Huntress*, by Kate Quinn, bombed Nazi targets and were highly respected and well equipped.

In some novels, such as *El tiempo entre costuras* (*The Time in Between*), by Spanish author María Dueñas, the war is more a backdrop for the exploits of the captivating heroine than a horrendous reality for victims of the Nazis. But all of these works contribute to a new image of women as agents of victory during the war, not simply pining Penelopes who wait at home for their men to return.

In several of these books, the war functions as a catalyst for self-examination and the exploration of interpersonal relationships. In *The Women of the Castle*, for example, Jessica Shattuck tells the story of three war widows who take refuge in a decaying Bavarian castle during the last years of the war, only to find that their differing backgrounds and life experiences make it impossible for them to form a lasting bond. Marianne von Lingenfels, the owner of the castle and widow of a courageous member of the anti-Nazi resistance, is the self-assured, self-righteous leader of group, but circumstances ultimately force her to question some of her decisions after it is too late to do anything about them.

In other novels, the war provokes an exploration of the past. In *The Rabbit Girls,* by Anna Ellory, the protagonist Miriam Winter is caring for her widowed, bedridden father, Henryk, in Berlin when she discovers a concentration camp number under the band of his watch. Henryk occasionally calls out the name "Frieda," and while rummaging through her mother's belongings, Miriam finds a cache of letters signed by Frieda sewn into the hem and seams of a Ravensbrück prison uniform. This triggers an exploration of her father's history, including his relationship to Frieda. Her discoveries lead Miriam to a new understanding of her own identity and inspire her to confront her abusive husband.

Sarah's Key, by Tatiana de Rosnay, is a different kind of novel of self-discovery. When Nazi collaborators arrest a Jewish family in the Vel' d'Hiv roundup in Paris, in July 1942, their ten-year-old daughter locks her younger brother Michel in a cupboard and keeps the key. She thinks she will soon return to let him out but instead is deported to Auschwitz. When she at last escapes and returns to the apartment, it is too late to save Michel. Feelings of guilt destroy not only Sarah but also an American journalist living in Paris named Julia Jarmond, who is writing a story about the Vel d'Hiv collaboration, considered one of the darkest moments in French history. Investigating the story, Julia learns that the apartment she and her French husband Bertrand are about to occupy had belonged to Sarah's parents and that Bertrand's family obtained it when the authorities confiscated Jewish property. As a result, Julia begins to reexamine her place in France, her relationship with her husband, and the silence and denial surrounding the collaboration.

In *The Tuscan Child,* by Rhys Bowen, the protagonist's voyage of self-discovery leads to a happy ending. When her estranged father, Hugo, dies, Joanna Langley returns to her childhood home in the English countryside. While organizing Hugo's affairs, she finds a letter addressed to Sofia in which a beautiful Tuscan child is mentioned. Hugo had parachuted to safety in Italy during the war, and Joanna assumes he had an affair with Sofia and that the child is her half brother. Anxious to find out the truth, she travels to the village in Italy where her father hid until the end of the war. The Tuscan child turns out to be something quite different from what she suspected, but in Italy Joanna matures. She learns about the treacheries of war, acquires a new self-confidence, and even finds romance.

In fact, romance blooms amid the horror in several of these novels. In *The Tattooist of Auschwitz,* by Heather Morris, a Slovakian Jew named Lale Sokolow is given the task of tattooing identification numbers on the arms of thousands of his fellow prisoners. One of the inmates awaiting a tattoo is Gita, with whom he immediately falls in love and whom he eventually marries.

The war is a unifying experience for a small community in Guernsey in the ingenious and lighter-hearted epistolary novel *The Guernsey Literary and Potato Peel Society,* by Mary Ann Shaffer and Annie Barrows. In 1946, a young writer named Julia Ashton travels to Guernsey to meet Dawsey Adams, a member of the Literary and Potato Peel Society, and learns that the society was a cover for townspeople breaking the curfew during the German occupation. While there, Julia discovers some of the town's darkest war secrets, and also falls in love with Dawsey.

Other Genres, Other Wars

Although the Holocaust predominates much contemporary war writing by women in the United States and Europe, elsewhere, other conflicts provide literary inspiration. From Bosnia to Iraq, Cuba to Rwanda, Vietnam to Argentina, women are writing about their wartime experiences in fiction, plays, and poetry. The corpus of contemporary women's war writing is far too immense to itemize here, but a few outstanding examples deserve mention.

The Mexican Revolution has inspired a prodigious amount of literature, and women are among the foremost of the war's interpreters. *Los recuerdos del porvenir* (*Recollections of Things to Come*) (1964), by Elena Garro; *Hasta no verte Jesús mío* (*Here's to You, Jesusa*) (1969), by Elena Poniatowska; *Arráncame la vida* (*Tear This Heart Out*) (1986) and *Mal de amores* (*Lovesick*) (1996), by Ángeles Mastretta; and *Como agua para chocolate* (*Like Water for Chocolate*) (1989), by Laura Esquivel are five of Mexico's most celebrated novels of the revolution.

Garro depicts the small, traditional, Catholic town of Ixtepec, in southern Mexico, during the period of revolutionary turmoil. When the town is occupied by federal troops led by Francisco Rosas and Justo Corona, the revolutionary forces move to shut down the churches and execute agrarian activists, eventually provoking the Cristero, or pro-Catholic, rebellion. Garro describes the central role women played in the movement, organizing *brigadas femeninas* that sometimes fought with the men and sometimes assisted them by providing support services, such as delivering munitions.

Poniatowska's *Here's to You, Jesusa* is one of the most powerful portrayals of women as active participants in the revolution in Mexican literature. At five years old, Jesusa loses her mother and embarks on a nomadic life with her womanizing father. When he and her brother join the revolution, Jesusa goes with them, serving with a cavalry unit. Pedro Aguilar, a brutal, domineering captain, practically forces her to marry him, and his abuse causes her to seethe with resentment. After the war, she finds herself alone in Mexico City, where she constantly tangles with the police. Based on Poniatowska's interviews with Josefina Bórquez, an actual *soldadera* (woman soldier), this novel captures the mentality of the tough, defiant woman of the revolution and is perhaps the best example of witness literature in Mexican war fiction.

With Mastretta's novel *Tear This Heart Out,* the focus switches from the slums of Mexico City to a lower-middle-class household in post-revolutionary Puebla, where memories of the war still permeate the atmosphere. Catalina Guzmán, only fifteen years old, leaves her parents' modest home to marry a retired general who is twenty years her senior. Domineering and lecherous, he soon finds himself involved in corrupt political schemes and is even accused of murder. Despite the idealism of the revolution, Catalina is her husband's pawn, silenced whenever she ventures an opinion and constantly belittled. Barriers for women were supposed to fall during the revolution, but as Mastretta shows, in post-revolutionary Mexico, women were still deprived of educational and work opportunities and subjugated to their husbands.

Lovesick, which takes place during the revolution, also features a heroine caught in a web of restrictive social values, but Emilia Sauri is a true rebel. The daughter of a Mayan herbalist and pharmacist, Emilia learns his craft and yearns to become a doctor. When her childhood sweetheart and lover Daniel Cuenca leaves for the front, Emilia joins him and practices medicine among the war wounded, observing firsthand how war destroys the soul as well as the body. One of her mentors is the peace-loving Dr. Zavala, whom she eventually marries, although she still loves Daniel. The novel highlights the position of Mexican women during the early twentieth century—restricted professionally and also emotionally. A woman in love with two men, Emilia must choose between them and suffers the psychological consequences.

Like Water for Chocolate, by Laura Esquivel, is ostensibly a classic love story in which a parent obstructs the desires of a young couple. The de la Garza family, owners of a ranch near the Texas border, consists of Mamá Elena and her three daughters, Tita, Rosaura, and Gertrudis. Tita and

Pedro Muzquiz are in love and want to marry, but the despotic Mamá Elena declares that according to tradition, Tita must remain single and take care of her. In order to be close to Tita, Pedro marries her sister Rosaura and moves into the house. The revolution raging around them provides the backdrop for the story: revolutionaries repeatedly overrun nearby towns and ransack the ranch, and then Gertrudis takes off on horseback with a rebel soldier. An extraordinary cook, Tita defiantly devises ways to communicate with Pedro by means of her culinary talents. Throughout the novel, the revolution serves as a metaphor for the tensions within the household. The repressive Mamá Elena represents the repressive government led by dictator Porfirio Díaz and his successors, while Tita and Gertrudis represent the insurrectionists.

The wars in the Middle East have also inspired a substantial amount of writing by women, although much of the material written in Arabic has not been translated into western European languages. One memoir written directly in English is *Sharon and My Mother-in-Law: Ramallah Diaries* (2004), by the Palestinian author Suad Amiry, who recounts the travails of Palestinians living under Israeli occupation. Amiry describes outbreaks of violence, arrests, bullying by soldiers, checkpoints that impede free travel, a shopping spree in anticipation of a deluge of Scud missiles from Saddam-led Iraq, and the endless bureaucratic snafus that plague everyday life in Palestine. In one of the few comical episodes in the book, Amiry's puppy Nura is granted a Jerusalem passport, to visit an Israeli veterinarian, that Amiry herself has been unable to get.

The Vietnam War has also inspired dozens of novels, short story collections, poetry chapbooks, memoirs, and plays by both Vietnamese and American women. One of the most poignant is *When Heaven and Earth Changed Places: A Vietnamese Woman's Journey from War to Peace*, by Le Ly Hayslip, in which the author recounts fighting between American and Viet Cong troops in Ky La, her native village. Another is *Unfriendly Fire: A Mother's Memoir*, by Peg Mullen, which recounts the author's efforts to cope with the death of her son from friendly fire. Mullen exposes the government's obfuscation of the facts regarding deaths from friendly fire and argues that the war in Vietnam was senseless. *Don't Mean Nothing*, by Susan O'Neill, is a collection of short stories that reflect the author's experiences as a U.S. Army nurse. The stories reveal the psychological stress of nursing under desperate conditions and the strength and compassion of the women who performed this service. A prodigious amount of poetry also came out of the Vietnam War, much of it antiwar protest pieces by both women and men. As numerous studies and anthologies of Vietnam War poetry exist, I will not discuss it here.

The works mentioned in this overview represent only a tiny fraction of the war-related writing produced by women from the beginning of the twentieth century. This smattering, however, should be sufficient to give pause to anyone who might ask, "What? Do women write about war?"

Collateral Damage

Collateral Damage is comprised of eighteen selections by professional women writers representing different areas of the world: Brazil, Cuba, El Salvador, Guatemala, the United States, Romania, Chile, Sierra Leone, France, Germany, Spain, Iraq, China, Rwanda, Sri Lanka, and Australia. At the beginning of each essay, the nationality of the author and the country she writes about appear in parentheses after her name. Each selection is preceded by a short essay in which the author explains the motive and context of her war writing. The selections are of different genres: essay, poetry, fiction, theater, memoir, reportage. Some are poetic and lyrical. Others are academic. Yet, despite the variety of styles and forms, commonalities abound. Subjects such as sexual violence, the brutalization of innocents, the anguish of displacement, and the fear of mothers for their children appear repeatedly in the works of writers from different countries. Images of women waiting for their absent loved ones are frequent. "Women are always the ones who wait," begins Marjorie Agosín's poem "Women." Yet some pieces depict women who display agency and initiative, such as Alma, protagonist of the short story by Carolina Rivera Escamilla, and the women activists in the article by Trudy Mercadal.

Although sadness permeates many selections, not all of them are devoid of joy. Domnica Radulescu describes a gathering in Bosnia in which, despite the falling bombs, people are "dancing the waltz and delivering baby girls." Michèle Sarde describes the elation of a French Jewish family at seeing American soldiers arrive in Paris at the end of World War II. Florinda Ruiz describes a family dinner in which the roasted pig set out on the table reminds her of the cadaver of the dictator Francisco Franco—a scene that, although macabre, is also hilarious. And Marjorie Agosín sings that in the midst of war, "A light was also there / Memory also persisted, there in the darkness."

With the exception of Miyoko Hikiji, a veteran of the Iowa National Guard who served in Iraq, the women whose work appears in this collection have not fought in wars. I have included Hikiji's essay and poetry, as well as Nancy Sherman's essay on sexual violence in the military, to provide a wider view of women's wartime. Still, the focus of this book is on how war affects *civilians,* in particular, women. Many anthologies of veterans' writing already exist, and such publications provide useful and necessary insight into the consequences of war for combatants, but the objective of *Collateral Damage* is not to duplicate their efforts. The selections included here highlight women who have experienced war as "collateral damage," unintended sufferers of military operations.

Some of the writers represented in this anthology (Mukasonga, Forma, Al-Taiee, Rivera Escamilla) know war firsthand. When war erupted in their homelands, they either fled under excruciating circumstances or stayed and coped with the ensuing violence and disintegrating social structures. Others (Agosín, Sarde, Ruiz, Radulescu, Ganeshananthan) experienced war vicariously, as part of their family histories. Although they did not live through war themselves, they grew up hearing stories that left them traumatized and yearning for understanding. One (Qiu) began studying the effects of war as a mentoring project, only to be drawn into the topic and making it her own. Another describes a war without invaders, but not without battles: Betty Milan lives in an area of Brazil so violent that she has come to see it as a war zone—a place where one is never safe, and no one is to be trusted. Some writers (Sherman, Mujica) were drawn to write about war because they had loved ones in the military or, in the case of Duarte, because she worked with the military. For some (Mercadal, Evans), war raises ethical issues about their own countries' interventionist policies.

Much of this writing falls into the category of witness literature because the writers bear witness to situations they themselves have seen or drawn from the firsthand testimonies of others. In the case of Carolin Emcke, a German war correspondent, bearing witness to the ravages of war is both a political and a moral commitment. Emcke seeks out conflict zones and describes the effects of war on civilians in areas as disparate as Kosovo, Nicaragua, Lebanon, Pakistan, and Afghanistan.

Our Selections

The first three selections in this anthology (Agosín, Sarde, Qiu) deal with World War II from different perspectives. In her poetry, Marjorie Agosín evokes her great-grandmother's escape from Vienna, a city with a substantial Jewish population that was destroyed by the Nazis. "You loved your prosperous and welcoming city, Helena . . . ," writes Agosín, but "Soon they began building massive bonfires / In which to burn all the Jews in the city." In other poems, she ruminates on war in general, especially the plight of women, which is always the same, no matter what the conflict: "You could have been the housewife of Sarajevo / The cellist from Sarajevo / The disappeared girl in Buenos Aires / The child soldiers of Cambodia / The old woman raped in Bosnia." And yet, Agosín ends with a ray of hope, a confidence that light will eventually shine through the darkness.

Michèle Sarde's selection is an excerpt from *Revenir du silence,* a fictionalized biography of her mother, Jenny. Sarde recounts her family's experiences during the German occupation of France, starting with the arrest of Jenny's brother Marcel—a Jew and a resister—and ending with the liberation. For the family, the effects of living in constant fear are devastating. Sarde captures magnificently the terror that she, as a young child, felt at the approach of German soldiers. The memory is so vivid that "I could tell you the color of the sky, the summery light of a fine morning, the dazzling hues of the wildflowers and the sound, at first muffled, then louder and louder, of fourteen jackboots hammering the sloping road to Corrençon, awakening a terror that has haunted my nightmares ever since." The young Sarde embodies the very concept of collateral damage. Although she survived and went on to achieve success, the trauma of war continues to haunt her.

Peipei Qiu writes as a researcher who has read and listened to countless testimonials from comfort women, sex slaves who were conscripted or captured during World War II to serve the Japanese Imperial Army. Considered objects to be used and discarded or disposed of, until recently, these women were simply absent from the collective memory. They were fragments of the detritus of war—unknown, unheeded, and forgotten.

The next five selections focus on Iraq. Miyoko Hikiji is an American veteran, but her poetry and prose do not depict the glories of battle. She writes of fallen comrades, of the need to tell their stories, "Because if I forget to honor Sissel's memory by failing to tell his story, then Aaron James 'George' Sissel would just be a number—one of 6,979." She writes of struggling to readjust to civilian life, of PTSD, of being a woman soldier. Her poetry is introspective and quiet. It conveys her pride for having served and her alienation from a society that doesn't share her experience.

My own stories are inspired by my experience of having a son at war.

The two included here are part of a collection, *Imagining Iraq*. The narrator, Jacqueline Montez, is the mother of a Marine fighting in Iraq. While he is away, Mrs. Montez imagines obsessively his life in Ramadi. To help ease her loneliness and anxiety, she rents out rooms to veterans, who tell her stories about their deployments. In "Imagining Iraq," a young Marine describes a senseless death that comes to encapsulate for Mrs. Montez the futility of war. "The Call" depicts a mother who is so angst-ridden over her son's deployment that she becomes suicidal. The "collateral damage" in these stories is not only the countless unintended victims of the Iraq war, but the mothers and fathers of soldiers for whom the stress of having a child at war causes emotional and even physical harm.

Thanks to the widespread images of war on television and the internet, as well as in print media, war is a shared experience. The deluge of information can have a desensitizing effect, but it can also raise awareness of the brutality of war, as people who have never been in a war zone experience war more intimately than ever before. The playwright Christine Evans is from Australia, an ally of the United States in Iraq. Her play *Greetings from Fallujah* conveys with enormous power and sensitivity how war destroys childhood.

Nancy Sherman has written extensively on moral injury, that is, harm done to one's conscience due to a real or perceived transgression. In the excerpt from her book, *Afterwar: Healing the Moral Injuries of Our Soldiers,* included here, she discusses the effects of military experience on women soldiers. The "collateral damage" of which she speaks is the injury done to conscience, self-esteem, emotional health, and moral well-being that can result from war and military training.

The selection by Ghusoon Mekhaber Al-Taiee deals with the diverse responses of Iraqi women to the presence of ISIS in their country. Whether they resist or embrace ISIS, argues Al-Taiee, women suffer under insurgent control. Many are "collateral damage" in a literal sense: they have died or been wounded in the fighting. But others are "collateral damage" in another sense: they have been brainwashed by ISIS to the point that they have lost their moral compass, and if they begin to express doubt about their commitment, they are severely punished, even killed.

The two next selections address wars in the Balkans. Carolin Emcke, a German foreign correspondent, observed the effects of war on the people of Kosovo and included her reflections in a series of letters to her friends, which she compiled into a book, *Echoes of Violence*. In the selections included here, she focuses on women and children—war widows, rape victims, and an emotionally disturbed little girl.

In contrast with most of our other authors, Domnica Radulescu finds joy among the rubble. In Bosnia, where her story takes place, "collateral damage" is all around. Snipers pick off innocent children. Bombs destroy entire neighborhoods. People are blown up while walking down the street. The newspapers have mostly all been shut down, yet a determined group of friends doggedly puts out a newssheet. At one of their gatherings, they play music and recite poetry. And then, one of them goes into labor and has a baby! You might call it "collateral bliss"!

The two selections that follow deal with wars in Africa. Aminatta Forna also describes a pregnancy in wartime, but here, the atmosphere is somber. Soldiers have overrun the narrator's town in Sierra Leone. They have shot large numbers of men. The women take precautions to protect their families. They send Adama away because she is pregnant, but the narrator stays, planting food and baubles in plain sight to distract the invaders. Then she hides. Forna builds tremendous tension in "The Box"; her reader can almost feel the closeness of the soldiers, smell their sweat, hear their joking. In a war, women are prey, and Forna makes us feel the angst of the hunted. She also raises questions about bringing new life into a world filled with danger.

Scholastique Mukasonga's moving selections from her memoirs, *The Barefoot Woman* and *Cockroaches,* describe vividly the horrors of the ethnic genocide of the Tutsi in Rwanda. The scores of relatives she lost in the war can hardly be described as "collateral damage." As she clearly explains, they were intended targets of a Hutu army determined to exterminate a segment of the population. The "collateral damage" are people like Mukasonga, who fled the massacres but will be forever haunted by feelings of guilt for having survived.

The Spanish photographer and poet Florinda Ruiz chronicles the violence that has beleaguered Spain from the persecution of the Moriscos (1609) until the Civil War (1936–39) and the Franco dictatorship. She then turns her attention to the current mass migrations from the wars in Africa, which too often result in drowning due to flimsy boats and overcrowded quarters.

In her novel *Love Marriage,* V. V. Ganeshananthan casts light on the Sri Lankan Civil War (1983–2009), in which the insurgent group known as the Tamil Tigers fought to create an independent Tamil state but eventually lost. In the excerpt included here, Ganeshananthan describes how her family fled the violence and escaped to the United States.

The last five selections all portray different aspects of violence in Latin America. In "Alma at about Four-thirty in the Afternoon," Salvadoran writer Carolina Rivera Escamilla describes the insurgent activities of a group of young students fighting the corrupt Salvadoran regime with ties to the United States. Rivera takes us inside the insurgent cell as the members plan different moves, such as blowing up a bus. Although these teenagers are idealistic, they are also naïve, and inevitably, one of them gets killed.

The article by Trudy Mercadal, an American who grew up in Guatemala, examines the violence and corruption in her adopted country as revealed in the recently discovered Guatemalan National Police Archives. The Archives shed light on the crimes committed by Guatemalan political operatives during the civil war (1960–96). Mercadal highlights the role of women, who were often the targets of abuse, in pursuing the perpetrators of crimes committed in the name of the government. She then reviews steps taken to bring about reconciliation.

Carmen Duarte's piece, an excerpt from her novel *The Ship That Took Us to War,* depicts Cuban soldiers on their way to fight in Angola. The Peruvian American journalist Marie Arana describes the Angolan war as "a proving ground between two hostile powers—a grisly, brutal conflagration by proxy between Africans armed to the teeth by the Soviet Union and those fitted out by the United States . . . It was a stubborn, perversely homicidal, seemingly never-ending bloodbath, and as a result, Cuba would pour half a million men into the country."[5] In Duarte's excerpt, the soldiers hardly mention politics. They are young men on their way to a war they don't understand or particularly care about. What they do care about is the young civilian female singer assigned to the ship to provide entertainment. The harassment by one of the officers becomes so unbearable that the girl is forced to take desperate measures.

The final selection, "War in the City," by Brazilian author Betty Milan, may seem out of place in this book, as it does not deal with an armed conflict between defined factions. Yet, São Paolo is a war zone. Arana writes that "Of the fifty most violent cities in the world, forty-three are in Latin America . . . There are scarcely more violent societies than those of Central America, Brazil, and the vast territory of South America gripped by corruption and the drug trade."[6] She traces the long history of war in the region from the precolonial Indian cultures to the recent civil wars and concludes the present violence that plagues Latin American cities has its roots in the war culture that has pervaded the region for centuries. Milan and her fellow urban Brazilians are indeed the "collateral damage" of wars that have been going on since before Columbus. They live in a state of perpetual anxiety, unable to walk the streets or drive their cars without fear of assault. Yet rather than addressing the problem, argues Milan, the police offer suggestions on how to disobey the law.

It would be impossible to include examples of every genre and style of women's war writing in one anthology, or to represent every area of the world that has produced great women authors who write about war. What I have attempted to do with *Collateral Damage* is open doors to further discussion of the topic: How do women experience war, personally or vicariously, and how do they convey that experience in their writing?

Notes

1. See Abhik Maiti and Deep Naskar, "The Dark Renaissance of the War Poetry: A Comparative Analysis between the Poetry of the Two World Wars," *British Journal of English Linguistics* 5, no. 2 (April 2017): 76–95.
2. "The Other Veterans: Soviet Women's Poetry of World War 2," *World War 2 and the Soviet People: Selected Papers from the Fourth World Congress for Soviet and East European Studies, Harrogate, 1990*, ed. John Garrard and Carol Garrard (London: Palgrave Macmillan, 1990), 77–97.
3. See Penny Colman, *Where the Action Was: Women War Correspondents in World War II* (New York: Crown, 2002), viii.
4. We/News, October 16, 2002, https://womensenews.org/2002/10/female-correspondents-changing-war-coverage/.
5. *Silver, Sword & Stone: Three Crucibles of the Latin American Story* (New York: Simon and Schuster, 2019), 182.
6. Arana, *Silver, Sword & Stone*, 241, 247.

COLLATERAL DAMAGE

Marjorie Agosín

MARJORIE AGOSÍN (Chile) is Professor of Latin American Studies at Wellesley College and an award-winning poet and human rights activist. She has authored nearly forty books in diverse genres—from poetry to short stories, essays, and memoirs—on human rights and social justice and the consequences of war. Her works deal with the dirty wars in Chile and Argentina, the Holocaust, and human rights violations on the Mexican-U.S. border. Among her books are *Ashes of Revolt* (essays) and the edited anthologies *A Map of Hope: Women Writers and Human Rights* and *Writing Towards Hope: Human Rights in the Americas.* Her most recent books are *Las Islas Blancas / The White Islands,* poems about the extermination of the Sephardic communities during the Nazi Occupation, and *Memorias trenzadas / Braided Memories,* poems inspired by her great-grandmother Helena Broder, who escaped Nazi violence in Vienna to settle in Chile.

Why I Write about War

Sometimes I ask myself why I write about inevitable things, like war. After all, war has been with us since time immemorial. War destroys civilizations, which we rebuild only to destroy them once more. I think my obsession with writing about war has to do with a desire to express the inexpressible, the incomprehensible, and to rescue memory from oblivion.

Wars and campaigns of intolerance have affected my family directly for generations and have led me to write about their experiences. For instance, my paternal relatives escaped from the horrors of the pogroms in Russia. Their houses were burned and their belongings confiscated. They fled from a frightful war. They traveled by foot to Turkey and spent a couple of years in Marseille, where my father was born.

My maternal family was, for the most part, exterminated by the Nazis at Auschwitz. They were Austrian and Czech Jews. Only my great-grandmother Helena, her two sons, and a first cousin survived. The cousin emigrated to Sweden. Helena fled Austria during the infamous Night of

1

Broken Glass in 1938 with her son Mauricio. They traveled first to Hamburg and then to Chile, where they were reunited with Helena's other son, Joseph, who had moved there earlier. Helena lived with my family when I was a child. She hardly ever spoke. Mostly, she sat on our balcony shrouded in silence, looking out at the sea with a vacant gaze. Sometimes it seemed to me that she was searching for something within the shadows of that turbid space that only she could see.

I have been thinking about the consequences of war since Helena came to live with us when I was nine. I remember imagining my dead relatives who perished in the concentration camps, while I ambled through our house in Chile, going up and down our staircase in silence. Those ghosts dwelt with us, reminding us with their eerie presence not to forget about them or the horrors they endured. Ever since, it has been my mission as a writer to rescue people like my unfortunate relatives from oblivion.

I have written extensively about the trauma of the dispossessed and the persecuted, especially of my people, the Jewish people. Like a number of other minorities, the Jews have suffered systematic prejudice throughout the ages. As far back as the Middle Ages in Europe, they were forced to live in ghettos, segregated from everyone else. In my work, I attempt to understand prejudice by studying the exclusion of people. I ask myself repeatedly why humanity always seems to follow the path of intolerance instead of tolerance and love.

The Holocaust has been the focus of much of my poetic work. I travel to cities where Jewish culture used to be vibrant and where now there are only plaques outside buildings and schools to remind us of the thousands of innocent citizens who were taken from those places to the concentration camps. I write about those persecuted people. I try to communicate with them through my poetry, and I ask them where they are now. When I visit those cities, I recognize the cyclical nature of war and persecution, and how quickly we forget the devastation they leave in their wake. We must remember that the past is an integral part of our future. Forgetting is pernicious, and we fall into its grasp time and time again only to repeat the same mistakes.

My poetry has crossed countless thresholds in search of the obscured memories of those who have died in war and as a result of intolerance: from the Jews to the disappeared in Latin America. I have tried to dream about spaces of absence in order to reclaim and rename them. Writing about war constitutes, in part, an attempt to eradicate pain and recover the innocence of those who lost their lives. The majority of my work evolves from those forgotten spaces where I endeavor to recover the voices, the identities, and the history silenced by the void. Perhaps one of literature's purposes is to recover the destinies of those whose lives were cut short because of war and hatred.

Writing about war is not fruitless, even though it may sometimes seem that way, given that war persists in spite of poetry. A poem may not be able to break the vicious cycle, but it can act as a form of resistance and a reminder of other ways of being. Sometimes I write about beautiful things like water, forests, and flowering trees, but my imaginative compass inevitably leads me back to darker places filled with pain, fragmented lives, absence, and silence.

I keep writing about war because it is bigger than I am. It pursues me, it destroys me, and obliges me to be reborn over and over again in my words. Through poetry, I endeavor to combat the ugliness of war and the ruins it leaves behind, along with the senseless pain of the loss of our humanity. My ultimate goal is to remember in a way that honors those who have been senselessly lost to war and persecution, and to resurrect beauty and love; to recover, by way of a poem, a voice that looks for, and recounts, what humanizes us and restores our dignity.

By recovering the voices of people like Anne Frank and the disappeared in Latin America, I attempt to return the victims of war, dictatorship, and persecution to life in order to tell them that they did not die in vain. I also write about survivors like my great-grandmother Helena Broder, who witnessed the savagery of the Nazis in Austria but managed to escape. The poems that follow address the devastation of Helena's beloved Vienna as a result of the Nazis' war against the Jewish people. Even though the city, as Helena knew it, was pilfered and destroyed, hope lived on in my great-grandmother's strength and perseverance.

Your City's Sidewalks

I have come to Vienna to find you,
But all I hear is the echo of tortured voices,
All I see are your son's hands covered in acid
After scrubbing the streets of his city,
All I feel is the yawning Viennese night,
The night thick with fear.

Bonfires of the Soul

You loved your prosperous and welcoming city, Helena . . .
Roasted chestnuts on sunny winter days filled with promise.
Soon they began building massive bonfires
In which to burn all the Jews in the city.
Your neighbor spat on you as you walked by.
You, crestfallen, said hello in return.
Vienna was delirious,
Delighting in burning Jews.
You stopped talking to the woman who sold flowers and herbs.
You became more and more alone,
A foreigner in your own land.

The Jewish Women

You paid your taxes,
Handed over your jewels,
Your life in a suitcase,
So they would let you leave.
Other Jewish women, those who remained,
Were hunted by the Nazis.
They were old women.
They burned them,
They shaved their heads,
They dismembered them in the camps of ash,
They sold the gold from their dead teeth
In this city that has come to welcome me.

Treacherous Vienna

Dark Vienna,
Somber Vienna,
Vienna where the dead howl,
Vienna where at night you can still hear
Echoes of the deceased, of the living.

Vienna where they pounded on your door,
Stole your voice,

Took your son away.
He scoured the dark sidewalks with acid.
Everyone laughed at the laboring Jews,
At the Jews in that city that robbed them of their name and their light.

Vienna with its murderous hands,
With its eyes blind to the pain of others.
Repressive Vienna,
Adeptly deceitful Vienna,
Elegant and vulgar Vienna,
Somber Vienna.

You sewed stars of David.
Your hands, stars.

The Echo of Fear

The echo of that night,
The deafening noise,
The wicked wind assailing your eyes,
Clawing at your hair,
Leaving you breathless.

That night,
The wind conspired with the din of breaking glass,
The Night of Broken Glass sliced into your soul,
Glass showered your face,
History shattered,
The world came crashing down.

You descended the iron staircase
In that elegantly treacherous Vienna,
That elusive Vienna,
The insidious wind sought to hinder your way,
To slice through your fingers,
To entangle you in its sinister madness.

Your will to live was so radiant
That you conquered the wind

And those who reveled in your pain.
You travelled fearless and beautiful toward the southern seas.
In your hair, fireflies illuminating the way.

Justice

> Compassion and truth met;
> peace and justice kissed.
> —Psalm 85:10

The ferocity of the winter had not
Yet arrived in the cities.

Like a sunflower, the fall with its colors
Still ruled the sky.
Couples played among the leaves,
While lovers dreamt
About luminous rivers
And love was like
The texture of water.
There was so much light in that city
Beloved by all.
Some children climbed among the trees,
Wanting to collect stars.

But suddenly, upheaval gripped the streets.

Death arrived at the most unexpected places.
At a bar where people used to offer a toast
To the city of light.
At a concert hall where a piano
Shattered into a thousand pieces
Like abandoned bodies.

It was in Paris and in Istanbul
In New York City and
In a neighborhood in Kabul.
They were everywhere

And we were everyone.
The upheaval also erupted
In a marketplace in Beirut
Where women carried children
And sweet dried fruit,
And where pomegranates appeased faith.

The words fell silent.
Throats dried up.
Pianos split open in
A heartbreaking wail.

Language became vulnerable.
We didn't know how to name them.
The ones who were thirsty for death
Lost and without a compass.

The upheaval was not only there.
It was felt in the whole world,
In houses big and small.

The sky cried ashes of tears.
The meadows were drenched in a fall sunlight
And were blanketed by black clouds
That eclipsed the earth.

A young girl's head was cut off
She could have been Dalila,
She could have been Marie
And her hair fell among the leaves
In the parks of Paris,
It fell in the markets of Beirut
Looking like a ring of fire.

They killed little Tatiana in mid-air.
Her doll also died in her hands
Both lost amid the rubble.

And the sky ceased being the sky.
The heavens became a shawl of tears
A howl, the scale of a sobbing universe.

And we wondered if this was our world
Or if perhaps it was another
If it was the other way around?

Or if we had entered the most evil zones
Where words are bereft of meaning.

And suddenly everything was immersed
In the deepest silence.
Only death
Among the streets
Among the boulevards
Among the cornices of Alexandria
And the narrow streets of Tunisia.

Death carried black banners
From so much bloodthirsty killing
It had also lost its breath and voice.
Death became entangled in itself
And fell in its own trap
The void
Of senseless pain
The carnival of deranged blood.

Death feared itself.
The earth also decided to swallow it.

And the children lay hidden
In the abandoned parks, perhaps dead
Among the leaves that turned
Ashen gray.

Look at the black cloud dancing in the world.
Look at the black cloud.

And where was Justice?
Had it gone away?
Had it moved to another place?

Where was the woman who carried
The tablet of hope?
Where was the noble goddess
Of bountiful generosity?
The woman who appeared in dark nights
To guide lost travelers?

And we ask ourselves if there will be
A lighthouse to give us shelter?
A place that will protect us?
A country?
A city?
A forest?

The world suddenly fell silent.
The universe stopped singing.
The crickets, the wind, the waves
Stopped bursting,
Stopped being.
Did we have to begin to name it again?
How would we be different from the past?

Suddenly Justice returned.
She appeared radiant and barefoot.
She had fallen asleep like all of us.
Ingenuous and sometimes comfortable,
Innocent and other times arrogant
In her innocence.
She also feared not being able to be as before.

Justice spoke and said:
"There will be no vengeance or hatred,
Nor will there be oblivion.

We will return to play in the
No longer abandoned parks.
We will dance again in the hills
Of our cities.
We will go joyfully to the markets and
Our baskets will fill with the
Offerings that the earth grows and provides.
Barbarism will be transformed into beauty.
Justice will dress in strands as golden as the sun
Like the light that rules over the planet.
Children will not kill other children.
The children will play on seesaws, on swings,
And with the stars.

And Justice will be made with words
That will be words again.
Tolerance and solidarity
Empathy and goodness.
Affectionate words
Beautiful words
Fluorescent stars
Fireflies."

Justice disappeared within the foliage.

And suddenly the children appeared
Jumping on the leaves.
And a young girl said that
She liked to count the stars.
Another invited us to her home by the sea
Because the lighthouses had returned,
And the wise old women told
Stories on the rocks.

It seemed like the world had turned around,
It had returned to its place.

We decided to remain on the side of beauty.
To confide in the night and the day.
We decided to touch the light,

And attend the concerts of the
Water and the earth.
And imagine cellos like deep forests
And pianos like a cascade of living water.

We chose life
And the paths of the possible.
To embrace living symbols
To love the silver butterflies and the monarchs
To love the thunder and the storm
The abundance of stars and of poetry.
Not to be afraid to live among those
Different from ourselves.

Justice suddenly appeared again
Without the weights
She had carried before.
She seemed like a floating bride,
Like a fairy predicting good signs.

Justice smiled,
Saying that this will be the road.

We will achieve more
When there is no more hatred or fear.
When oblivion makes way
For luminous memory.

And above all, when we will repair
The fallen bodies
The mutilated voices.
And the children's gaze
Like a river of fear.

We will achieve for the now
When the wolf talks with the lamb
Just as the ancients had written.
And when the light within you
Will be your safe harbor.

Before departing, Justice in all her
Beauty and lightness of being said:

"There will be no more hostile roads of fear.
The cities will open
Their enormous, glorious avenues
With pedestrians walking confidently
Among the museums and cafés,
Among the concert halls and their homes.
And the sky will once again be
A galaxy of possible magnitudes.
The children will count the stars again
And draw the Milky Way."

Justice promised that beauty
Would bathe the fields with poppies,
Where grenades and blood had once been.
And that the rain would cleanse
The universe.

Justice departed without weights.
She danced barefoot throughout the earth
And rose toward the sky.

A Woman Dreams between the Thresholds

You could have been her
The girl amid the rubble
The girl dissolved by the haze of fire and hatred
But, you were not her.

You turned the corner of good fortune
Luck and its premonitions accompanied you.
But, could you have been her?
The girl amid the rubble?

Anne Frank sleepwalks through the streets of Amsterdam
Dressed in blood and gold.

You could have been the girl from Pakistan
With a bullet wound in the head.
Punished for wanting to read, to write and to be.
You could have been that woman
On the corner steeped in wrath.
Time and again her husband beat her in the night
Joined together for so many years
By the persistence of his assaults.
It wasn't your turn, said the neighbor
Who thought about denouncing you at midday
When the Santiago city police
Came looking for you.

But you were not there
You had gone to speak with the surf
Were recently learning how to
Revive the soul
You always approached the sea as the universe
You and the sea
The sea and you
Linked in a symphony of generous words
Because you believed in wonder and in the magic of kindness.

And on the road you encountered an old toothless woman
Who told you heroic and fragile stories
Did you listen to her words
Or was it your love that saved you?
You listened to her with the wisdom of an older child
And you and she travelled along a map drawn in sorrow
She told you that her village no longer existed
That only the geography of pain marked her face
And you kissed her fallen eyelids
Her hand like a burned and wounded forest.

And perhaps you never arrived at the city of Sarajevo
But imagined it on a canvas of anger
Or in a poem dressed in pain
Perhaps someone told you that before searching for food.
The women painted their lips in red and purple.

And clothed the children with pages from books
Dostoyevsky, Victor Hugo, Neruda
Everyone clothing the children in memory and War.
To dispel the horror on the face
To aim for beauty and not oblivion.

And when you heard the word, Srebrenica,
Your body bristled with terror.
What could be done with the magnitude of hatred?
What could be done with the invisible abundance of love?

They had told you so many things
And you were not in the cities of fear.

Your story was simply another.

Bosnia was just an illusion
You had heard about Cambodia
And Vietnam
About Rwanda where the women embroidered
The names of their dead on their dresses
And Argentina where the women embroidered
Their names in their scarves
About the children who feared
Their own sleeping eyes at night.

Did someone tell you about the disappeared?
They were your age
They enjoyed going to cafés and singing at midnight
About the things of love
They played guitar
They sang the International
They did not fear the police
They just loved poetry.

But you did not go to the café,
That night you covered other distances,
You settled for the still frailty

Of an open book, like a serene leaf
From a festive magenta autumn.

When they called at the door you were not there
Your terrified mother with the unkempt hair
Came out and denied your whereabouts.
But you could have been there
You could have been the housewife of Sarajevo
The cellist from Sarajevo
The disappeared girl in Buenos Aires
The child soldiers of Cambodia
The old woman raped in Bosnia
The one who wove blankets for her dead
The one who lost her voice and history
Until you came to sing it.

And what was history?
A game of chance?
A game of one type of cruelty over another?
Or perhaps the possibility of empathy?
Of finding beauty amid the hopelessness
The honor to call them by their names
The forgotten ones
The disappeared
The mutilated
The ones erased by history.

You refused the silence of the unjust
You opened their lips and their words
You learned to speak with the dead
To listen to their footsteps
And to save them a place at night
You were a Bridge and a Gaze
You were an open heart
Never sealed by cruelty.

One day you left with your voice hanging on your shoulder
Like a poet carrying bread

And you found yourself
Without crossing thresholds or borders
You were the little girl from Bosnia
That they raped and later scattered among the rubble
And she also cried out because you recognized her
Or perhaps you were one of the widows from northern Chile
Who searched for some little bones
A hand, a shoe, a flower between the words of the dead.

And each time you came back more clearly
They confused you with the angel of justice
The angel of memory
The angel of empathy.
But you looked around
And gathered histories
You embroidered them with the lighter side of your heart
And you did not look at the void
Only at the zones of pain.

A light was also there
Memory also persisted, there in the darkness
And you saw a resemblance in everyone
To the child soldier
To the young girl in Bosnia
And to the seeking mother.

And you found yourself in them
And they lived again in you.

In the night
You listen to them
And fill the celestial dome with stars from all the heavens
It seems that you have named them
It seems that the angels of hope
Mapped trails for your eyes.

You have received the grace of truth
You are all of them
And they are you.

Maker of words
Seeker of bodies.

Dreamers of stories.
Weaver of justice.

Women

Women are always the ones who wait
On the outskirts of cities,
On tempestuous paths.
They await the arrival
Of the children of war,
They wait on the side of arid roads,
On riverbanks of dry rocks,
Like the parched water itself.

They await arrival,
They bring blankets to cover the children who survive,
And those who never come home.
They are always waiting
Amid the light and the shadows,
Amid the winds of misfortune,
Amid memorials of oblivion.
They wait . . .

They are women made of water,
They are women made of wheat.
It is always the women
On the sides of roads,
On the paths of memory,
Women caressing their unborn children,
Rocking them, singing to them, making them false promises
Of a blue future.
With those children soon to be born,
The women await the day they will give birth
And they welcome the children alone,
And alone with them
They embroider the story of a new world.

The women search for those helpless children
Who crossed the rivers with parched throats,
Who are no longer stories or stones,
To save them from oblivion.

Women in love,
Those sweet women who taste like a sweet river,
Women who sit on the shores
Awaiting the promise of a single caress,
Women who yearn for a single kiss,
Women who hope they will no longer be beaten,
That they will not be maimed.
They await their husbands hoping not to be punished.
Women who crave a moment of love,
Acknowledgement in a glance,
A stirring in their souls,
Who want to be seen for who they are,
Who want someone to read their souls.

Elderly women who watch over their daughters
So no one slashes their hearts,
So no one mutilates them
And leaves them on the banks of arid rivers . . .

Women praying for their dead,
Women praying for their living,
Women in the time of wakefulness and dreams,
Women desperate in the face of heartbreak,
Women of the world united by a smile,
By hands that caress,
By lips that speak other languages,
By hands that wait to embrace.

That is who we women are:
The noble guardians of memory
Who lovingly wait,
Women who love in the lost heaths of memory,
Women who recognize the faces of their loved ones,
Women awaiting a train, a ship, a word, a caress, a clear breeze . . .

Women who wait for night and day,
Radiant women who wait for you on the paths of light,
Women who stand up from amid the swells and the mighty waves
To spy the shore,
The privileged horizon of life.

> *All poems translated from the Spanish by Alison Ridley, except
> "Justice" and "A Woman Dreams between the Thresholds,"
> which were translated by Celeste Kostopulos-Cooperman*

Michèle Sarde

MICHÈLE SARDE (France), professor emerita at Georgetown University, is a specialist in twentieth-century French literature and gender studies. She is a novelist, biographer, and essayist whose work has been translated into English, Italian, Dutch, Spanish, Japanese, and Russian. Her biographies include *Colette: A Biography,* for which she received an award from the Académie Française; *Vous Marguerite Yourcenar* (You, Marguerite Yourcenar); and *Jacques the Frenchman.* Among her essays are *Regard sur les Françaises* (Perspectives on Frenchwomen), for which she received prizes from the Académie Française and the Académie des Sciences Morales et Politiques, and *De l'Alcôve à l'arène* (From the alcove to the arena). Her novels include *Histoire d'Eurydice pendant la remontée* (Eurydice ascending), nominated for the Goncourt Prize, and *Constance et la cinquantaine* (Constance at fifty). Her fictionalized memoir *Revenir du silence* (Returning from silence) was awarded the WIZO (Women's International Zionist Organization) Prize for France for 2017. A sequel, *À la recherche de Marie J.* (In search of Marie J.), appeared in 2019. Michèle Sarde's work focuses mainly on women, the relationship between the written word and life, as well as personal and historical memory. She has been decorated by the French government with the Orders of Academic Palms, Arts and Letters, and National Merit.

Why I Write about War

The Second World War is distinct from other wars in two ways. For one thing, it was a war against civilians as much as military combatants. Thus, women were victims as well as men. For another, under the influence of Hitler and the Nazis, it became a racial war—Aryans against other peoples who had to be subjugated, like the Poles, or exterminated, like the Jews.

The selections below are taken from *Revenir du silence: Le Récit de Jenny* (provisional English title "Returning from Silence: A Novelized Memoir"). These episodes revolve around the Amons, a Sephardic (Spanish-Jewish) family from the Ottoman Empire who emigrate to France in the 1920s and are caught in the upheaval of the war. The narrator and author in this excerpt is a child, Michou, who was born shortly after the outbreak of war. However, the protagonist of the tale is an adult, Jenny, the narrator's mother. The vision of the war is therefore that of two women, the mother who lived through it and relates her experiences to her daughter, and the daughter, a child of the conflict and distant witness, who has chosen to write about it.

To establish the context of these excerpts from a long and eventful story, we should first identify the members of the family. Michou, the author and narrator, is the daughter of Jenny, who is the wife of Jacques and the sister of Marcel. Marie is the mother of Jenny and Marcel.

It is the summer of 1944, the year preceding the end of the war (May 1945), in a small village in the French Alps. Occupied by the German army, the Wehrmacht, and controlled by their police, the Gestapo, the French fall into three groups: those who collaborate with the Nazi occupiers; those who fight with the Resistance, directed from London and elsewhere by General de Gaulle; and those who just suffer and wait for the war to end.

Jenny's twenty-year-old brother Marcel is one of those who have chosen the Resistance and joined the Maquis (men and women waging guerilla warfare against the occupiers in remote areas of France). Consequently, he has taken off into the mountains to fight the German army with his brothers-in-arms. This confrontation ends in defeat, as the resisters do not receive the reinforcements they were expecting from the Allies. The maquisards then return to the village, which in the meantime has been taken over by Germans. The occupiers have obtained, perhaps through forced denunciations, the names of Marcel's collaborators. They detain Marcel first, as he is first on the list by alphabetical order.

Marcel is extremely brave, but also an imposter. To reinforce his position as his mother's favorite and get care and food from her, this young music aficionado has forged letters from great musicians praising his "musical genius." These letters are still in his pockets when he is arrested by the German commander, Major Schultz, an orchestral conductor in civilian life. The hoax saves Marcel's life, before the incredulous eyes of his sister and his niece Michou. It is Michou who much later records this extraordinary event in writing.

The scene in which Jenny accompanies her brother into the tent of the German soldiers the day before their final retreat—and finds herself a lone woman standing before hundreds of men—is emblematic of the role of women in war. Witnesses and victims, widows and orphans, they hand down the memories of the actors, that is, the soldiers and the resisters, nearly all of them men. It is the men who lead the battles and direct the extermination operations, but it is often the women who record their stories.

Translated from the French by Bárbara Mujica

From Returning from Silence

MY FIRST CHILDHOOD MEMORIES

Marcel's arrest . . . My first childhood memory, the first in a sense of an "official" and legitimate memory in my eyes—because I have never forgotten it since the day it happened, on August 7, 1944. For I can now put a date on it. It was morning. I was playing with other children outside Fleur des Alpes. And I recall precisely the bouquet I was gathering. I'd picked bluebells, buttercups, daisies, and poppies, which I clasped carefully so that those ever-so-delicate petals would not come off their stalks. I was concentrating on my bouquet when, from far off, I heard the characteristic crunch of our ogres' jackboots.

At what moment in my childhood did I identify the enemy and grasp the danger he represented? I was born with the war and the hunt for Jews. When did I begin to feel afraid? Was it the day after the botched arrest of my father in September 1942, when those two French policemen came at dawn and rang the doorbell of our apartment on the rue César-Franck? Was it when the German sentry refused to let me cross the demarcation line with my parents? I wasn't three at the time. Was it during the round-ups in Marseille, in January 1943, when the terrified screams of neighbors who'd been caught mingled with the bellowing of the Germans carrying out their orders? Was it in December of the same year, in Nice in the grip of Brunner and his men, brutally driving their victims to the Hotel Excelsior, before dispatching the mother of Ninon and her brother Jako to the train bound for Drancy and onward in sealed railcars to Birkenau? But I was only four, and the only memory I have of that Christmas month was the cradle wrapped in pink muslin, with its cute sleeping doll.

One can never be sure where memory is concerned. But timelines can help. Just before that singular day in the summer of 1944, there was the lunch on July 14 while bombs were falling, and the singing of our enemies marching past our windows on the 21st. Not really coherent memories, just bits and pieces, hazy; I could not have localized or identified them before I began my research.

I remember nothing of my father's and my young uncle's return to the welcoming rooms of Fleur des Alpes a few days earlier. But that morning of August 7, 1944, is as clear in my memory as the day my own son was born. I could tell you the color of the sky, the summery light of a fine morning, the dazzling hues of my wildflowers and the sound, at first muffled, then louder and louder, of fourteen jackboots hammering the sloping road to Corrençon, awakening a terror that has haunted my nightmares ever since.

In a flash, I dropped my bouquet and rushed to the stairs in Fleur des Alpes. I raced up them two at a time, as fast as my little legs could mount the steps, which seemed so high, barely stopping to pick myself up before racing up to the second floor. I had to pause a moment on the first-floor landing. The ogres were on my heels. Their footsteps were drawing near. I grabbed the handle of the door on the right to catch my breath. I held on with all my strength, thinking they couldn't snatch me away from behind because I was holding on so tightly—me, a little girl not yet five, against these Nazi giants.

Then I continued upward to the second floor. I reached the landing in a twinkling of an eye, then hammered frenziedly on the heavy wooden door, on the other side of which were Jenny, Jacques, my uncle Marcel, and Marcel Janowski, who'd come around for a visit.

"Papa! Germans!"

The door opened quickly, then closed. I barely had time to see my father get out his papers and the neighbor slide under the bed when already a call came through the door.

"Open up! German police!"

I sat down cross-legged, my favorite position. And from my few centimeters above the floor I lifted my head in the direction of these goliaths scarcely able to fit through the door. There were seven of them. Seven members of the German military police carrying submachine guns, bursting into the tiny apartment.

"Amon, Marcel? Papers! . . ."

My uncle drew the documents from his pocket.

"Get your things and come with us!"

They didn't even glance at my father, who trembled as he waited his turn. Marcel calmly packed some clothes and left with them.

Marcel was the first to be arrested because his name began with *A*. Others, young and not so young, were apprehended in their homes. All night, the German army marched to the tune of its famous warrior song, while never ceasing to hunt down the maquisards. No one could sleep a wink. Early next morning we learned that around seventy or eighty men had been picked up and taken to the old school, now a prison. It stood next to the Hotel Splendid, where the Kommandantur had set up its head-quarters. All these people were members of the Compagnie Philippe, like Marcel. All had been arrested by name.

From this it was deduced that the Germans had a list of the company's members that included the maquisards' real names in alphabetical order. The French considered them to be members of the regular army. For the Germans, they were mere terrorists: they would have been better off keep-ing just their *noms de guerre* as resisters.

"Why did the Germans have the identities of the Compagnie Philippe and not the others?" Jenny wonders still. "There was rumored to be a traitor. There were so many informers, voluntary or under torture! In any case, the youngsters arrested with Marcel all belonged to the same company. Most of the men lived in Villard-de-Lans. In some of the farms where young men had hidden in the woods, the Germans had politely asked the inhabitants to hand over their sons, saying they had noth-ing worse in store than being sent to work in Germany. Elsewhere, they threatened to burn down the farm, eliciting this distressing confession to the priest, Abbé Vincent, from a father who had given up his son: 'What can I do, Father? It takes a century to build up a farm and only twenty years for a boy to grow up to be a useful worker!'

"Suspicions of an informer were never verified, but the whole story of the Vercors is steeped in mistrust. In addition to the normal sources, the Gestapo and the Militia, there was also the SD, the military intelligence, which was highly effective; there were informers, willing and unwilling; confessions extracted under torture; reports of gossip; recklessness; care-lessness; cowardice; personal hatreds and jealousy."

For Jenny, and even more for Marie, the long wait and deathly anguish began all over again. They brought food to their prisoner in the school building every day. The guards were fairly easygoing, one a Bavarian who perhaps had a few things on his conscience, and a Pole who'd been forcibly conscripted. They too listened to the English radio and knew they were fighting a losing battle. The game was up. The prisoners were interrogated daily in turn by Major Schultz.

The youngsters agreed among themselves to say they were students who had come up to Villard-de-Lans on vacation to escape the bombing of their towns after D-Day. Some of the older ones were released. Then came Marcel's turn to be interrogated one morning.

In the afternoon, Marie asked the sentry in her halting German why her son hadn't been released while others had.

"Just go to the Kommandantur to ask them why! *Gehen Sie . . . Gehen Sie zur Kommandantur! Los!* Go on . . . Go on . . ."

"Shall we go?" asked Marie.

"Yes, let's," replied Jenny.

The Kommandantur was next door. Jenny trembled but went in head held high.

THE EXECUTED OF THE COURS BERRIAT

"Madame, your son is not eighteen years old. He's twenty. He is not a student. He is a dangerous terrorist whose main concern is to evade compulsory labor in Germany. We're going to kill all terrorists. The first thing they deserve is a bullet in the head."

The two women had gone into the lobby of the Hotel Splendid. It was teatime. All was quiet in the Kommandantur. Officers were sitting at round tables, drinking fruit juice or beer and eating biscuits. The women were greeted cordially, almost. They were ushered to a table. Major Schultz joined them immediately and uttered these brutal words politely, with the utmost refinement.

Marie blanched. She didn't need to muster her faltering German. Major Schultz spoke perfect French with a faint, barely detectable accent. She responded with a gesture.

"I know, I know. You're his mother. And the young lady with you is not a friend but his sister. I too have a mother, and a sister . . . You see, Madame, I've interrogated your son. He's a charming fellow. A genuine musician. I talked music with him, German music, which I love above all in the world . . . Beethoven . . . Bach . . . Handel . . . Haydn . . . Wagner . . . Above all Beethoven . . . I must tell you, Madame, that I'm a conductor in civilian life. Yes. A conductor in Leipzig . . . I've read his letters. The ones found in his pockets when we searched him. Munch! Ansermet! The greatest musicologists! All praise him! Music! It's greater than war, music. War is a horrible thing. But music . . ."

The German major paused. As if the notes of a symphony lingered in his ears, then:

"Yes. A horrible thing! . . . Alright . . . We're not going to destroy them, these young people! I'd like to pardon them and send them to work on the railroad in Grenoble. As for your son . . . I can't let them shoot a boy who could one day become one of the glories of his country."

"Major Schultz got up," says Jenny, "and gave us a kind of military salute as he showed us the way out, leaving us dumbstruck. We got out as fast as we could, my mother—Marie—and myself. If I hadn't been there myself, I would never have believed it. Actually, no one did. That episode, and the ones that followed, were dreamlike.

"The next day, we thought English radio had gone mad. We had nothing to go on but hearsay since we no longer had a wireless. All we knew was that there had been a flurry of cryptic messages repeated over and over, such as 'The huntsman is hungry . . . Nancy's got a stiff neck . . . Don't knock the cripple over . . . No horseplay in the morning . . . Sherry is a Spanish wine . . .' Operation Dragoon had just begun on the night of August 14–15, 1944. Another Allied landing. In Provence, this time. With seven French divisions under General de Lattre de Tassigny.

"In Villard-de-Lans, we were back to waiting. With a lump in our throat. Torn between joy at hearing of this new landing and fears for Marcel and the others still being held in the school. And we couldn't leave the village, as it was barricaded at either end.

"Then, out of the blue on August 21, Marcel, our young maquisard, and a Jew!, was released into the village square in Villard with a safe-conduct allowing him to go outdoors during the curfew. The conductor from Leipzig had spared the composer-genius. Along with another fellow. As for the rest of the prisoners, there were only twenty-one left."

Jenny pauses. There is a slight tremor in her voice, but she carries on: "The major told their families that they'd be working on the railroad in Grenoble . . . which was being bombed, but, well . . . there was a chance they'd survive. They were locked up in the prison in Grenoble. Then we had no more news of them. We thought they'd been sent to work in Germany. And then . . . and then . . . a mass burial site was found with their corpses. Inside Grenoble itself, on the cours Berriat.* All dead. All twenty-

---

* A broad street in Grenoble.—*Translator*

one. No, just twenty. Young Gilbert Soroquère was spared because he had been alone in a cell whereas the others had been two in a cell. That odd number had saved him. He'd been overlooked. The others were executed by firing squad. In Grenoble. They'd been taken from the truck, one by one, and executed. There's a monument to them now: *Les fusillés du cours Berriat,* the Executed of the cours Berriat. I returned there after the war and shed the tears I'd held back at the time.

"As for Marcel, he'd had the luck of the devil. His prank had saved his life. 'I can't let them shoot a boy who could one day become one of the glories of his country.' Major Schultz, or rather the Leipzig conductor, had kept his word. For him, music took precedence over war. Then war had returned to the fore and he had ordered the execution of twenty-one twenty-year-old boys: I knew all of them and used to call them by their first names."

For years, like Jenny, I thought Major Schultz had pardoned Marcel because he had believed in his genius and had condemned the other twenty because in his eyes or ears they had none. We know now, thanks to the work of local historians, that these young prisoners in Grenoble were not intended for the firing squad. They had been taken from their cells on August 14 and put into a truck, quite possibly bound for the village. That same day, at 11:50 in the morning, two German soldiers had just been shot in the cours Berriat. No one claimed credit for the attack, quite possibly it had been the FTP-MOI,* or a criminal shoot-out involving the militia.

Baying for reprisals, the Germans decided to shoot the hostages. Fate pointed its finger at the twenty maquisards from the Compagnie Philippe. The men being held in the Bonne barracks were executed in late afternoon, on the corner of cours Berriat and rue Ampère, near the bridge over the River Drac. The first four were brutally pushed out of the truck and machine-gunned. The others watched in horror as their comrades were slaughtered, knowing they were next. Each was murdered in turn, one after the other, in groups of three or four.

Twenty corpses, each aged twenty years, lay on the sidewalk at the corner of the cours and the street.

Doubts linger as to the circumstances: Were these young men taken from their cells to be shot, or were they simply crossing the road at the

---

* FTPF, Francs-Tireurs et Partisans: armed resistance organization created by members of the French Communist Party. MOI, Main d'Oeuvre Immigrée: a resistance group made up mainly of immigrant workers. — *Translator*

wrong moment? Were they machine-gunned three at a time, four at a time, or all together, like birds? Had she known, Jenny would have appreciated this finding that potentially absolves Major Schultz of responsibility for the shooting.

On the evening of that famous Monday, August 21, Marcel made a point of thanking the Polish and Bavarian guards who had wanted him released. Marie insisted:

"You can't go back alone. Your sister will go with you."

For the third time during the war, Marcel's sister confronted her adversary. The first time was in the prison at Fresnes, then at the Kommandantur in Villard, and finally in the tent of the last occupiers.

Jenny says: "It was eleven in the evening. The two of us set out at night into the mountain, with no light, without really knowing where we were going. These low-ranking soldiers weren't living in the Hotel Splendid, unlike the officers. They were bivouacking under a huge tent in the middle of nowhere, where it was completely dark. Marcel showed the sentry his safe-conduct. The sentry lifted a tent flap and I found myself, the only one of my kind, facing these dozens of men.

"No one can imagine what it was like. Almost pitch-black! There were perhaps two hundred, three hundred guys, not saying a word, with tiny candles flickering around them. Of course, they mustn't be seen. They could have been bombed. So, Marcel thanked his Pole and his Bavarian. Then I pulled him by the sleeve to cut matters short. It was a scene I'll never forget. Really, it was like a hallucination. All these silent men, motionless, in that twilight atmosphere, with those little lights, like candles in a church. And there was I, the only woman facing them.

"We went out into the night. Next day they had gone, leaving behind them the corpses of seven hundred French. On Tuesday, August 22, there wasn't a German to be seen in Villard-de-Lans. They had moved out without a sound, like shadows. They had cleared out in silence, with no marching band, no singing. Leaving us free!

"For us, the war was over."

LIBERATION . . . AND A JEWISH GODFATHER

Tuesday, August 22, 1944. As if by magic, the enemy had vanished, though no one had seen them leave. The barriers barring access to the town were gone. All was quiet. The town square in Villard-de-Lans was deserted. At Fleur des Alpes, Marcel, free once more, slept late. Jacques and Jenny walked out into that lovely dawn of peace. Suddenly, climbing the steep path leading to the square, Jenny felt a presence behind her. She spun round: another soldier! Jacques shuddered, then:

"He's an American! Jenny . . . An A-me-ri-can!"

An American . . . AT LAST!

"I was beside myself!" recalls Jenny. "I rushed to embrace him! Suddenly, people thronged the square. They were shouting for joy, weeping, dancing. Our liberators had arrived. Everyone wanted to talk to them, touch them, kiss them, thank them.

"A woman approached the first soldier I'd seen, begging him, in English at first, 'Please, *monsieur* . . . would you agree to be godfather to a newborn child?'

"'I'd like . . . I'd love to . . . but I'm Jewish—*Juif!*'

"'Never mind, the baby is too!' came the reply.

"And the next day, August 23," says Jenny, "we all held a party for the baby and its American godfather, both Jewish. And for the rest of humankind."

Translated from the French by Rupert Swyer

Peipei Qiu

PEIPEI QIU (China/USA) holds the Louise Boyd Dale and Alfred Lichtenstein Chair professorship at Vassar College, where she served as adviser to the Class of 2021, chair of the Department of Chinese and Japanese, and director of the Asian Studies Program. A scholar of Japanese literature and Asian studies, Professor Qiu is the recipient of many honors and grants, including the National Endowment for the Humanities Fellowship, the Japan Society for the Promotion of Science Fellowship, the Japan Foundation Dissertation Research Fellowship, the Columbia University President's Fellowship, and the Japan Foundation Fellowship for Researchers. Her publications include *Bashô and the Dao: The Zhuangzi and the Transformation of Haikai* (2005), *Chinese Comfort Women: Testimonies from Imperial Japan's Sex Slaves* (2013), and many research articles. Professor Qiu's scholarship has been published in English, Japanese, and Chinese and has drawn international attention.

Why I Write about War

As a Japanese literature professor, I had never imagined that one day I would write about war. Therefore, I was not very surprised when media reporters asked why I would write a book on wartime sexual violence. The book I wrote, *Chinese Comfort Women: Testimonies of Imperial Japan's Sex Slaves,* was published by three university presses at a time when geopolitical tension between Japan and China was escalating. Understandably, the media reporters' questions implied that my writing might be motivated by nationalistic emotions or state politics. My answer, however, was a surprise to them: my writing about the war was inspired by one of my students.

During the 2001–2 academic year, an Asian studies major at Vassar College, Lesley Richardson, wrote her senior thesis on the "comfort women" redress movement in South Korea and Japan, and she asked my colleague Seungsook Moon and me to be her thesis advisers. "Comfort women" is a euphemism used by the Imperial Japanese military men to refer to the women and girls who were coerced into becoming sex slaves of the military during Japan's aggression in Asia from 1931 to 1945. These women were subjected to multiple rapes each day. They were violently abused, and many were killed. However, the end of the war failed to bring justice for these women, and the postwar social, political, and cultural environments kept the survivors in silence until the 1990s, when women's groups and human rights activists in South Korea and Japan brought international attention to the issue and encouraged the survivors to speak out. Lesley's thesis examined the historical, social, and cultural contexts that allowed the establishment of the sex slavery system and the international movement that emboldened the victims in South Korea and Japan to reclaim their voices.

While working with Lesley on her thesis, I noticed that, although there was a large number of publications in English on the Korean and Japanese "comfort women," little was available about the ones who were drafted from mainland China. This lacuna seriously impaired understanding of the scope and nature of the "comfort women" system, as Chinese women comprised one of the largest victimized groups. Because these women were nationals of Imperial Japan's political enemy, their experiences reflected the darkest end of the spectrum of military sexual brutality. At the time, nationwide investigations on Japanese military "comfort stations" had taken place in China, so I hoped historians would fill this void soon with new scholarship in English. However, even four years after Lesley had graduated with her award-wining thesis, there were still few publications in English about Chinese "comfort women." I became increasingly concerned. The narratives of Chinese "comfort women" that I had read constantly came to mind. These women, treated as war supplies by the Imperial Japanese military, were brutally tortured and exploited during the war. Then, when the war ended, they were shamed or even persecuted as traitors by their own patriarchal societies. Their demands for an official apology and compensation were denied, and one after the other, the aged survivors died without seeing justice served. I felt that something must be done to make their stories widely known. Seeing that Japanese officials' continued denial of Imperial Japan's war crimes sparked widespread anger among its Asian neighbors, I believed that in order to achieve true reconciliation, a fuller understanding of the human sufferings caused by the war would be indispensable.

Hoping to bring to light their untold stories, I began researching the "comfort women" in the summer of 2006. A friend of mine who knew I was struggling with medical issues was very concerned. "Are you sure you want to write about such a difficult subject?" she asked. "Don't you know that the author of *The Rape of Nanking* died after she wrote about the Nanjing massacre?" Frankly, I wasn't sure if I could handle this project at the time. I was not a historian by training, and my health condition made it very difficult for me to travel internationally for field research. Two voices were debating in my mind. One said, "This is not your field, and it is too politically challenging to write about. You should concentrate on your current project on the Daoist classics." The other said, "These women's sufferings must be made widely known. Since you have the language skills required for the research, you should help tell their stories to the world." In this debate with myself, I thought about the days I spent working with Lesley on her senior thesis, about how deeply she cared about the human suffering that was so distant from her in time and space. I asked myself how I, a person who came from the land where the atrocities and misery had happened, could shy away from the project simply because it was not my field? The answer was clear, and I made up my mind to write about the Chinese "comfort women."

Learning the methodologies of the historian along the way, I worked nights and weekends on the research, juggling it with teaching and administrative duties and my other research projects. The process was intellectually and emotionally demanding. Frequently, I could not hold back tears when listening to and translating the survivors' testimonies and reading about the brutality they had experienced. Writing about the wartime trauma became particularly difficult during the times when my medical condition worsened and when my mother fell ill and passed away. At times I worried whether or not I would have the energy to complete the book. However, these courageous comfort station survivors who lived through hideous atrocities and went on fighting for justice gave me the strength. I was also immensely encouraged by the numerous researchers, activists, legal specialists, and volunteers in China, Japan, Korea, and around the world whose work informed my own, and whose compassion and commitment to justice inspired me to carry this difficult project to fruition and to continue researching and writing about Chinese "comfort women" after the book was published in 2013.

Documenting the history of the "comfort women" was an arduous task. Since the "comfort women" redress movement arose, ultranationalists in Japan have launched increasingly intense denial campaigns and fiercely attacked publications that expose that dark phase of history. In order to provide irrefutable evidence of the atrocities against the "comfort women," I dug into a staggering amount of material in Chinese, Japanese, and English. To offer a more objective and layered description of the proliferation of the Japanese military comfort stations, I used the eyewitness accounts of both Chinese civilians and military men published during the war. To acquire additional information, I also delved into the writings and documents produced by former Japanese military men, as well as reports and diaries of foreign nationals who witnessed the war atrocities in China. In collecting testimonies of survivors and eyewitnesses, I collaborated with and received support from many Chinese researchers, including Su Zhiliang and Chen Lifei at the Research Center for Chinese "Comfort Women," legal specialist Kang Jian, Chen Junying of Zhanjiang Normal University, Liu Guanjian at the Nanjing Museum of the Site of the Lijixiang Comfort Stations, Zhao Yujie at the Jilin Provincial Archives, and independent researchers Zhang Shuangbing, Chen Houzhi, Liu Changyan, and Li Xiaofang. In the book and my other writings on Chinese "comfort women," I tried to present the personal narratives of the survivors in the context of the war, reflecting the correlation between the expansion of the comfort stations and the progression of the Japanese invasion of China. This was later recognized as a major historiographical contribution, as my work was among the first to integrate the testimonies of the "comfort women" into military history.

Looking back, I am immensely grateful to the courageous survivors, my collaborating researchers, colleagues, students, friends, and my family. Their support made it possible for me to engage in this challenging research and writing. In today's world, the rape of women is still being used as an instrument of armed conflict, and the sexual exploitation of women continues to be common. It is particularly important and meaningful for women to write about war and to document the atrocities and sufferings war brings about. Through our collective efforts and writings, we can sustain the transnational endeavor to prevent the recurrence of war crimes against humanity.

Chinese "Comfort Women"

On September 22, 2017, a new "comfort women" monument, *"Comfort Women": Column of Strength,* was unveiled near the St. Mary's Square in downtown San Francisco. The inscription, engraved on a plate in five languages, begins with a quotation from a Japanese military comfort station survivor:

> Our worst fear is that our painful history during World War II will be forgotten.
> —former "Comfort Woman"

> This monument bears witness to the suffering of hundreds of thousands of women and girls, euphemistically called "Comfort Women," who were sexually enslaved by the Japanese Imperial Armed Forces in thirteen Asia-Pacific countries from 1931 to 1945. Most of these women died during their wartime captivity. This dark history was hidden for decades until the 1990s, when the survivors courageously broke their silence. They helped move the world to declare that sexual violence as a strategy of war is a crime against humanity for which governments must be held accountable.

> This memorial is dedicated to the memory of these women, and to eradicating sexual violence and sex trafficking throughout the world.

"Comfort Women" is one of the many "comfort women" memorials built in different countries in the past decade. Since the Japanese military comfort station survivors broke their silence in the early 1990s, the "comfort women" justice movement has gone international. However, the ultranationalists' attempts to whitewash Imperial Japan's war atrocities have also accelerated. In recent years, the struggle between the transnational movement to commemorate the lives of the comfort station victims and the denial campaign to erase that dark page of history has turned into a memory war. On the one hand, civic groups and advocacy organizations in different countries placed the memory and memorial of the "comfort women" at the center of the movement after the Japanese courts dismissed the survivors' legal demands for an official apology and compensation from the Japanese government. On the other hand, Japanese officials publicly requested the removal of the "comfort women" memorials, claiming that the "comfort women" issue has been resolved.

Has the issue been resolved? On December 28, 2015, Tokyo cut a deal with Seoul, under which the Park Geun-hye administration agreed to launch a foundation with a ¥1 billion (approximately $8.3 million at the time) contribution from Japan to carry out projects for the needs of "comfort women" survivors, and the Abe Shinzo administration announced that "this issue is resolved finally and irreversibly" with this agreement.* However, immediately after the announcement, critics and activists called for the cancellation of the accord, pointing out that the Japanese government still refuses to recognize its legal responsibility and has denied that the women were forcefully recruited for the military comfort stations. They also noted that the deal was reached without consultation with the victims in South Korea, and the process did not even include other countries that have large numbers of victims. One condition the Japanese government required for the settlement is that the South Korean government take measures to remove the "comfort woman" statue near the Japanese embassy in Seoul. This requirement outraged the participants of the "comfort women" justice movement.

The international dispute concerning the history and memorial of "comfort women" accentuates the power of memory and the importance of having these women's stories told. It also reminds us of the ongoing struggle between individual human rights and state politics. It has been a disturbing reality that although there have been a large number of survivors' testimonies and research findings from different countries and regions, and although even some Japanese court judges recognized the allegations made by the former "comfort women" plaintiffs, Japanese government officials continue to insist that Japan has not confirmed any objective sources proving forceful recruitment of the "comfort women."[†]

The denials have been focusing on two main points from the beginning: one, the women were not forced into the comfort stations by the Japanese military; and two, these women were prostitutes, not sex slaves. It is true that women and girls were brought into the Japanese military comfort stations in different ways and that their experiences there varied. This has been used by Japanese rightists and ultranationalists to deny the atrocities and the criminal nature of the "comfort women" system. However, investigations since the 1980s have shown clearly that the vast majority of the "comfort women" were taken into the military comfort stations

---

* Ministry of Foreign Affairs of Japan, "Announcement by Foreign Ministers of Japan and the Republic of Korea at the Joint Press Occasion," accessed December 10, 2019, https://www.mofa.go.jp/a_o/na/kr/page4e_000364.html.

† See, for example, "Press Conference by the Chief Cabinet Secretary Yoshihide Suga," Prime Minister of Japan and His Cabinet website, accessed December 9, 2019, https://japan.kantei.go.jp/tyoukanpress/201409/5_a.html.

by force and that the brutal treatment these women suffered amounted to slavery. This is particularly evident in the experiences of women abducted from the Japanese-occupied areas, of which Chinese women constituted the largest group.

China was Imperial Japan's greatest enemy during the Asia-Pacific War, and the widespread belief existed among Japanese troops that vicious acts against enemy nationals were a normal part of war. This mentality furthered the Japanese soldiers' violence against Chinese women. Many of the Chinese "comfort women" died as a direct result of the abuse or untreated illness; others were murdered as punishment for attempting to escape, killed as amusement for the Japanese soldiers, or eliminated to destroy the evidence of crimes committed by the military. Only a small number of the victims survived, but they were silenced in the postwar social political environment. Thus, the profound sufferings of these women remained largely unknown to the outside world for decades after the war ended. The Japanese military's deliberate concealment and destruction of relevant evidence, and the lack of a thorough investigation by the Chinese government and the International Military Tribunal for the Far East (IMTFE) immediately after the war, also contributed to the lasting injustice.

One important point I wanted to elucidate with my work was that the "comfort women" system was a war apparatus. It was created for Imperial Japan's military aggressiveness and made possible by the war. The Japanese troops began to set up comfort stations in China's Manchuria and Shanghai regions in the early 1930s, as soon as the Japanese army occupied northeast China. After the outbreak of full-scale war in 1937, Japanese forces directly conscripted women or used local collaborators to draft women. They rapidly expanded the military "comfort women" system, keeping the colossal sexual slavery apparatus running until the end of the war in 1945. While Japanese military leaders claimed that the purpose of the comfort stations was to prevent mass rape and the spread of sexually transmitted diseases among the soldiers, the testimonies of the "comfort women" themselves show that the system actually institutionalized systematic rape and sexual violence on a massive scale.

Investigations in China reveal clearly the militaristic nature of the "comfort women" system and the Japanese military's use of violence in drafting women. My research shows ample evidence that the vast majority of Chinese "comfort women" were literally abducted from their homes when Japanese forces occupied their hometowns, and the abductions were often accompanied by the brutal killing and torture of the women's family members and neighbors.

Hao Yuelian, a native of Wuxiang County, Shanxi Province, was only fifteen when two Japanese soldiers broke into her house and gang-raped her. It was an early summer day in 1943, and her parents had gone to work in the field. Hao Yuelian was scared to death and could not utter a word when the soldiers violated her. Having no means of escape, she hid under a quilt after the soldiers left. However, more soldiers tore into her house before sunset and dragged her out to the main road, where they tied her to a row of local men and women. Armed soldiers then herded them all to a Japanese military stronghold at Nangou Village. That night she was locked in a room alone and given no food.

The following day, Hao Yuelian and the other women and girls were taken out of their rooms and forced to watch the soldiers interrogate the captured local men. The soldiers ripped off the men's clothes, poured water into their mouths and noses, and pressed their bellies with wooden bars until water gushed out of their mouths and anuses. The soldiers repeated the torture to force the men to provide useful information. However, these villagers did not know anything the soldiers needed and said nothing. Accelerating the torture, the soldiers burned a piece of iron red hot and used it to scorch the men's bodies. Smells of burned human flesh permeated the air. The men screamed and began cursing the soldiers. The soldiers then let out four military dogs to maul the men to death. Hao Yuelian and the other women collapsed on the ground.

That evening, a Japanese man examined the bodies of Hao Yuelian and other girls and women. Three women were sent home after the examination. The rest were locked in a dirty room and raped repeatedly. After that, the soldiers came to rape the women continually whenever there was no battle. Hao Yuelian soon became very ill, her lower body bleeding. Yet, the soldiers continued to rape her. The sexual abuse lasted for about a month until the soldiers abducted additional women from another village as replacements. In order to get her out of this hell, Hao Yuelian's family paid a ransom to the occupation army. At that time, Hao Yuelian was already too sick to service the soldiers, so the troops took the money and allowed her to be taken home.

Two months later, before Hao Yuelian was fully recovered, she was once again kidnapped by Japanese soldiers and taken to the stronghold at Nangou. This time, she was locked in a room that had a pile of hay in it. Every evening a group of soldiers would come to the room and gang-rape her. Within a month Hao Yuelian's body was severely damaged. Lying on the ground, she was unable to move. Thanks to a villager who happened to pass by and saw her, Hao Yuelian's father and older brother found out where she was detained. They secretly got her out when the soldiers were not around and carried her home. Hao Yuelian was bedridden for months.[*]

Hao Yuelian is representative of Chinese "comfort women," whose experiences highlight many previously concealed aspects of the system. One is the ransoms the occupation army forced the victims' families to pay. Since the emergence of the "comfort women" justice movement, deniers have been insisting that these women were prostitutes who made money at the frontlines. However, investigations in past decades in China have shown that not only were the majority of the women abducted and not paid, but their families were often forced to pay large sums to the Japanese troops to ransom them back. There were also cases in which the occupying troops took the ransom, yet continued to hold the woman captive, or else the ransomed woman was kidnapped again, as in Hao Yuelian's case. These appalling atrocities against women and other civilians were made possible by the wartime context and the absolute authority of the occupation forces.

It should be noted that even though some "comfort women" received money when they were recruited or were given a percentage of the service fees in the comfort stations, they were held captive and forced to provide sexual services to the soldiers continually. Thus, the monetary payment does not change the coercive nature of the "comfort women" system. In an article published in *Guangxi funü* (Guangxi women's journal) in 1941, the reporter Wang Bizhen wrote about a military comfort station at Tongcheng, Hubei Province. This article was one of the few I found that were written when comfort stations were still running in the middle of the war. According to this report, the Tongcheng comfort station divided the "comfort women" into three classes: Japanese women were first class; women from Japan's colonies were second class; Chinese women

---

[*] This summary is based on my conversations with Hao Yuelian and her adopted daughter on August 5, 2018, and her testimony collected in Zhang Shuangbing, *Paolou li de nüren—Shanxi Rijun xingnuli diaocha shilu* [Women detained in the strongholds—Investigation records on the Japanese military sex slaves in Shanxi Province] (Nanjing: Jiangsu Renmin Chubanshe, 2011), 167–68. I would like to thank Mr. Zhang Shuangbing for his kind help during my visit of Hao Yuelian.

were third class. The women from Japan and its colonies were assigned to service the military officers, whereas local Chinese women serviced the soldiers. The Japanese military men who used the comfort station had to purchase a ticket. The first-class tickets were 1.4 yuan; second-class, 0.8 yuan; and third-class, 0.4 yuan. Although the money the soldiers paid to purchase the tickets was supposed to be given to the "comfort women," after many layers of exploitation, very little was left for the women. In addition, all the medical expenses were charged to the "comfort objects" when they became sick, and the money the women received was not even enough to pay one medical bill. The article also states that most of the "comfort women" in the station were drafted from local areas. During her days in service, a "comfort woman" was raped by some sixty soldiers. She was forced to smile when being raped, and if she showed any unwillingness she would be stripped naked and whipped ruthlessly, and she would not be permitted to go home for three weeks.[*] The hierarchical nature of the payments and the conditions described in this report are remarkably similar to those set forth by the military comfort stations in other countries under Japanese occupation. In his book on this subject, the Japanese scholar Yoshimi Yoshiaki exposes similar conditions, described in the "Regulations for the Operations of Comfort Facilities and Inns" (1943) by the Malay army administrative inspector.[†] Documents such as these, which were written when the "comfort women" system was still in operation, show clearly that the comfort stations were not ordinary brothels; they were set up for militaristic purposes and controlled by the Japanese military. It is remarkably revealing that in her article, Wang Bizhen uses the term *weianpin* (comfort object) to refer the women, clearly distinguishing them from prostitutes.

The second dark fact revealed in the narratives of the Chinese "comfort women" is the massive abduction of local women in the occupied regions by Japanese Imperial forces. Besides the formal comfort stations established in urban areas, numerous makeshift comfort stations were set up by small military units. These were established in all sorts of places seized by the Japanese troops: temples, churches, civilians' houses, or simply spaces in a military barracks or stronghold. Zhang Shuangbing, a schoolteacher

[*] Wang Bizhen, "Weiansuo li de nütongbao" [Women in the comfort station], *Guangxi funü* 17–18 (1941): 36.

[†] Yoshimi Yoshiaki, *Jûgun ianfu* [Military comfort women] (Tokyo: Iwanami Shoten, 1995), 145–46.

who identified the first comfort station survivor in China in the 1980s, conducted investigations at four counties in Shanxi Province and wrote a book on the women detained in Japanese military strongholds. His findings show that each Japanese military stronghold in the region regularly detained five to six, or sometimes over a dozen, women as sex slaves. Their detention usually lasted for about ten days to two months, although there were also cases in which women were enslaved for more than a year. Zhang estimated that if one stronghold regularly detained five to six local women with a frequency of replacement every twenty days, then the number of women victimized in one military stronghold in one year would be about one hundred.* During the war, the Japanese forces built an extremely large number of strongholds in China. The researcher He Tianyi, at Hebei Provincial Academy of Social Sciences, reports that by the end of 1943, in the southern Hebei region alone, the Japanese army had built 1,103 strongholds. He suggests that the number of Chinese women enslaved in Japanese strongholds in northern China alone could have been between one hundred thousand and two hundred thousand.† The comfort facilities set up in barracks and strongholds prove undeniably the Japanese military's direct involvement in drafting "comfort women" by force.

The massive abduction of Chinese women for comfort stations escalated in 1937, around the time of the Nanjing Massacre. Wartime documents of the Japanese military police unearthed at the site of the Headquarters of the Kwantung Army Military Police in Changchun (the former capital of the puppet state Manchukuo set up by Japan) show that from the very beginning of full-scale warfare, the Japanese military systematically implemented the "comfort women" system and drafted women from both the Japanese empire and the occupied regions in China to be the soldiers' sex slaves. Among the Kwantung documents preserved in the Jilin Provincial Archives in Changchun, there were two reports on "comfort facilities" in Nanjing and its vicinity merely two months after the Nanjing Massacre. The reports were submitted by Ōki Shigeru, commander in

---

* Zhang Shuangbing, *Paolou li de nüren*, 1.

† See He Tianyi, "Lun Rijun zai Zhongguo Huabei de xingbaoli" [The Japanese military's sexual violence in northern China], in *Taotian zuinie: Erzhan shiqi de Rijun weianfu zhidu* [Monstrous atrocities: The Japanese military "comfort women" system during the Second World War], ed. Su Zhiliang, Rong Weimu, and Chen Lifei (Shanghai: Xuelin Chubanshe, 2000), 254–68.

chief of the Japanese Military Police Regiment of the Central China Detachment, on February 19 and 28, 1938. According to the reports, Nanjing City had 25,000 Japanese soldiers and 141 "comfort women" at the time. The number of soldiers per "comfort women" was 178/1. At Zhenjiang, a smaller city near Nanjing, the number of "comfort women" was 109, and 5,734 Japanese military men used the comfort stations during the ten-day period February 1–10, 1938. During the next ten-day period, the number increased to 8,929. The reports also show a rapid increase of the numbers of "comfort women" between the two reporting periods: at Xiaguan, the numbers increased from 6 to 17 in ten days; at Danyang, from 0 to 6; and at Wuhu, from 25 to 109. One of the reports also indicates that at Wuhu there were 48 Japanese, 36 Korean, and 25 Chinese "comfort women"; at Danyang, the troops recruited local women due to the insufficiency of "comfort women."[*]

Investigations since the 1990s indicate that there were more than forty comfort stations in Nanjing under the Japanese occupation. The buildings of the largest comfort station still remain today. I visited the site in Liji Alley in 2017. Preserved by the city as a museum, the site comprises multiple two-story buildings, indicating the huge size of the former comfort station. Large Japanese comfort station sites did not exist only in large cities. In the summers of 2018 and 2019, I traveled to sites on the Chinese continent, from the Hainan Island and Sanzao Island facing the South China Sea, to Dongning County and Sunwu County, at the northeast borders. Although the county seat of both Dongning and Sunwu were small towns, multiple comfort stations were created there during the war, when the Japanese army constructed gigantic fortresses near the border to defend it from the former Soviet Union. The Shengshan Fortress at Sunwu County, for example, extended over 350 square kilometers, and the Japanese army had 17,570 soldiers stationed there.[†] Local researchers

---

[*] Jilin Provincial Archives, Quan zong, J315. The photocopies of the files are published in *Tiezhengrushan: Jilin-sheng xin fajue Riben qinhua dangan yanjiu* [*Irrefutable Evidence: Studies on the Newly Discovered Files on Japanese Invasion in Jilin Province*], ed. Zhuang Yan (Changchun: Jilin Publishing Group, 2014), 119–26. I would like to express my deep thanks to Ms. Zhao Yujie, senior research archivist of the Jilin Provincial Archives, for her assistance to my research at the archives.

[†] Xu Zhanjiang, Yang Bolin, Zhao Jiang, Yang Yanhong, comps., *Riben Guandongjun Huoermojin (Shengshan) Yaosai* [The Japanese Kwantung Army Shengshan Fortress] (Hulunbuir: Neimenggu Wenhua Chubanshe, 2011), 1 and 91.

have found four sites of the comfort stations at Sunwu, each of which reportedly had 50 "comfort women." In addition, there was a Military Club, which kept 20 women who could sing and dance to entertain the high-ranking officers. Today in Sunwu, only the building of the Military Club still remains—a two-story edifice with a cafeteria, a bar, and a dance hall on the first floor and more than twenty rooms on the second where the military officers raped the "comfort women." Local people reported that the "club" was managed by an old Japanese man and had Japanese, Korean, and Chinese cooks to serve different kinds of food.

The luxuriousness of the Military Club at Sunwu contrasts dramatically with the comfort facility sites I saw in Shanxi and Hainan Provinces, where the Japanese soldiers seized the villagers' cave dwellings or houses, or simply used a room at the military base for sexual enslavement. In 2017, I visited a survivor, Chen Liancun, at Baoting County of Hainan Island. Her experience of being abducted to a military comfort station was very similar to that of Hao Yuelian. Chen was thirteen when she was first raped by Japanese soldiers on the mountain near her home village. At sixteen, she was abducted by Japanese soldiers and detained at the Jiamao military stronghold. She was forced to do laundry and other work during the day and service the soldiers at night. She tried to escape from the stronghold but was recaptured and beaten until she passed out. Soon Chen Liancun became too sick to move due to the continual torture, so the Japanese soldiers let her be carried home. However, not long afterward, she was abducted to the military barracks again and enslaved until the defeat of Imperial Japan. The stories of Hao Yuelian and Chen Liancun reveal clearly the brutal reality of the "comfort women" system and the war.

The trauma of the "comfort women" did not end with the war. When I met Hao Yuelian in the summer of 2018, she was in very poor health and lived with her adopted daughter. The Japanese soldiers' sexual violence had severely damaged her body and left her sterile. She told me that she has had nightmares every night: she sees Japanese soldiers chasing her in her dreams. Her adopted daughter showed me a chopping knife next to her bed. Hao Yuelian refused to let anyone remove it because she was in constant fear of being violated. I took a picture of that knife. I was unable to hold back my tears. Hao Yuelian passed away on September 28, 2018, at the age of ninety-one, not long after my visit.

The brutalization of the "comfort women" should not be forgotten. War atrocities cannot be denied. It is in the hope of facilitating a deeper understanding of the sufferings of the hundreds of thousands of women whose lives were ravaged by military sexual violence that I write about war and tell these stories. Now warfare and sexual violence against women still ravage the globe. As we struggle for a more just and humane world, we must remember and draw strength from the voices of the "comfort women."

Miyoko Hikiji

Mıyoko Hıkıjı (USA) served on active duty and with the Iowa National Guard for nine years, earning sixteen military decorations. Her transportation company received the second-highest unit decoration—the Valorous Unit Award—for extraordinary heroism during its deployment in support of Operation Iraqi Freedom in 2003–4. Her book *All I Could Be: My Story as a Woman Warrior in Iraq* (2013) details her year with the 2133rd Transportation Company. Her interviews and book reviews have been featured by NPR, Armed Forces Radio Network, *USA Today, Marie Claire, AARP Magazine,* and *Stars and Stripes.* As a continuation of her service, Miyoko Hikiji has been involved in politics as a lobbyist for veterans' legislation and as a former Iowa State Senate candidate. She is also a member of the U.S. Global Leadership Coalition's Veterans for Smart Power. Miyoko lives in Urbandale with her two daughters, Grace and Noelle, both amazing storytellers.

Why I Write (about War)

When we start with the numbers, we forget their stories. When we stop telling their stories, we fail to honor their memories, and when we fail to honor their memories, we are no longer a grateful nation.

We are a grateful nation. Every citizen who spends a moment in still silence, whispers a prayer, visits a gravesite, or attends a remembrance event demonstrates that we are a nation that has not forgotten the sacrifices of the servicemen and servicewomen of the United States Armed Forces, or their families or communities that have lost the most precious commodity this country still produces—patriots.

A patriot is passionate about defending the liberties and luxuries of her country. A patriot puts the needs of others above self. A modern-day patriot grips tightly to ideals that never go out of season: loyalty, duty, and courage.

In the last decade of war in Iraq and Afghanistan, the number of fallen patriots totals more than seven thousand. I don't know how to describe seven thousand pair of boots without feet, helmets without heads, or bodies without souls. I don't know how to describe rifles without two hands on the grip and stock. I don't know how to articulate the heart-piercing reverence of Arlington National Cemetery. But nearly that same number, almost seven thousand veterans and their dependents, are buried there every year. I don't know how to talk about a number, but I do know how to tell you a story.

Aaron James "George" Sissel was born on Valentine's Day in 1981 to Kirk and Joallyn Sissel. He lived in Tipton and graduated from high school in 1998 and enlisted in the Iowa Army National Guard the following fall. He did his basic training and heavy vehicle job school at Fort Leonard Wood, Missouri. After the September 11 terrorist attacks, Sissel volunteered for Force Protection Duty, where he met his fiancé, Kari, and me. Sissel worked the overnight shift; I worked the first. When we changed over the guard shift, I always noticed that everything was squared away. It was wintertime, so he'd warm up the Humvee and top off the generator with fuel. But he also cleaned the guard shack and completed the paperwork. Not every guard did this; not everyone cared. And now that the gates of Camp Dodge are no longer protected by body armor and M16s, and no terrorist has ever infiltrated its gates, plenty could argue it never even mattered. But it mattered to Sissel; and it mattered to me, because it wasn't every day I got the privilege to work alongside a soldier with that level of care and pride. And all those qualities, along with his easy smile, made him easy to like. He was the type of friend you were glad to have nearby. He was a true patriot.

In 2003 he answered the call again, deploying with the 2133rd Transportation Company to Iraq for a year where his above-and-beyond-the-call-of-duty performance was recognized by General Roger Shultz, director of the Army National Guard at the time, with the general's coin. But his highest military decorations—the Purple Heart, Army Commendation Medal and Bronze Star—were awarded only after making the highest sacrifice a soldier can make—his life.

It was the Saturday after Thanksgiving, November 29, and the good people of AAFES (Army and Air Force Exchange Service) had just put out the Christmas cards at the Post Exchange at our forward operating base (FOB). It was the rainy season in Iraq, cold and windy, and the fine desert sands turned into seas of muck and mud. Everything was a depressed gray.

I was coming from FOB Quinn near the Syrian border, heading north on the main supply route returning from a supply convoy mission. Sissel was returning from a mission at FOB Tiger, driving south on the same road, when his convoy was ambushed. Sissel and another troop's .50 gunner were killed. Sissel's co-driver, Gottschaulk, sustained a debilitating injury as a bullet passed through his ear and exited his eye. I listened to the radio transmissions and messages sent over the movement tracking system laptop. My convoy couldn't get there in time; neither could the Medevac helicopter.

Sissel died in the northwestern sands of Iraq at the age of twenty-two. He never got to marry Kari and start his family. I did. I have two beautiful daughters now. And I don't dare take them for granted. I don't want to walk a single day without the kind of care or pride Sissel showed me. These extra days of life have extended into sixteen years now since my buddy died. Time has created a continuous pressure on my conscience to do more, live more, be more, and tell his story more—even on the days I'm not sure I can. Because if I forget to honor Sissel's memory by failing to tell his story, then Aaron James "George" Sissel would just be a number—one of seven thousand.

I write because the depths of despair and loneliness related to death can never be overstated. I write to keep the memory of myself young and strong alive. I write to remind myself that I'm constantly evolving alongside my truth and that who I can become, well, that's as simple as crafting a story I'd want to live and diving into it. And some of my biggest life shifts have occurred on days I did just that. I write to feel, and to relate and connect with humanity, with those who share the same emotions under different circumstances. I write to sit at the center of my true self, because that is where peace lives.

I Am an American

Well, I did want to get out of town. I needed money for college too, but it was much more than that.

I was three months past my eighteenth birthday and I had a big dream, to see the world and have grand adventures . . . to belong to something much bigger than I could imagine. To be all I could be. I wanted to be a soldier. What I didn't realize was that I'd become a *female* soldier.

1995, the year everything turned green. At Fort Jackson, South Carolina, my starched-stiff drill sergeants shouted, "What makes the green grass grow, Private?" "Blood. Blood and guts makes the green grass grow,"

I shouted at the tire in front of me as I skewered it with my bayonet. And with the tire, my individuality also died. My race, my poverty, my religion died. The only thing that mattered was my strength on the team, except when I heard: "Don't let that female soldier pass you!" or "No female's gonna finish this ruck march!"

By 2003, I'd finished my share of runs and ruck marches. Now it was time to put it all to the test. I was on my second mission in Iraq—a night patrol enforcing Ramadi's city curfew, a presence that kept insurgents from burying roadside bombs. The patrol chased a car down an alley, into a dead end. With surging adrenaline and no power steering, I pulled my truck forward and back, inch by inch, to get out of the alleyway and back inside the safety of the wire with two Iraqis from that car, zip-tied and guarded in its cargo area.

"That's the last time I drive with you!" my co-driver said back at base camp. "I'm not getting killed here because of a female soldier." As if he was the only one who was scared. As if I hadn't done my part on the team that night.

A year later, I stepped off my C-130 freedom bird onto American soil. A few folks had heard an overseas flight was arriving so waited to greet us. Scattered down the tarmac in twos and threes they clapped as we walked past. A gray-haired woman at the end of the line, wearing a red, white, and blue sweater, held out her cell phone and said, "Call your mom. Tell her you're home."

Thank God America cared, I thought. But that pride, that gratitude, the security of that moment was hard to take with me—to Iowa State University, where I finished school, to my suburban neighborhood, where I'm raising my two daughters, to my civilian job fully equipped with inboxes and meetings and deadlines.

Earlier this year, in my kids' school, I noticed a hallway lined with photos of other parent-soldiers (no females, of course) headlined with bubbly, bulletin-board letters spelling out "We Support Our Troops." Like the principal's voice over the intercom, the walls announced with authority that the school was patriotic. But the administration didn't roll out the red, white, and blue carpet when I arrived to discuss a policy that was negatively impacting my girls. Being mission-focused and short-tempered, I cut straight to the tough questions and demanded answers. The school staff lobbed bureaucratic niceties back, talking to what I suspected they thought was my PTSD instead of to an impassioned, assertive parent. They were anything but supportive to this patriot. If being a veteran is respected at my daughters' school, I wouldn't know it. After all, I'm a *female* veteran, and while throughout my military career I was supposed only to be green, the truth is, I was always something more.

Every chance I get to redefine the face and the faith of service members and veterans as more than male and female, I take it. Whether that's teaching a veterans' writing class, running for public office, or sharing my story in a book edited by a woman I've never met, I say "yes."

So, I did get that great adventure after all, and it is bigger than I ever imagined. I am all I can be. I am. An American.

PTSD Dating

Post war dating is a battle
But first things first
Yes, I'm a veteran
Before women were allowed in combat zones
I already had been
I was a Tomboy as a kid
But that's a whole other poem
I'm not a lesbian
And I survived sexual assault, twice

As if those nine uniformed years weren't enough terror
Welcome to PTSD date night
When he arrives at my AO at 1730 hours
He backs into the driveway to park
As if dinner were a mission
Dinner is a mission
Everything is a mission
And this is how we begin accomplishing our evening

I greet him with a hug and ask
"How you doin' brother?"
And he responds
"Did you take your meds?"
I lock the two deadbolts on my front door
That keeps my insurgent anxiety beneath the threshold

We roll out from home base
Into rush-hour traffic
I force my eyes to glance at him
Instead of staring out the passenger window
Searching for threats over sights that
Are no longer there

We experience time accelerated
Pulse quickened
Adrenaline spiked
Breaths rising
Pupils dilated
Mind focused

By the time we get to the restaurant
We have already been through so much
Never since convoying across the Iraqi desert
Have I gotten into a vehicle to just "go for a drive"
No longer is there joy in the ride
Only joy in the arriving

We ask the hostess for the table in the corner
Sliding in seats
Side by side, shoulder to shoulder
Our backs to the wall
In a defensive position
Though sitting, we move at hyper-vigilant speed

While the rest of the diners sprawl across booths
Swinging legs and sipping Cosmos in slow motion
We are the sky marshals
Our minds at 40,000 feet, moving 500 mph
We want to join their inertia

Beer helps us descend
Tame the fireflies of our minds
Turning down like a dimmer switch
Our look-twitch-trigger electricity

Better than taking out the light bulbs altogether
By pills in bottles from VA hospitals
In brown paper bags to camouflage our shame
The ads told us reaching out was an act of courage
As if we, watching our buddies die in the sands
Needed courage defined

PTSD isn't about courage; it's endurance
It isn't about shouting from the mountaintop
I'm hurting
It's about after traversing a monolithic mobilization
Calculating your compasses' back azimuth in order to
Navigate your way back down

We waited for hours on hold, weeks for appointments
For shrinks who quit their jobs
We got busy signals when dialing the suicide hotline
And were given a rainbow of pills that made us truly crazy
Sertraline, Tradazone, Vilazodone, Alprazolam
Paroxetine, Zolpidem
There was no pot of gold at the end of them

The razor blades could not wait
Their desire to cut a springboard across our arteries
An escape hatch for demons to leap to their death
Before we took our own

We became amateur pharmacists, or magicians
Splitting pills, skipping doses, subbing in shots of tequila
Because close is good enough in horse shoes
And hand grenades
And we were expert pin pullers

As uncomfortable as we are in our own skins
We feel normal, together
Camaraderie renewed
The closest feeling I know to happiness
I don't know if this kind of love touches the un-uniformed and un-war
    torn

We slip into acronym-speak
OIF, FOB, M16, ROE, KIA
A fubar foreign language that makes
What they describe more palatable

We bite through our hamburgers
Dip freedom fries
Chase down beer number two
And are just starting to feel alright

Sometimes when we let down our guard
We awake in the green zone
Jocularity, vulgarity
"Remember that dumbass private?" he says
Everyone has a "that guy" story
That platoon sergeant, sloppy as a soup sandwich
That captain, tore up from the floor up
And us, well, we were just trying to survive it all

We are full
There is no weapon to shoulder as we exit the building
But there are heavy burdens strapped across our backs
Lamplight has replaced sunlight
Smell of night crushes old memory herbs
Renewing the flavors of sand and sweat

He drives me back to my threshold in silence
I unlock two deadbolts and let some night in
"You gonna be alright sis?" he says
His arms encircle me and press the air from my body

I am left with a sleeping pill and nine hours of darkness
To refill my lungs
A small dog, probably out for its last potty break, yips
Its owner yells, "settle down"
We're trying, I whisper
A garage door opens, car doors unlock with a 'beep-beep'
Headlights travel across my bedroom wall and fade away
I drift

Then silence, finally
Dead silence

Year of Change

1976, our nation's bicentennial
So that's what my father called me: his bicentennial baby
And it was on the last day of that year
I was formed from the earth
By the fingers of my mother's right hand
And the fist of my father's left
Pressed together into slurry
Kneaded by poverty and public education
Rolled into coils of years
That became my first vessel of adulthood

1995, the Chinese Year of the Pig
An animal that is easy to fool and likes it that way
So that's what my mother called me: foolish
And it was the fourth day of April in that year that I left her home
And moved into the South Carolina barracks of Mother Army
Her day-to-day dictates shaped me into a pot
That carried water along miles of forced ruck marches
Contained the ricochet of rifle shots from targets downrange
And held my breath during timed drills to don my gas mask

2003, Iraq
My pot, strong and smooth, was ready for the kiln
The armored cavalry hardened me by fire and blood and I came out
     steel
So that's what they called me: Brave Rifles!
And it was on the 403rd day of the following year I came home
My total strength tested
Pulled apart by the guilt of living, when fifty fine riflemen had not
Compressed by a series of itch and twitch
Memories of sand fleas and mortar rounds left me scratching my arms
On guard duty in my bedroom tower from noon to midnight

2010, Lucky Seven
Cracked and chipped, unable to hold even a tear, my pot had no purpose
So that's what they called me: broken
And so it was after seven years of vodka bandages, angry outbursts,
    insomnia and the same ol' story, I started my search for people who
    repaired pottery
Pills and appointments and pages of awful truth and uncomfortable
    confessions
Were going to lift my pieces back into place
I'd be the vessel I used to be, like new
A fresh outlook and paint, and no one would even know the cracks were
    there

2017, The Big 4–0
A woman with a complicated history that never gave up on herself
So that's what people call me: an inspiration
And so it was on New Year's Day, the first full day of my 40th year of
    life, that I started a new story that I never get tired of telling
My scars, I painted with gold, and show them to the world
They are the luxury of the wisdom of my experience, and I cherish them
My pot, repurposed, no longer open to be filled to the rim
It now rests, enveloping the time and space of this moment
Knowing that there is nothing more to be done, but only to be

Someday, the end will come around to meet the start
So that's why they call it: circle of life
And so it will be, from the earth I will return to, a new life will begin
From a mother's fingers, a root, a seed, an egg . . .

Tip of the Spear

The tip of the spear
I was, we were
Our lungs an expanding balloon in endless inhale
Driving into Middle Eastern sands, an unknown land
With metallic dust of bombshells
And charbroiled, oil-smoke clouds
The war on terror
Hanging on our horizon

We breathed it in, toxicity
In pants and gasps and cries
As the dust settled deep in our souls
Particulates seemingly too small to matter
But oh! Picking one forbidden fruit
Can banish you from your heaven
That is the knowledge
That your naked being
Is good

I left the desert, a 6,000-mile exhale
Of angry adrenaline smoke
Putrid stench of souls wasting away
In fear, in death
An unblinking gaze
Screening rock-heart denial

Undetectable mist
Sand grains like powdered sugar
Stowaways in my cargo pockets
Under fingernails, along my scalp
No bathing ritual could rid me of its residue

It became a fixture on my mental landscape
Like the thin-air peak of Mount Damavand
Reflecting in the Caspian Sea
An image that is not the water
Yet the water cannot deny the mountain
To lay across its surface with each sunrise
Imposing its powerful foreboding beauty

Breathing became possible
By psychiatric oxygen cocktails
That turned vivid memory scars into
Lines in a history book, borrowed from a shelf
Held by the reader in two palms and ten fingers
That do not recognize they penned that past

Feet that do not fall asleep
But leap off the cliff into unconsciousness
For hours in darkness
The mind does not agonize
Or ponder, for that matter
Or count stars or sheep or blessings

It is turned off, practically dead
A temporary suicide
White noise, no information
Not even to convey timely breaths
And a steady heartbeat
No! I am not present to experience peace
Only un-medicated war

When the potency of pale blue and white wanes
I rattle my bottles in search of more survival
Skipping
Like a game of hopscotch
Along a razor-thin rim of an erupting volcano
Dangerously close to melting
Back into the earth that made me

As I bury the sharp memories
Of days, not too long-ago days
When donned in rifle, ruck and camo
I kept watch

There are times I unearth them
A grave robber of my past
To examine what remains
What matters
What, if any, of it
Was holy

These words
Are the teeth and jawbone
That identify me
I offer it to you

Will you place it under your tongue?
And say a prayer
For peace

Four-Letter Word

I used to think about my pen as a blood letters razor
Where sanguine, inexpressible, adrenaline-shaking, snake-pit-deep
    emotions
Make shapes into words into meaning
That I shoo off like hoodlums on Halloween night
Saving my pumpkin from being smashed on the street

The bloodletting metaphor fails like the medical practice
An oozing, weak literary fatality
For blood cannot be separated into "good" and "bad"
Much like brain activity, "good" and "bad" don't inhabit separate spheres
All are intermingled, tangled and connected

Now I'm not a doctor, and I won't play one in this poem
The physical matters but the philosophical reigns
To imagine myself lying open, spilling blood
Says I'm a patient, just another drop of evil from a cure

That on the other side of pain, sweat and ash
A phoenix of good life awaits resurrection
This ink on the page, I declare from Mount Author
Is my madness, my glory, my therapy, exclamation point

I've climbed that mountain, to find no such treasure
No rest for my grip, no fountain of health
So instead, from the brink
I have this to say

I am no longer at war with myself
I have no battles left to win
I have no thing yet to prove
I have a new treatise

I approach the "bad" inside with an extended hand
OK, I say, there's only one body
You want a different approach, more choices
Bent boundaries and a faster exit strategy

We do it, some of it
We both win, sometimes
We team up
We watch each other's backs

We find goodness in our common ground
There are not more lines in the sand
There is no more "good" or "bad"
There is a cease-fire in judgment
I refuse to label my weaknesses as weak
My sleeplessness as hopelessness
Or my tiredness as toes on the edge of giving up
This is more than a positive spin
There is no turning turds into rainbows here

But I've decided to think things anew and through
A weakness can be one of my lesser super-strengths
My sleeplessness energy for living
And tiredness, well, that's from swimming long and hard
In a can-do pool

I'm not exorcising demons
Or dying
Or puking up my guts
For vulture bloggers and ergonomic armchair shrinks
To pick through so they can tell me what I just ate

I know what my hands have held
And what my tongue has tasted
I'm telling you right now
Those crows are digested and I'm searching for a better meal

I want my words to be salve on wounds
And this paper the moccasins on tired feet

My sentences the arms that wrap around the lonesome
And my punctuation the water drops from a washcloth on feverish
    foreheads

I will no longer allow my stories to crumple into compression bandages
They've been twisted enough
The bright-red blood has stopped

I'm tired of war metaphors
I use them only because I understand them
And sometimes it feels damn good just to know
That I know something

But this new diet of mine
Requires a full course in linguistics
What fool brings a chicken à la king MRE to a five-star restaurant?

I'm out of the foxhole
My words refuse to take cover
I have no noise discipline
Even when I'm silent
My message shouts like a drill sergeant
At 0400 hours
But instead of "shitbag, get up!"
It screams "Hey, take my hand!"

My hate
Has circled the drain
I'm pumped
With liquid love

Not Southern Comfort, ya'll
Not Starbucks double shot,
You morning bloodshot-eyed optimists

I'm talking about the Living Water
I'm talking about all that bad
Being covered by all that good

So that, finally, for once you can believe
It's gonna be alright

Fuck is not the only four-letter word that works in all situations ya'll
In fact, it's a bad way to describe damn near anything fucked up
Fuck can't explain a damn thing
Fuck can't get you closer to true meaning

When you want to really get your hands dirty
And describe what's right in front of you
Maybe it's time we threw out all the props
And costumes and lighting

Stand naked in the spotlight of human LOVE
Cause if you tell me it's hate that makes a man do crazy shit
I'll say
No, it's the absence of LOVE

Or it's good looks that makes a woman shine
I'll say
No, it's the presence of LOVE

LOVE doesn't bleed ya'll
Between the blue lines on this page
Are not the scribbling of red, white and plasma

This here
This is a song
It's a round
You gotta join in

This song
You can carry in your pocket
It's on every jukebox phase in life
And will never cost you more than the change you got in your pocket

It's a LOVE song
You can dance to it Saturday night
And pray to it Sunday morning

I hope this song never leaves your head
I hope it drives you to love like crazy
If your nightmares wake you up at two
Let it be the lullaby that gives courage for your eyelids to close again
      until sunrise

Cause the Sun is gonna rise
And it wants to shed light on your new beginning
It wants to be that clean air that fills your lungs
When you sleep with the windows wide open

This LOVE is gonna guard your door
It's gonna cover you like a battle buddy you can always trust
So, bask in it
Let it burn its way into your soul
Until there's starlight under your fingernails
And comets cruising through your veins

And when your LIGHT is so big it's ready to burst
Be a firework of LOVE in someone else's night
Be the flash and the bang that bolts them upright from the table
And makes the blood letter drop his razor
So they know . . .

There can be peace
That they are filled with goodness
And that while hate exists
LOVE rules

Then teach them to sing

Bárbara Mujica

BÁRBARA MUJICA (USA), professor emerita of Spanish literature at Georgetown University, is a novelist, short-story writer, and essayist. Her novel *Frida* was an international bestseller and has appeared in eighteen languages. *Sister Teresa* was adapted for the stage at The Actors Studio in Los Angeles and published in Spanish in 2017. *I Am Venus* was a winner of the Maryland Writers' Center National Fiction Competition and a quarter-finalist in the ScreenCraft Cinematic Novel Competition. Mujica's collection of stories, *Far from My Mother's Home* (2017), was published in Spanish in 2019. Mujica has won numerous prizes, including first prize in the 2015 Maryland Writers' Association (MWA) national fiction competition for "Jason's Cap," about a suicidal veteran. In addition to four other prizes from the MWA, she has won the E. L. Doctorow International Fiction Competition, the Pangolin Prize, the Theodore Christian Hoepfner Award for short fiction, and the Trailblazer's Award from Dialogue on Diversity. Her essays have appeared in the *New York Times*, the *Washington Post*, and hundreds of other publications. Since her son, a U.S. Marine, returned from Iraq in 2008, Mujica has devoted much of her energy to serving veterans. In 2015, she received a Presidential Medal from Georgetown University for her work in this area. Mujica's latest scholarly books are *Women Religious and Epistolary Exchange in the Carmelite Reform: The Disciples of Teresa de Ávila; A New Anthology of Early Modern Spanish Theater: Play and Playtext; Teresa de Avila, Lettered Woman;* and *Women Writers of Early Modern Spain: Sophia's Daughters.* The selections included here are from her short story collection, *Imagining Iraq* (2021).

Why I Write about War

When the United States abolished the draft in 1973, I rejoiced. If I ever had a son, I thought, he wouldn't have to go to war.

I grew up after World War II hearing stories of Nazi concentration camps and American pilots downed over the Pacific. When I was a little girl, we had air-raid drills in case the Reds dropped a bomb on us. Then came Vietnam. Some of my schoolmates were drafted and returned home weird, maimed, or not at all. The newspapers carried images of caskets with the remains of American servicemen and articles about napalm and My Lai. How was it, I wondered, that the government could whisk away your son, send him halfway around the world, and return him in a box? I was terrified of war. I had nightmares.

My son Mauro was born during the Reagan years. It was a time of optimism and relative peace. The draft had ended, and I shoved the matter of military service to the back of my mind. But when the first Gulf War began on August 2, 1990, my worries returned. Our neighbor Justin enlisted in the Marines. When he returned from Iraq, I watched how my son listened, enthralled, when Justin spoke of his deployment. When I was a little girl, ten-year-old boys played cops and robbers, but my son and his friends played "get Osama." They hid behind bushes and leapt out from behind garbage cans to ambush an imaginary Osama bin Laden. One afternoon, when Mauro was in high school, I came home from work to find a Marine recruiter in the living room. Fortunately, one of his teachers, an elderly Jesuit named William Elliott, convinced Mauro to go to college first and then apply to Officer Candidate School (OCS). When Mauro entered OCS shortly after starting college, I thought I was off the hook for four years. By graduation, I was sure, my son would have changed his mind. But on September 11, 2001, Mauro and his buddies watched from the roof of their dorm as terrorists flew an airplane into the Pentagon. Mauro decided to drop out of college and enlist.

"No!" I begged. "Finish your education first!"

"I've got to do this, Mom," he told me. "I know you're scared, but you protected me when I was a little boy, and now I've got to protect you."

What could I say? He believed his country and his family were in danger. He knew that Osama bin Laden, founder of Al-Qaeda and mastermind of the World Trade Center attacks, continued to threaten America. The news media reported on Saddam Hussein's abuses and his weapons of mass destruction. Mauro and thousands of other young people prepared to answer the call to service. I respected Mauro's moral conviction and his courage. Fortunately, when he contacted the Marines, they gave him the same advice that Father Elliott had: stay in college and go in as an officer.

When the invasion of Iraq took place on March 20, 2003, Mauro still had more than a year left of college. "It will be over by the time he finishes," I told myself.

But when he graduated in May 2004, the war was still going strong. He was commissioned as a second lieutenant the day after he received his diploma, and he left for Ramadi, in the heart of the Sunni Triangle, the following year.

At first, Mauro emailed often, sending photos of the sun gleaming over the Euphrates and colorful souks. Then the messages became irregular and cryptic: "You won't hear from me for a few days. I'm busy." The news in the papers was horrifying. As the casualties mounted, I became addicted to the news, reading three newspapers a day and surfing the internet for reports on Iraq. Whenever something happened in his area, I'd dash off a frantic message: "Just send word that you're OK." In a few days, the answer would come: "I'm OK. Stop reading the papers." My husband started hiding the *Washington Post,* but I read it online, along with a slew of other publications. I would sneak downstairs at midnight and turn on the computer.

I was terrified. War was no longer an abstraction or a philosophical question. It was something real and close, something that could shatter my family. Returning soldiers told me stories about Al-Qaeda tactics, how Al-Qaeda intimidated civilians by planting bombs on their property or decapitating children to terrify their parents into submission. My brain filled with images of bodies blown to pieces and toddlers with no heads.

Whenever I heard of a Marine dying, I'd feel horror, then relief that it wasn't Mauro, and finally guilt over my relief. Somewhere, I knew, a mother and father were weeping. I kept a backward calendar: 280 days until he's scheduled to come back, 279, 278 . . . Of course, we didn't have an exact return date, so it was only an estimate. I prayed a lot. I became obsessive about calculating survival rates: about a half million have served, and 3,000, 3,040, 3,080 . . . have been killed. The chances of Mauro making it back are good, I told myself. But Anbar Province, the stronghold of Sunni resistance to the Shiite-dominated Baghdad government, was a dangerous place, and, anyway, percentages don't matter if it's your kid who's wounded or killed. Mauro didn't tell me when his close friend Fitz died in an IED explosion. I read it in the newspaper. In Washington, the *Post* ran stories about the Bush girls—what clubs they went to and with whom, what they wore, what they ate. It was a cruel reminder that most of the politicians who were sending our kids to war were making no equivalent sacrifices. Later, when the Bushes were planning Jenna's spectacular wedding, all I could think about were the thousands of military families who had had to plan funerals.

While Mauro was in Iraq, I suffered a stress-related stroke and lost partial vision in my right eye. I decided not to tell my children. They had enough to worry about.

After Mauro returned from his first tour, he said very little. It was clear from his clipped responses to my questions that he didn't want to talk. Out of some eight hundred men in his battalion, fourteen died. In a single attack on Mauro's platoon, one Marine was killed and six others lost legs. Mauro went to Walter Reed Hospital to visit the wounded. I found out from newspapers and other sources that he had saved the life of a journalist, pulled two Marines out of a burning vehicle, and dismantled an IED. I'm glad I didn't know about these events while they were happening. Hearing about my son's heroic deeds did not put my mind at ease. I knew he was going back. More disturbing still, he wanted to go back. "You have to fix what you break," he told me. "The only reason for invading a sovereign nation is to leave it in better shape than you found it."

I found him changed. He had lost his bravado. His commitment hadn't faltered: in order to make sense of sacrifices like Fitz's, we had to secure a lasting peace. But he thought we were going about it in the wrong way. When he talked, which was rarely, it was about the need to confront the root causes of the insurgency and the need for economic development. "It's a war that can't be won solely with weapons," he said. Once back on base in California, Mauro studied Arabic and read extensively on the Middle East and Islam. By living and working closely with Iraqis, he believed, the Marines would be able to foster a healthier relationship with the people. This might facilitate some new economic development projects that would help to stabilize conflicted areas by giving Iraqis a vested interest in keeping things calm.

When Mauro returned to Iraq in April 2007, he expected to find Ramadi violent and chaotic, as he had left it. Instead, thanks in part to the "surge" and the Sunni Awakening Councils, the area was relatively quiet. Mauro was assigned to a police station in the Thaylat district, where, as the U.S. commander, he managed a base of ten Marines and between two hundred and three hundred Iraqis.

At first, people distrusted the Marines. Many had lost relatives in the violence. People averted their eyes and walked on when they met U.S. soldiers. The streets were empty and garbage-strewn, and the souk was moribund. Mauro encouraged his men to build relationships with Iraqis. That meant getting used to new customs. As the platoon commander, he set the example by eating with Iraqis, seated on the floor and scooping up food with his hands from a common dish. He fasted for Ramadan and broke the fast each night with a different family. He bought livestock to be sent to the mosque to feed the poor. He observed that Iraqi men hug and kiss each other. These gestures contain no sexual innuendo, but they made the Americans uncomfortable. "As guests in their country, we just had to get used to it," he explained.

In order to stimulate economic activity, Mauro directed the men to buy all their supplies in the souk. As they saw Americans circulating freely in the marketplace, local people began to assume that security had improved. Little by little they ventured out to the stalls. Mauro worked with the local authorities to rebuild schools and get a dysfunctional hospital up and running. He negotiated with the elders to include a woman representative in the town council, something that had never been done before. At the women's request, the Marines and Iraqis worked together to start a transportation system and build a park. With State Department cooperation, they started a Grameen bank so that women could take out microloans and start businesses. At the time, I didn't know about these activities. I assumed he was still in combat.

Mauro's second tour ended in 2008. We celebrated at his favorite restaurant. He entered graduate school. Everything will return to normal now, I thought, but a year after my son returned, I was still sleepless, depressed, and prone to recoil at loud noises. I'd awaken during the night thinking he was still in Iraq.

"It's PTSD," my doctor Mary told me.

I laughed. "Impossible. He's the one who went to war, not me."

"You were there in your head," she said.

She explained to me that the psychological trauma caused by steady, intense worry can indeed trigger PTSD.

I didn't believe her. My ordeal seemed insignificant in comparison with those of other mothers. After all, my son was home and safe.

"Channel your emotions," Mary told me. "Get involved. Volunteer."

I didn't need convincing. I was extraordinarily grateful for Mauro's safe return and was already looking around for ways to express my gratitude. After checking the Georgetown website, I realized that my university had no apparatus to facilitate the transition of veterans to civilian life. I began visiting administrators, urging them to provide services to our veteran community. Around the same time, the student veterans themselves were organizing the Georgetown University Student Veterans Association (GUSVA). I became their faculty adviser, and began to take GUSVA officers with me when I paid my visits. These young men and women were smart and articulate, and they were speaking from their own experience. Working with administrators and faculty, we were able to establish a Veterans Office at Georgetown. When we started, there were fewer than two hundred student veterans on campus. Now we have over a thousand.

Mauro continues to be reticent about his war experiences, but he did allow me to interview him for an article.* Even then, though, he avoided topics he thought would upset me. On the other hand, often campus vets would plop down in my office and talk for hours.

"My son never tells me these things," I'd say to them.

"We never tell our mothers either," they'd respond invariably.

By listening to their experiences, I have come to understand to what extent the consequences of war extend beyond the casualty figures we read in the newspapers. One young man told me that his mother became so stressed she could no longer cope with marriage and left her unsupportive husband. Another spoke of a sister who had to be hospitalized. A female Army veteran described the trauma her children experienced when she deployed to Afghanistan. Although we have at last begun to take seriously the psychological effects of combat on soldiers, we rarely hear about their loved ones. Yet, the anxiety produced by the deployment of someone close can result in depression, physical ailments, even suicide.

I began to write stories based on these soldiers' experiences. Thinking back, I realized that all my novels deal at least tangentially with war—*The Deaths of Don Bernardo* with the War of the Pacific; *Frida* and *Lola in Paradise* with the Mexican Revolution; *Sister Teresa* and *I Am Venus* with the wars of religion in the sixteenth and seventeenth centuries. People tell me that I write effectively about war. Soldiers ask how I can capture the horror of battle without ever having been a combatant. But, of course, I have spent decades imagining war.

As I compose stories, I am able to step away from the horror and concentrate on the craft of writing. I am able to appreciate the beauty in the camaraderie among soldiers and the affection many of them express for their Iraqi counterparts. I can even see the humor in some of their situations—for example, the collusion of an officer and his men to rescue a dog. Listening to their experiences has enhanced my understanding of the challenges our veterans face when they return home and of the stress

---

* Bárbara Mujica, "Tours of Duty: A Mother's Story," *Commonweal*, June 9, 2009, 11–16.

their families endure. As a woman and a mother, I wanted to hear about Iraqi women. I imagined how *they* felt when their sons went to war, when their children were prevented from going to school or were kidnapped and abused as a means of intimidating the populace. Writing about war has enabled me to face and scatter my demons, to show that our soldiers do more than shoot and destroy, to connect with other military mothers and, through fiction, share their stories with an audience.

Although I bring to my current project some of the strategies I have used in my novels, writing about Iraq is different from writing about the Mexican Revolution or the Thirty Years' War. It is a form of catharsis that has freed me to heal and move forward.

Imagining Iraq

He spoke in a monotone, as though reciting a prayer learned in childhood, and he never looked me in the eye.

"We were in a little village outside of Al-Karmah," he began, "about sixteen clicks northeast of Fallujah. Karmah, ha! What a dumb name. It was the most violent city in Iraq."

"I thought that was Fallujah."

"This was worse. At least there's a wall around Fallujah. Here there was nothing. No protection at all. The bastards could walk right into town and attack our patrols. IEDs, mortar attacks, all that shit. We lost so many guys . . ." He fell into silence.

I sat there waiting. "Want some more coffee?" I asked finally.

"Nah . . . yeah, sure. Why not?"

I got up and took the pot off the stove.

He sipped his coffee slowly, as if reluctant to go on.

"Al-Karmah was an Al-Qaeda stronghold, a tribal safe haven."

Another pause.

"After the Awakening—you know, when the Sunni sheiks finally decided to work with the Marines instead of Al-Qaeda because Al-Qaeda was too fucking violent—things changed. People started to report the smugglers. We'd go into these little villages, and the people would tell us where the weapons caches were. A lot of them had lost family members to Al-Qaeda, see? Somebody didn't go along with what Al-Qaeda wanted, and the next morning the head of one of their kids would show up on their doorstep. They were brutal bastards, Al-Qaeda. They'd cut off kids' heads to intimidate their parents. I liked the Iraqi people well enough, the ones I met, but the terrorists, I never felt an ounce of regret about taking one of those guys out."

It was the longest snatch of language I'd heard from him since he'd moved in, and the first time I'd heard him swear. Corey Frater almost never talked, and when he did, he was polite and soft-spoken. If he said *damn* or even *jerk,* he excused himself first. "The guy was . . . excuse me, ma'am . . . but the guy was a real jerk."

I'd had a room to let, and he answered my ad. I liked him right away. A brawny young vet with blond hair, impenetrable blue eyes, and a square jaw, he reminded me of the men in the recruiting advertisements: "The few. The proud. The Marines." And he reminded me of my son Ignacio.

"Naturally," I said. "That was your job: to stop Al-Qaeda."

"Yeah," he said. "To stop Al-Qaeda."

He slouched down in his chair. His jaw tightened slightly, and I didn't know whether he was going to go on. The aroma of coffee filled the kitchen, giving the place a warm, cozy feel, but I knew he was a million miles away, in some godforsaken village on the outskirts of the inappropriately named city of Al-Karmah.

"It's actually a beautiful place," he said abruptly. He laughed. "When the sunlight glimmers on the river, it's breathtaking. Parts of the Tigris-Euphrates valley are so green. It's where the Garden of Eden was. Sometimes I thought, if I have to die over here, this is a good place."

A frisson shot up my arm. I wondered if my son had ever had that same thought.

"Sometimes we parachuted in. We'd sneak into a village at night to gather information. But that day we went in by truck. We made a lot of noise, too much noise. There were six of us—five Marines and a terp . . . you know . . . an interpreter, named Hakim. Except for the part that's irrigated, it's all sand. Sand everywhere. A great big sandbox. We called it moon dust. It was so fine and silty that it got into everything—under your nails, into your nose, into your skin. You had to be careful it didn't get into the engine because it could wreck your truck. We had to change air filters all the time." He fidgeted with a napkin and then sipped his coffee.

"We were supposed to move in for a few days and scout around. Who was with us, who was against, that sort of thing. We had intelligence that there'd been some insurgent-sympathizers in the village and that they'd hidden weapons somewhere. A favorite place was the school. If there were bombs in a school, you didn't want to go in because then they'd set them off and kill a bunch of kids. They knew the Americans didn't want civilian casualties, especially not children, so that's where they'd hide their hardware, the bastards."

I scrutinized his face for traces of anger, but in spite of his harsh words, he appeared composed.

Suddenly he sprang up. "I'm sorry, ma'am. I shouldn't be bothering you with this."

"You're not bothering me at all," I countered. "It's interesting. Please go on."

He hesitated, nodded, and then shrugged. I wondered what he was thinking. It was obvious he didn't like to talk about the war. Before then, I had no idea where he'd been, what he'd done. Now I learned that he was a staff sergeant, a recon guy in charge of a small team of Marines, and a master freefall parachutist. His specialty was dropping in behind enemy lines in the dead of night to gather intelligence with all kinds of fancy surveillance equipment.

"Have some more coffee, Corey," I said, getting up. "I have some blueberry muffins too. Want one?" I didn't want him to stop talking. My own son had never told me anything at all about the war, and I was ravenous for information. I opened a package of muffins and put them on a plate, wondering what it would feel like to jump out of a plane at 29,000 feet. Does your stomach float up to your throat? Are you terrified your chute won't open? Can you breathe normally? I speculated about whether Ignacio had ever plunged into enemy territory that way. I thought not. He was an infantry Marine. He strode up to a house and kicked in the door. At least, that was my understanding of things.

"This time we didn't parachute in," he said, as though reading my thoughts. "Of the five Americans, Jake was the only one who hadn't done this gig before, and he made me a little nervous. The rest of us, including Hakim, had been together for weeks. Each guy knew his job and everybody else's. Unless we met with resistance and got into a firefight or something like that, these operations usually went off like clockwork—especially now that the Sunnis were mostly cooperating. It was Jake's fault we made too much noise. I told him to slow the motor, to cool it, but he was determined to roar into town: 'We're Americans and we're here to save you!' That kind of shit. I was afraid he'd frighten the folks and cause bad feelings."

"Did he?"

"Yes, but not with the Humvee."

He sat for a moment staring into space, lost in the depths of his memory.

"Another muffin, Corey?"

He blinked and started, as though awakening from a trance. "A man came out to meet us. He was one of the village elders. In a community like that, a stranger draws attention. Hakim explained our mission to him and told him we'd be there for a few days. We were gathering information, and we needed a base of operations. Could he find us a house?"

I imagined the elder: a wizened old man with shrewd ferret eyes in a brown, lackluster face. I imagined him wearing a long, colorless dishda-sha and a red-and-white checked keffiyeh—the kind of headdress Arab men wear to protect themselves from the sun. (I knew what a keffiyeh was because Ignacio had emailed me pictures.) I conjured up the man's small but sturdy frame, his leathery skin, his dusty sandals, his gnarled hands reeking of sheep dung and aniseed. He stood enveloped in the implacable Iraqi sunlight against a blue, motionless sky, bereft of even a single languorous cloud. Ribbons of light reached out of the heavens and splintered into the distant Euphrates. I had spent years imagining Iraq, wondering what it was like to tread that silty sand under the relentless, blazing sun, carrying sixty pounds of gear on my back, plus weapons. My son had done it. Corey had done it. And with a mother's obsessiveness, I had created and re-created in my mind the experiences I thought they had lived through. But, of course, I couldn't know what it was like . . . not at all, not really.

"Was he angry, the elder?"

"He didn't seem angry. He showed us to the home of his son, Ali. He thought it would be appropriate for our needs, he said."

"His own son? How generous. He must have been on our side."

"By then, most of the Sunni sheiks were."

I hesitated. "Can you tell me what the house looked like?" I was afraid that if I asked too many questions, he would shut down again, and maybe this time he'd refuse to go on.

"It was pretty large for a rural house, but then, Ali was the son of an elder. When you went through the front door, you found yourself in a sizeable main room. That was the plan of most of the houses. Off to the sides were the kitchen and bedrooms. You could access the main room from any part of the house. There were no doors. Americans think privacy is a big deal, but Iraqis don't. The floors were concrete and there was almost no furniture. People sit on the floor to eat, the men first, and then the women and children. We looked around and decided the place was perfect for us. I asked Hashim to thank Ali and his father and promised we'd take good care of everything.

"Of course, Jake had to go and say something stupid. 'Nice digs for a bunch of towel-heads,' he said. There was another guy, Dave, a radio operator. He turned around to Jake and snapped, 'Shut up, you moron.' He'd taken a dislike to Jake from the beginning."

"Did you meet the family?"

"They were all there: Ali, his wife, Farrah, and four children. Ali was the one who talked to us, of course. He came out to greet us with his two little boys. I guess they were about nine and six or seven. The wife and two little girls stayed in the kitchen. The tiniest one—she couldn't have been more than three—hid behind a barrel and peeped out at us. She was the cutest little thing, with enormous brown eyes, puffy cheeks, and a captivating smile. Her name was Leyla. I wanted to pick her up and squeeze her. She and her sister, who was about five, would catch my glance and burst into giggles. I wished I had a teddy bear or something to give her. I put my hand in my pocket and found some candy—we always carried candy to hand out to the children—and the older girl tiptoed out of the kitchen and took it from me. Then she turned around and scampered back, shrieking with laughter."

Corey was smiling broadly. For a moment he had abandoned his reserve and let himself go. But then he drifted back into melancholy.

"It was a sheepherding area, and all the men were shepherds, so of course they had a dog. It was out in the pen, a beautiful herder, tan and black with huge brown intelligent eyes. It looked as though it were smiling at us. Iraqis don't usually get sentimental about pets the way we do, but a shepherd needs his dog, and Ali clearly loved this one. The family was going to vacate the house for us—they would be staying with cousins—but they were going to have to leave the dog behind. I never caught what his name was, but we called him Raj.

"David said we could feed him our MREs, since that's all that military grub was good for anyway. We all laughed, but then Jake made a crack about using the dog for target practice. Dave was really getting pissed. 'Shut the fuck up, you asshole,' he snapped. I'm sorry, ma'am, but that's the way Marines talk."

"That must have been awful for the family! Imagine having to hand over your house to a bunch of foreign soldiers."

Corey sighed. "I know. I felt terrible about it. And they were so gracious. Imagine, before they left, Farrah spent hours cooking. She left us enough food for a week! Even meat! And, you know, meat is a luxury."

I imagined Farrah, invisible under her long abaya, her head covered with a hijab, scurrying around her kitchen to prepare food for foreigners, only to have to abandon her house afterward.

"'Don't worry about the dog,' I told Ali when they left. 'We'll take care of him.' Little Leyla gave me a big smile and stuffed a fig into my hand. 'I think she likes you,' Ali told me. He said it in fractured English, laughing."

Corey took a sip of coffee.

"It must be cold," I said. "I'll get you a new one."

He shook his head. "Please don't bother, ma'am. Cold coffee's not the worst thing I've ever dealt with."

"Of course not, but . . ."

He wasn't listening. He'd slipped back into gloom. His dejection wasn't perceptible in his eyes or his mouth, but only in that slight tightening of the jaw—and the silence.

Suddenly I felt embarrassed. I had urged him to talk out of . . . what? Greed. Greed for what? Vicarious experience. I ached to know what I could never know: what it was like to be there. I'd been selfish, and I felt contrite.

"You don't have to go on," I said softly. "I can see it brings back bad memories."

He turned to me and shrugged. "No big deal," he said in that offhanded tone soldiers use when they try to convince you that something truly horrific hasn't affected them. "No big deal." The stoics. The real men. The tough guys. The few, the proud, the Marines. Ignacio used that tone too, when his best friend and future housemate got blown to smithereens by an IED.

"After they left, the dog became restless." Corey was clearly determined to finish the story. "He missed them, and he didn't like that strange people were living in the house.

"Dave went out to calm him down. 'It's okay, Raj,' he kept saying. 'Come on, Raj, let's play ball!' But we didn't have a ball, so he threw a stick instead. 'Go ahead, Raj! Go fetch it.' Gradually Raj got into it. He ran after the stick and brought it back a couple of times. Dave and I gave him some MREs and roared with laughter when he gobbled them up. Dave snickered. 'See?' he said. 'I told you that stuff wasn't fit for human consumption!'

"At dusk Raj grew distressed again. He paced and barked and whined. He knew something was wrong. Ali hadn't taken him out with the sheep, and the family hadn't come back from wherever they were. By nightfall the dog was miserable. 'Shut that fucking dog up or none of us will get any sleep,' Jake kept complaining. 'Put a blanket over your head, asshole,' Dave fired back.

"But by the third night, all of us were frazzled. Raj had a sharp bark that pierced you like a bullet, and his whining sounded like the howl of a coyote. He was driving everybody nuts, even Dave. All night long he yapped and yowled.

"But then, suddenly, the barking stopped.

"When I got up the next morning and went out to the pen, there was Raj, dead, lying in a brown pool of blood. Jake had put a silencer on his gun and gone out and shot him."

Corey's voice quivered slightly, and his eyes looked faintly swollen.

"I opened the pen and stood there looking at that poor animal, the one we'd promised to take care of. 'What the hell's the matter with you, you idiot?' I said to Jake. 'Why'd you have to go and kill the fucking dog? These people were nice to us! This could have been a productive experience, man. Winning hearts and minds and all that crap, remember?'

"Jake just stood there with a warped grin on his face. Suddenly Dave flew at him with a snarl. He punched him in the jaw so hard I thought he'd kill him. Jake stumbled and then went crashing into the sand. For a moment he didn't move. But then he pulled himself up. He gawked at us awhile and then burst out laughing. He just roared with laughter. His whole body was covered with blood and dog shit."

Corey pursed his lips and looked blankly at the opposite wall. "I'm sorry, ma'am. I shouldn't have told you. I don't know why I did."

I longed to reach out and squeeze his hand, but I knew better.

"It's just that . . . It was such a lovely family. They were so friendly, so anxious to cooperate. And then the fucking moron . . . sorry, ma'am . . . and then Jake goes and kills their dog." I sensed his rage, even as he struggled to regain his stoic demeanor.

"Thanks for the coffee, ma'am." He stood up, took his cup to the sink, and washed it, careful to keep his back toward me the whole time.

I grasped then what I hadn't before: Raj was the whole war—the lost buddies, the wailing children, the sudden explosions followed by intense darkness, the sirens in the night. Raj was the senseless death of innocents and the tears shed in secret by so many soldiers—Corey, Dave, Ignacio . . . all of them. Raj was the Iraq I just couldn't fathom, just couldn't imagine, no matter how hard I tried.

The Call

Every time Cándida López saw a strange car in the street, she reviewed in her mind the most efficient ways to commit suicide. If Riqui were dead, two Marines would knock on her door and recite some canned speech, the same speech they always gave when they told a mother her child had made "the ultimate sacrifice." Then they'd go out and have a beer. And what about the mother? Pills, thought Cándida. Just drop off to sleep and never wake up. Or carbon monoxide. "Too bad I don't know how to use a gun," she said out loud.

But what if Riqui were injured? There would be a call, probably from some hospital in Baghdad or the medical center in Landstuhl. A lot of the guys airlifted to Landstuhl never made it home alive. Or else they came back too battered to lead normal lives. She'd read all about it in *La Opinión*.

The doctor had told her to stop reading the news, stop watching Univisión, stop listening to the radio, but she was addicted. She checked the Net ten, maybe twelve times a day. Whenever a bomb went off or a plane went down, she got down on her knees and prayed. "Please, Holy Virgin, don't let it be Riqui."

"What's the point of checking the news?" her friend Carolyn chided. "All it does is upset you."

"I know," sighed Cándida. She felt enchained in a prison of helplessness.

"I heard about a grandmother who joined the Army," she told Riqui before he left. "She went over to Iraq to cook for the troops to be near her grandson. What if I did that?"

"Forget it, Mom!"

"Riqui . . ." Cándida felt as though a rough-edged stone were lodged in her throat. "You're my only son, my only child . . ."

"Everything will be fine, Mom. The guys all protect each other."

"*Dios te oiga, hijo.* I hope God is listening."

The phone rang. Cándida flinched. She stood there staring at the black object hanging on the wall as though it were a dead rat.

Finally, she picked up the receiver. "Hello?" she said.

"Hey, Cándida. It's Carolyn. You okay?"

Cándida exhaled in relief.

■

When she'd left El Salvador in 1985, the civil war was raging. The FMLA was ambushing anyone with a cow or a radio and putting a gun to his head. Private property was evil, they said. Whatever you had belonged to the revolution.

"We don't have to worry," insisted Cándida's husband, Ricardo. "We don't have anything they want." But he was wrong.

One night, as Cándida was putting the children to bed, she felt strangely uneasy. Suddenly, an explosion sent her reeling. There were only two rooms in the minuscule house, the bedroom and an all-purpose room for cooking, eating, and everything else. That's the room that had a door, and someone had shot it open.

"Hide!" she ordered.

Riqui, then three, dove under the cot, but it was too late for eleven-year-old Nélida. The soldiers—a gang of ragtag thugs who called themselves guerrillas—were already in the room. One of them grabbed the girl and pulled off her dress, while the others threw Cándida to the floor. Then they undid their pants and took turns.

When Ricardo got back from his Uncle Raúl's house, the first thing he noticed was that the chicken coop was empty. He stopped in his tracks and scrutinized the yard. Feathers and eggshells and human feces were strewn everywhere. Ricardo's temples started to throb and his fingers turned icy. The door to the house had been blasted to pieces. The pots and pans that normally hung on the wall were missing.

He found his wife hysterical and writhing with pain. His inert daughter was sprawled in a pool of blood. Cándida was babbling something—boys, rape, *Virgen María*. He couldn't make out the words, but he'd already grasped what had happened. Next to Nélida lay a shattered, bloodied statue of the Holy Mother. It had been the only object of beauty in the house. They'd smashed it over Neli's head, probably to silence her, or maybe just for fun.

Ricardo crumpled. Their beautiful child—her wide, tiger eyes; her smooth brown skin; her full lips and budding body.

They buried her in the village cemetery. Ricardo held little Riqui in his arms and watched his uncles and cousins lower the casket into the ground. He was a poor, insignificant man, but he wasn't going to let those brutes get away with this crime.

"I'm going to join the army," he vowed. "I'll take care of them."

"The government soldiers are just as brutal as the guerrillas," countered his cousin Juan. "What you need to do is get out of here. Find a coyote who'll sneak you through Mexico and over the U.S. border."

"Who has money for a coyote?"

"We could pool our resources."

"How much could all of us put together? Coyotes charge three or four hundred dollars a head." Ricardo inhaled on his foul-smelling cigarette.

"At least enough for Cándida and Riqui," said Uncle Raúl. "Or if not, you can borrow money from Tello. He's financed a lot of people. They pay him back once they get there. I hear you can make forty or fifty dollars a day in the U.S. A day! Imagine! You'll be able to pay Tello back in a couple of months!"

Tello was the owner of the only store in the village of San Teófanes. He sold everything from chicken feed to beer to ladies' panties.

Uncle Raúl lit a cigarette with trembling hands. His skin was as fragile and crinkled as a used paper bag and his fingers, as knotted as ropes. But his mind was sharp. Ricardo was listening.

"You owe it to your son. You have to get him out of here."

"What if they get caught?"

"The coyotes know all the secret routes. After Cándida gets settled, you can follow."

"Holy Virgin," moaned Cándida. But she knew Uncle Raúl was right.

■

She crossed the border stuffed into the hidden compartment of a truck, her son tucked under her. The driver put them on a bus to Los Angeles, where a Salvadoran woman named Vilma, who routinely scoured the station for newcomers, offered them a room for one hundred dollars a month.

"I don't have that kind of money," Cándida told her.

"You will," said Vilma.

The barrio streets were strewn with garbage, and the walls covered with lurid graffiti. Everywhere men who reminded her of the hooligans who had raped her and Neli hung around smoking and spewing obscenities. They made her shudder.

Vilma got her a job in a restaurant washing dishes. Riqui went too, because she had nowhere to leave him. At night, she attended English classes at the local church. That's where she met an Ethiopian woman named Aisha who told her about a family in Beverly Hills that was looking for a live-in nanny.

"Get out of this neighborhood before it's too late," said Aisha. "Before the gangs get to your boy."

"He's just a baby."

"Exactly. There's still time."

Cándida had just escaped from a war zone, but the barrio was a war zone too. She took the nanny job.

"Stay in touch!" said Vilma when Cándida moved out. "Come eat tamales and *pupusas* with me on Sundays."

"I will," Cándida assured her.

And she did. She wasn't in the least homesick for San Teófanes, but she loved the familiar aromas of Vilma's kitchen. She loved hearing her local dialect and catching up on news. Vilma's little group gave her a sense of community in this new and alien country.

Beverly Hills was like some sort of fantasy—blocks and blocks of manicured lawns, soaring palm trees and crimson oleanders, driveways with exotic automobiles. Janine McGovern, Cándida's employer, was an attorney with too much to do, so it was up to Cándida to get the children off to school and care for the house. She and Riqui had their own room with a bathroom and a toilet that flushed. Before long, Riqui was in a neighborhood school free of marauding gangs. Everything would be fine, thought Cándida, as long as she could stay out of sight of the immigration authorities—*la migra*—and didn't do something stupid like apply for refugee status. Mrs. McGovern had told her that less than 3 percent of the Central Americans who applied got it. By applying, you only attracted attention to yourself.

"Sorry," she said. "Even though I'm a lawyer, I can't help."

In two years Cándida had learned passable English. "Don' forget you mat' book!" she called to David, Mrs. McGovern's ten-year-old son, when he left for school.

She took a second job in a little beauty shop on Beverly Boulevard, shampooing the heads of elegant ladies on Saturdays. She needed the extra money. She was saving up to bring Ricardo to Los Angeles. It was at the beauty shop that she met Carolyn, a beautician with frizzy blond hair and a heart of gold beating under an enormous bosom.

Every month, Cándida sent a money order to Tello to pay off her debt, and another one to Uncle Raúl to ease his burdens. Uncle Raúl couldn't write, but Tello occasionally sent a note with news from the community. Juan's wife had just had a baby girl. Raúl had bought a cow and two goats that he watched like toddlers. Ricardo had joined the army, and no one had seen him in months. Cándida went to church and lit a candle for her husband.

"*Virgen*," she prayed, "even though they abused you in our house, please don't abandon us."

Eventually the letters stopped coming. By now Cándida had paid off the debt to Tello, but she was still sending money orders for Uncle Raúl. She tried to call—telephone service was now available in San Teófanes—but no one ever answered.

She explained the problem to Vilma, who promised to ask around.

It took a few weeks, during which Cándida prayed a lot and cried a lot. When the answer finally came, it was devastating. Government troops had overrun San Teófanes, ransacked Tello's store, stolen Raúl's animals, and shot everyone but the few folks who had managed to flee. Now there were phones, but no one to answer them.

"And Ricardo?"

"Nothing about Ricardo."

"He might be dead."

"He might be," said Vilma matter-of-factly. "After all, it's a war."

"I will never, ever let my son go to war," said Cándida.

■

By 1992 the conflict in El Salvador was over. Thousands of Salvadorans headed back home, but Cándida decided to stay put. She'd left Mrs. Mc-Govern a couple of years before. Carolyn had convinced her to study for her high school equivalency diploma and a beautician's license. Standing over fussy ladies for hours at a time, mixing dye, combing curls, remembering who had just gotten a divorce and who'd vacationed on the Riviera was exhausting, but Cándida didn't complain. She had a little apartment in Santa Monica and a used Toyota. If only it weren't for *la migra*, she could relax. But *la migra* was a constant worry. What if they popped into the beauty shop and dragged off all the illegals? It would be a nightmare for her, of course, but also for the owner, who had been kind to her. And what about Riqui, now in fifth grade and more gringo than *guanaco*?

One day in 1997, Mrs. McGovern called her. There had been a terrible earthquake in Central America, and the U.S. government had passed a relief act allowing undocumented Nicaraguans and Salvadorans to stay in the country.

"Now I can get you a green card," said Mrs. McGovern.

"Well," said Cándida to herself, "I've been through my own personal earthquake, so maybe I qualify."

"Any news about Ricardo?" added Mrs. McGovern.

"No, ma'am. Nothing."

■

Cándida had just gotten up and turned on the radio when the blaring voice of the newscaster announced that a plane had rammed into the World Trade Center in New York. Cándida assumed some amateur pilot had swiped the wall. *"Idiota!"* she said out loud.

She switched to the music station, where they were playing *"Ni tú ni nadie."* Cándida hummed along, lost in her calculations of Riqui's school expenses—he had just begun classes at Santa Monica College. Suddenly, an announcer interrupted. A second plane had flown into one of the towers, he said, and a third was headed for Washington, D.C.

Cándida felt her stomach tighten. She remembered things. A presentiment of danger. An explosion. Guerrilla thugs stomping through the house. Neli's screams. The statue of the Virgin crashing to the floor. "No," she whispered. "No."

A few months later she returned to the apartment to find Riqui in the living room with a Marine Corps recruiter. "Oh, God," moaned Cándida. *"¿Qué es esto?"*

Riqui had grown into a handsome boy. He'd have been tall in El Salvador, but here he was average height, about five feet ten inches. He had the same tiger eyes as his sister, the same wide brow and smooth brown skin. His black hair draped over his forehead seductively. He grabbed a shock in his hand and smiled broadly at his mother.

"Take a good look, Mom, 'cause the next time you see me, I'll have a buzz cut!"

"You just started college, Riqui." She was struggling to stay calm.

"This country gave us a home, Mom. And now we're at war."

Cándida started to sob. "But we're not citizens," she said finally.

The recruiter, a tall black man with a no-nonsense demeanor, gazed over her head. "He's nineteen years old and a legal resident, ma'am. He can sign up."

The recruiter left. Riqui sat on the table, legs wide, eyes twinkling, already with that cocky Marine grin.

She had to admit she was proud. But she was also scared, so scared she felt nauseous.

"Listen, Mom," said Riqui, suddenly serious, "a long time ago . . . back there . . . you protected me. I couldn't defend you . . . or my sister." His voice was gentle. "But I'm never going to let anything bad happen to you again."

Cándida was still sobbing, and shivering like a sparrow in a winter wind.

"Look," said Riqui. "I'm going to show you something."

He went into his room and came back with a paper. Under the image of an eagle with outstretched wings were the words "U.S. Citizenship and Naturalization Services." He pointed to the text he had highlighted in yellow: "Special provisions of the Immigration and Nationality Act (INA) authorize U.S. Citizenship and Immigration Services (USCIS) to expedite the application and naturalization process for current members of the U.S. Armed Forces and recently discharged members."

"You see, Mom? If I serve, we can become citizens. No more worrying about *la migra* or renewing green cards."

"Don't do it for me, Riqui. I'd rather live in the shadows forever."

Days later the phone rang. When she thought about it afterward, it felt as though the whole scene had taken place in slow motion. It was the call she'd been expecting—and dreading. An official was calling from San Salvador. Ricardo was dead, he said. No details. That was the end of it.

Cándida steadied herself against the wall. Now her son was going off to war. Would there someday be another call? She had already lost her daughter and her husband. "Oh, Holy Virgin," she prayed, "watch over him."

The sleeplessness started even before Riqui left for boot camp. During the day, Cándida dozed on her feet. At night, she lay awake for hours, calculating Riqui's chances for survival. So far, only thirty-seven U.S. soldiers had died in Afghanistan. A tiny number. But if it was your kid who got hit . . . She started taking Excedrin PM—first one, then two, three, four. When she did fall into a fitful sleep, she dreamed of bombs and burning tanks. During the day, she contemplated suicide.

"Honey," said Carolyn, squeezing her shoulders, "you have to get some help." Furrows had formed over Carolyn's brow and around her eyes, and her chin had grown spongy. But her hair was still blond—she knew how to apply hair color, after all—and she was still as kind and caring as ever. Cándida thought she was lucky to have her for a friend.

The doctor wrote a prescription for Ambien, but it didn't help. In March 2003, the United States invaded Iraq, and in August, Riqui announced that he was being deployed. He was full of bravado. Lots of loud music and talk of kicking ass.

Cándida became morose and obsessed with the news. She began to suffer from shortness of breath. She prayed, but found no relief. Gloom clung to her like an ugly black leech. Strangely, at the salon, no one but Carolyn knew anything was wrong. Cándida somehow kept up appearances, even though she felt as though she were suffocating.

Every day, she emailed Riqui. Weeks went by without a response.

"Sorry, Mom, I've been working," he explained when he finally called her. He made it sound as though he were shuffling papers at an insurance office.

It was late January 2004, and she hadn't heard from him since Christmas.

"They'll notify you right away if I'm dead," Riqui had joked. "If you don't get a call or a visit, don't worry."

Every time she heard about the death of an American soldier, she felt guilty because she felt relieved. It was a relief that it wasn't Riqui, but awful that some other woman just like her would be mourning.

She felt guilty about other things as well. Riqui had put his life at risk to protect her. To get her citizenship, so she'd never have to worry again about *la migra* or the green card. "Don't bother about me, Riqui," she whispered into the shadows. "Just stay alive."

One night she took more Ambien than she was supposed to and then lay in bed staring into the dark.

The jangle of the telephone jolted her upright. A call in the middle of the night! She gasped for breath and clutched at the receiver.

"Hello?"

There was no one.

"Hello?"

Still, no one.

Cándida sat in the dark, hyperventilating. The digital clock with the bright-green numbers read 1:32. Finally, she hung up.

She spent the rest of the night waiting for the phone to ring. "They'll call back," she told herself. But they didn't. The same feeling came over her as the day Vilma had told her that Ricardo was probably dead. She was certain, absolutely certain, that this would end the same way.

But then, after a month, Riqui called.

"Are you okay?" Cándida asked breathlessly. "The phone rang one night . . . I thought . . . something might have happened."

"No, nothing has happened." His voice sounded decisive.

They chatted a few minutes about nothing, and then Riqui asked suddenly, "When did you receive that call?"

"January . . . it must have been around the twenty-fifth. It was 1:32 in the morning. I'm certain about the hour."

Silence.

"¿Hijo?"

"No, nothing." He said good-bye and told her not to worry, the way he always did.

But Riqui knew what had happened on January 25. It was a day he would never forget. Lieutenant Metzer had sent him to a town outside of Ramadi rumored to be harboring an al-Qaeda operative. His instructions were to observe what he could. He was to carry a military-issue cell phone with him to keep Metzer informed. He and four other Marines started out early in the morning, but right before they arrived, Riqui realized he didn't have the phone. He tried to remember where he'd left it. He thought back over the last few hours and recalled giving it to one of the Iraqi interpreters to make an authorized call. He thought the man had given it back, but now he wasn't sure.

At 11:32 a.m.—1:32 a.m. in Los Angeles—Riqui López's phone set off a bomb in Ramadi that killed one Marine and left three critically injured. Riqui would have been a casualty too if Metzer hadn't sent him on that mission. Riqui should have died that day. Somehow, the phone called his mother. How it happened, Riqui couldn't explain.

When Riqui left the Marines in 2006, the first thing he did was apply for U.S. citizenship. As soon as he got it, he could sponsor Cándida. One night, he took his mom out to dinner and told her the story about the phone.

Cándida felt as though the hand of God were stroking her cheek. "It was the Virgin calling to let me know you were okay," she said. "Only I didn't know how to interpret the message."

"Yeah, Mom," Riqui said, biting into a tamale. The truth was, he didn't know what to think. "I'm sure that's it."

Christine Evans

CHRISTINE EVANS (Australia) is a professor of performing arts at Georgetown University and a playwright, novelist, and librettist whose work focuses on war. Her plays have been produced in Australia, the US, the UK, Canada, Austria, and New Zealand. Selected production highlights include *Closer Than They Appear; Trojan Barbie; Weightless; Mothergun; Slow Falling Bird;* and *My Vicious Angel.* Playwriting honors include the 2020 George A. and Eliza Gardner Howard Foundation Award, the Jane Chambers Playwriting Award (2007), Plays for the 21st Century Award (2009), and the Rella Lossy Playwriting Award (2004). Her verse novel, *Cloudless,* was published in 2015.

Why I Write about War

The renowned Serbian theater company Dah Teatar says that it makes work "in dialogue with our times." This suggests an evocative way forward through the many pitfalls of socially engaged theater, the first of which is the diatribe. "Dialogue," by contrast, suggests flux, adjustment, and scope—a back-and-forth between artist, audience, and the complexities of "our times." It summons the difficulties, contradictions, desires, and terrors that ghost any profound conversation. And, in war as in love, timing is everything: Dah Teatar was birthed during Serbia's war of aggression that eventually tore Yugoslavia apart. This accident of timing— the collision of these artists with "our times"—irrevocably shaped the dialogue toward peace and complexity that the company has sustained in the twenty-five years since.

In a similar, if more cushioned, way, my life collided with another war of "our times" when I relocated to the US from Australia in 2000 to study playwriting at Brown University. One year later, two planes crashed into the World Trade Center, and the country slid into a disastrous and weakly justified war. The timing of my arrival, when everything about America was new and strange (and therefore visible, in a way that habit erases) forced me to grasp the interconnectedness of international events. The US invasion of Iraq pulled strings in Australia: my own country went to war in support of the Bush administration's invasion. Subsequently, greatly increased numbers of Iraqi, Iranian, and Afghan asylum seekers washed up on Australia's shores—often fleeing the very wars that the US, followed by Australia, had precipitated. In a chilling foretaste of wider international practices, they were demonized and detained indefinitely in hellholes in the desert while their claims for asylum were reviewed.

All of these events were made possible by rhetoric; by the ways the war and the people in it were framed.

This is why we need art: *to imagine things otherwise.*

■

I read Eliot Weinberger's magnificent prose poem "What I Heard about Iraq." I noticed the disappearance of Iraqi fates from the pages of the newspaper, and the foregrounding of tales of US soldiers. I noticed that journalists were "embedded" with US troops instead of reporting independently from the invasion zone—with a very few honorable exceptions, such as Anthony Shadid, of the *Washington Post.*

I noticed that the US had, for the first time, stopped counting the Iraqi war dead and refused to release images of the coffins of returned dead American soldiers.

This seemed ominous: bodies that disappear from public view also disappear from public memory. I remembered that Euripides (incidentally, a foreigner in Greece) once had a job tallying the foreign war dead. Afterward, he continued counting the bodies by creative means, bearing imaginative witness to those overlooked in classical drama: the women; the enslaved. I felt compelled to attempt the same.

The first full-length play I wrote on these themes, *Slow Falling Bird,* is set in an Australian immigration detention center and explores the dreams, fears, and white-nationalist fantasies underlying the terror of "floods" of refugees, arriving by water, in the driest continent on earth.

My next, *Trojan Barbie,* is a kind of car-crash collision with Euripides's *Trojan Women:* Lotte, a lonely English doll repairer, visits contemporary Troy on a tour for singles, only to find herself flung into a prison camp for women with Euripides's characters: Hecuba; Helen; Andromache. The two worlds—modern and ancient—barely recognize each other, and their fates are gruesomely distinct: my English tourist is rescued by the British embassy, whereas the "local women" are driven off in a truck and never heard of again.

I wanted these two distinct experiences of war—that of the English tourist and that of the women whose country is invaded by a superpower— to vibrate together in the same picture until the frame breaks.

As Judith Butler writes in *Frames of War*, the act of framing can itself be an act of war. To frame an event is to make it intelligible; it's also to shape the picture by virtue of what's left out. This means that simple reportage on events is an insufficient artistic response; it's not what we know but how we frame it that matters. I see my writing about war as an attempt to break the frame and reorder its contents so that what's usually left out—the women, the children, the civilians, the people who are not American—can come into imaginative focus.

My most recent play about war, *Closer Than They Appear*, directly stages the obscene and orchestrated separation of conjoined events: The fate of a US Iraq War veteran in therapy for post-traumatic stress is interwoven, in the same animated landscape (projected from the therapy tool Virtual Iraq) with that of a teenage girl, Zaynab, who blogs from Fallujah in 2003. For Michael, my US veteran, the landscape of war is a painful memory; for Zaynab, it is her actual home, under mortal siege.

The play published in this volume, *Greetings from Fallujah*, is a short mono-drama excerpted from this longer work, featuring this teenage girl. Zaynab wouldn't leave me alone; she demanded to have her own play, so here it is. She kept whispering to me:

Imagine
This could have all been different

Greetings from Fallujah

A ten-minute solo play in seven blog posts

CAST: Zaynab: An Iraqi teenage girl, blogging from Fallujah in 2003–4. She's Sunni, but not particularly religious, from an educated professional family. Smart, playful, full of life.

TIME & PLACE: Fallujah, Iraq, 2003–4.
Zaynab's lounge room, where she blogs to the world from her home— increasingly a war zone.

STAGING: This play could be performed in a bare space, with everything suggested by language and lighting shifts. Or it could be done with sophisticated projection design to suggest the landscapes and world of Fallujah. There are opportunities to create a world of echoes (recorded/live sound) and to mix live and recorded video.

ANACHRONISM: Though video blogs (vlogs) weren't around in 2003, I've taken poetic license in making Zaynab a vlogger.

POST #1

(*Crackling noise. We see Zaynab checking her webcam, trying to get online. And then . . . ta da! It works!*)

ZAYNAB: Wow. Finally online. It's been so bad this week. Electricity is off half the time. And we're all jammed in here with a sick baby. At night she turns into a baby demon and howls.

And I'm stuck at home because school's closed because of what happened to the Christian students. A group of men got hold of three girls after school and pushed them around because they dressed like sluts, that's what they said. So now—here I am! Trapped with my family!

Anyway, this will be short because Nasir and Mahmoud are both nagging me for the computer. They are really driving me crazy— Mahmoud always does, he's thirteen, but Nasir isn't usually this bad. Aunt Morouj, Cousin Nasir, and the baby are here because their house in Baghdad got blown up last week. So the house is crammed, everyone's on edge. Mornings—with one bathroom and nine people—we're all just trying not to scream at each other. My mother does scream sometimes. And the baby never stops.

(*In Arabic*) All right, all right! Give me a minute, I'm coming! (*In English*) So. Don't send us more soldiers. Send us some toothpaste instead. And soap! And candles, but not the ones that smell like food. (*Turning*) All right! I'm coming! (*A parting shot*) And men's deodorant!

POST #2

ZAYNAB: Online! Hello, Earth. Greetings from Fallujah!—Nasir is really annoying me. Today we've had electricity for four hours and he's been online for three of them. He wants to play war games online, can you believe it? Just go outside if you want to play soldiers, Nasir, I said, and he yelled at me and said I didn't know anything about the real world. And then he was mean about my essay prize.

I got an essay prize at school, we had to write about heroes. Everyone else did Ali Baba and Scheherazade but I'm bored with them, so I picked Hercules. Zeus's wife made him go insane and murder his own wife and children. And then he had to fight monsters as punishment, but it wasn't even his fault, the goddess just struck him to get revenge.

(Beat)

Everything's about revenge now, the car bombs and snipers and kidnappings and it's really hard to know who's doing what. The mud is getting wetter, that's the only thing that's clear.

Anyway, in my essay Hercules restores the ancient canals of Baghdad and the water gardens all bloom again. My dad says that Nasir and I will rebuild the country just like my Hercules, *he* liked my essay. *After it's smashed to bits,* said Nasir, he's so rude. He always talks about our "past glory," blah blah. He wants to be an engineer but he can't even finish school now so he just boils with rage instead. Dad told him, *be patient, the Americans hop around like fleas, they'll find a new adventure soon and leave us alone.*

—*Ha ha, just like Hercules,* I said. *Oh, so the Americans are your heroes?* said Nasir, then he stormed out. Even though it was nearly curfew. Nasir makes me sick sometimes. And Dad's worried about him too, I can tell.

Nasir was in the protest at the school last month, against the Americans using it as a base. That was very bad. The soldiers hid on a roof and shot at them. Everyone was screaming. Hundreds of people got hurt or killed.

Nasir saw people killed and his friend Khalid got shot in the leg. And then two days later there was another protest and they killed people again. So he's an idiot to go back out there.

Especially after dark.

(The light slowly fades. Zaynab looks around anxiously.)

Post #3

ZAYNAB: May 16, 2003. Hello, Earth, Greetings from Fallujah. Are you still out there? Anyone?

(Beat)

Tonight is the full moon! We can all see the moon. The same moon, all over the world. That's strange.

Well, you know what we did? We had a moon picnic! We were all in this strange mood, it's been quiet lately and we're not used to it, so my Aunt Morouj suddenly says, let's have a moon picnic! We all looked at her like she was crazy—she is sometimes—we can't get soap or candles but there's a huge market in Prozac—but no, she was laughing and said, let's go up on the roof. And suddenly everyone went crazy!

Dad dug out the blankets, I made my date and honey cakes, well we didn't have dates or honey but I put sugar in and they were still divine, and we went up on the roof. No bombs, no guns—a car backfiring made Mahmoud jump, that's all. Even Nasir was in a good mood, he was home for once. He made my aunt laugh talking about how he'd rebuild Baghdad with space-age robots and solar power—oh, listening to Nasir is like a roller coaster.

(To us, confidentially) He is not sensible like me and Mahmoud.

Tonight everyone was happy. The moon was so beautiful. And everyone, even Nasir, said my honey cakes were good. And that made me feel like crying. Because in truth they fell apart, they were just semolina and sugar cooked in an oven that kept shutting off so they weren't even cooked through.—Oh, and here goes the electricity. I can see the lights shutting off so I'm probably next.

(Blackout. The sound of cheerful Arabic pop music, then static.)

Post #4

ZAYNAB: Hello, Earth. Greetings from Fallujah. The mud is getting wetter every day but Al-Chalabi says the situation is "calm and improving." Huh. We've all been cooped up here and the baby demon cries all the time. The boys still go out, Dad tells them not to, but my cousin Nasir does what he likes now and Mahmoud follows him. And I have to stay here with my crying aunt and her crying baby and my mother who is taking Prozac by the fistful but won't give *me* any and nobody can go near the windows since the car bomb last week.

I hate babies. I'll never have a baby, especially in a war.

Anyway, things reached boiling point when the baby screamed and screamed, I was looking after it while Aunt Morouj slept, I shook it just a little bit to see if I could scare it quiet, but Auntie saw me and lost her mind and started shouting and slapped me, and I cried and my mother cried and my Dad said the house was full of howling females so he yelled at us to shut up.

So I decided to do Mahmoud's job that he has stopped doing and take out the garbage, just to breathe my own lungful of air. I was in a very bad mood and wishing the baby and Nasir and my aunt would vanish back to Baghdad, but they can't because their stupid house was bombed. Anyway, I stomped over to the garbage. It stank and it was overflowing so I wanted to hurry, but then I noticed a big round thing in the bin. It looked like a watermelon but it was reddish-purple, not green. I poked it with a stick to see what it was and it rolled over and I saw.

It was a boy's head. I felt completely calm, as if I was made of ice. I noticed the green-blue bruises on his cheek. How young he was, his top lip soft and downy above broken teeth. The curl of brown hair on his forehead. He was like a flower, truly, a little crushed but beautiful. His green eyes were open and they looked straight into me.

And then I realized. It was Khalid, Nasir's friend.

The furnace of Fallujah rushed back into my lungs and I retched. I ran back inside and couldn't talk, I just locked myself in the bathroom until I could stop being sick.

What kind of world is this? What did Khalid do? He looked right into my eyes. And I saw . . .

I am so, so, terrified of what Nasir will do when he finds out.

Aunt Morouj says we mustn't tell him.

But that's one of the things I saw in Khalid's eyes.

Nasir will find out.

And then we will reap the wind.

(*Static*)

Post #5

ZAYNAB: Greetings, Earth. Allahu al adheem. I don't know what to do, I don't know what to do. You hear that crying? It's my mother. It's my mother. It's my fault. I looked the wrong way, always Nasir, Nasir, Nasir. But Mahmoud is only thirteen. Was. My little brother! I can't think straight. Our hearts are burning to ash. Why? He just sold DVDs! He didn't have any enemies! Nothing makes sense.

And worse is to come. Yesterday they burned the bodies of the American mercenaries. They dragged them from the truck and hung them up on a bridge. Everyone says the Americans will take terrible revenge. All the men have to leave or they will be killed as fighters. Dad says we have to pack for the village right now. But my mother wants to stay and die in her own house.

If I could find the man who shot Mahmoud, I would tear him to pieces.

Write to me. No, don't write. Say prayers. Tell them people live here.

POST #6

ZAYNAB: April 3, 2004. Greetings from Fallujah. This might be my last blog. It's very strange—I feel outside of my own face. Like I'm watching myself on TV.

Is anyone out there? Are you going to watch us die on Fox News and CNN?

You should tune in to Al Jazeera. They get much better pictures of civilians.

Our TV's not working. The water's shut off. It's very quiet. The others are sleeping, I don't know how they can. I haven't slept in three days. But it's a relief that they're quiet. When Aunt Morouj and baby demon are awake, they *both* cry all the time now. Thank God, we can still get Prozac.

We shouldn't be here. We should have left. But Nasir has disappeared. My father went to find him.

That was two days ago. We don't know what's happened to them. So now it's just me, my mother, and Aunt Morouj and the baby. And it's too late to leave. All the roads are blocked off. The city's crouching. Nothing's moving. There's just this terrible waiting. Like rats in a cage.

I'm watching myself, a girl, in this fishbowl. I have that calm ice feeling again that I had when I found Khalid's head. But this time it's Nasir looking at me—I can feel it.

Nasir has such beautiful eyes.

The moon will rise again. Everything does. *Safra tawila.* I'm so cold.
(We hear footsteps running up the road, and up the stairs to the house.)
—Oh God, someone's coming. I have to put my scarf on.
(She looks in the camera/mirror/out to the audience, worriedly adjusting herself. A loud sound of the door smashing in. Zaynab turns. A frozen moment. White light. Blackout.)

(A moment, then static. Zaynab appears again, very calm, in a ghostly light. Her movements are slow. Perhaps she is doubled with her own projection. She smiles at us, gently. When she speaks, her voice has an echo, or delay, as if broadcast from very far away.)

POST #7

ZAYNAB: Hello, Earth. Greetings from Fallujah.

Can you see the moon . . . from where you are? All over the world. People see the same moon.

The moon will rise again. Everything does.

How strange.

Safra tawila. I'm so cold.

Tell them . . . people lived here.

(Zaynab's projected image lingers as Zaynab [live] slowly backs away and disappears. Then the image fades to black, too.)

End of play

Nancy Sherman

NANCY SHERMAN (USA) is a professor of philosophy at Georgetown University and was the inaugural Distinguished Chair in Ethics at the United States Naval Academy. The focus of her research is military ethics. Her books include *Stoic Wisdom: Ancient Lessons for Modern Resilience* (2021), *Afterwar: Healing the Moral Wounds of Our Soldiers* (2015); *The Untold War: Inside the Hearts, Minds, and Souls of our Soldiers* (2010); and *Stoic Warriors: The Ancient Philosophy behind the Military Mind* (2005). The selection below is taken from *Afterwar: Healing the Moral Injuries of Our Soldiers*.

Why I Write about War

My introduction to the psyche of the soldier goes back to my father and my childhood. My dad was a World War II vet who never talked about "his" war, though he carried his dog tags on his keychain for more than sixty-five years. I found them when I was cleaning up his effects the day he died. I was the closest of daughters. Yet somehow I never saw the tags all those years. Clearly, the war had never left him; he took it to the grave, but he always felt that his burden was private. And I suspect I obliged him. You might say we had our own "don't ask, don't tell" policy.

In time I came to realize that the burden of that policy was just untenable. No service member should lock up his war experience for most of his or her life. The burden ought to be shared some way. In my own case, I must have been unconsciously waiting for the right moment to start sharing his war. And thankfully, it came before he died.

It happened when I was appointed the first Distinguished Chair in Ethics at the U.S. Naval Academy in the mid-1990s. I was brought on to help "morally remediate" 133 midshipmen who were implicated in the biggest cheating scandal in the Academy's history. Shortly thereafter, I would help set up an ethics course for all midshipmen in their second year. I had been an academic for most of my career, focused on ethics and the emotions in ancient and modern philosophy. I also had a background and research training in psychoanalysis. But this was the first time in my life that I was a civilian academic in a military world. Although I was among officers and my dad was enlisted, I began to understand a bit more about his secret world. And he felt I now had the right street "creds" to make it safe for him to open up more. I started teaching and writing about the moral challenges of going to war and returning home. I have been immersed in that research ever since.

The issues couldn't be more urgent for a nation now fighting endless wars for almost two decades. The issues are especially urgent for service members and veterans struggling to understand whether their wars are just, how killing in war that appears discriminate and proportionate may nonetheless not be if the overall ends of war or interim goals for which they are fighting aren't. Indeed, they struggle with how to understand moral responsibility when moral conscience pits them against role duties and norms that don't easily tolerate moral skepticism or quandary. The justice of a war and its conduct is never easily decided, before or even after the fact. But that doesn't condone moral withdrawal, given the gravity of the subject—killing and the probability of being killed.

Soldiers whom I have interviewed over the years often talk about the guilt that they feel about eliminative killing or collateral harm or bad luck or losses that seem preventable after the fact. They are hounded by "could'ves" and "should'ves." Others speak of the moral dilemmas that come with displacing populations or toppling governments and leaving a vacuum for a more despicable regime than the incumbent one. Still others try to sort out the moral aftermath of fighting in areas where it is next to impossible to spare civilians or distinguish between a human shield that is voluntary or coerced. Others speak of command betrayal; many women speak about a patriarchal military that hasn't fully accepted women and doesn't take seriously sexual assault and harassment. The moral challenges of soldiering have always been complex. But they are increasingly so in the twenty-first-century asymmetric battlefield. Moral anguish is never magically lifted by insight and understanding. Nor should it be. But greater conceptual clarity about the moral terrain can play some significant role in helping to move beyond psychological and moral paralysis. Conversations that are both personal and substantive, and woven into friendships built on empathy and trust, can morally heal.

Much of my work in the classroom and in public lectures is geared toward building that trust in a way that can help disentangle the moral complexity of war. I view my work as not simply a contribution to war ethics but as a way of helping service members and civilians together understand the inner wars that can rage for years before it feels safe enough to speak. Destigmatizing post-traumatic stress (whether military-related or not) is an absolutely critical part of the healing process. But the diagnosis of PTS, and its treatment, typically involving some form of cognitive behavioral therapy and deconditioning, often eclipses moral injury. For PTS is a psychological injury primarily to do with deeply conditioned fear—a hair-trigger responsiveness to perceived overwhelming life threat. The sensitivity is hard to turn off once turned on. But while it's lifesaving on the battlefield, it isn't necessarily so at home when thunderclaps become gunshots, and potholes in neighborhood roads sure signs of buried Improvised Explosive Devices. PTS symptoms of hypervigilance, social withdrawal, and nightmarish flashbacks are familiar. They are harrowing, and those who suffer from them can try to turn them off by self-medicating with drugs and alcohol.

But moral injuries—injuries to do with perpetrating, suffering, or witnessing real or apparent moral transgressions (as well as a sense of massively falling short of moral ideals)—are not, at their core, fear responses to threat. Rather, they are responses to morally salient circumstances expressed in guilt, shame, a sense of betrayal, resentment, moral indignation, and the like. Desensitization is not the way to treat this kind of anguish.

The above moral emotions are what philosophers call "reactive attitudes." They record and express a sense of moral accountability. Some of the reactions can be misplaced, grandiose, aimed at only apparent violations that fail to track objective wrongdoing. Others track real transgressions. Some who suffer morally hold themselves strictly liable for outcomes for which they are not culpable. Others fail to take responsibility for the wrongdoings they have done. All this is reason to engage in moral philosophy with those who are eager and ready to reflect on their war experiences or learn from the experiences of others who have gone before them. And so listening to veterans and service members, helping them sort through the moral dimensions of their experience, has been central to my work as teacher and author. The idea is not to judge but to create a safe space for putting words and concepts on thoughts and mental states locked up deep within because the pain of feeling and acknowledging them is often too great.

Since my time at the Naval Academy, I have written something of a trilogy of books about going to war and coming home. *Stoic Warriors* (2005) grew directly out of my experience at the Academy. When I taught at the Academy, the Stoics resonated with midshipmen and officers alike. It was *their* philosophy. To survive the deprivations of military life required "sucking it up." Stoicism was just the ticket. Epictetus, the slave philosopher of the first and second centuries CE, became a folk hero of sorts. He was already known to some. Epictetus's short handbook *The Enchiridion* was the book that helped the then young naval officer James Stockdale survive seven and a half years as a POW in the "Hanoi Hilton," two years of which were spent in solitary confinement mostly in leg irons. (He served as a POW during the time that John McCain did.) Stockdale was to become the senior member of the chain of command of American POWs, and he told me during my lengthy interview with him that he endured by remembering Epictetus's Stoic tonics: "Some things are up to us and some are not . . . And if it is about one of things that is not up to us, be ready to say, 'You are nothing in relation to me.'" He had memorized *The Enchiridion*. It was his salvation in years of sucking it up in torture.

Yet despite Admiral Stockdale's legacy in establishing a place for *The Enchiridion* in all of the military academies, few trained in the academies knew other Stoic texts or redactions, even those highly accessible, such as the ones by Marcus Aurelius (himself a general), Seneca, or Cicero. In *Stoic Warriors,* I argue that this richer set of resources is critical for showing both the blessings and curses of being a Stoic. The book has had wide appeal not just within the military but also in the business world, where Stoicism has become its own self-help movement. The *Untold War* (2010) followed, as I started to see many of those I had formerly taught now coming home from war and morally anguished. In some cases, the issues had squarely to do with interrogation techniques and an American policy that condoned torture. *Afterwar* (2015), my most recent book, continues the mission to listen to service members and veterans tell their stories and, when apt, to help them probe the moral contours of what they have seen and done, or left undone.

I have listened to those stories with the ear of a philosopher and psychoanalyst but also with the ear of a daughter who always felt that she needed to understand more about what her father went through. In these works, I have aimed to write in a voice that steps outside the academy—and to be accessible to folks like my dad who lived through war but didn't analyze it academically. I wish to talk accessibly about visible and invisible wounds of war and ways to heal. And so I take up such topics as moral injury, PTS, resilience, military suicide and its prevention, military honor, guilt, and shame. And I do so always guided by the voices of those I have interviewed.

As I write these words in 2020, I am reminded that my incoming students at Georgetown have never lived in a United States that has not been at war. Still, few know those who have gone to war. The university must be a place for both sides to come out of their bunkers.

Due to my training in ancient philosophy, my work in military ethics is also always, in some fashion or other, informed by the ancients. *Stoic Warriors* relies heavily on the texts of the ancient Stoics who give us rich resources for filling out a Stoicism that might actually help us psychologically. *Untold War* and *Afterwar* draw on the philosophy of emotions and its connection with moral injury and repair. I am convinced that you cannot have a substantive conception of moral injury unless you appreciate the special class of emotions and emotional expressions through which we hold ourselves and others morally accountable.

It should not be surprising, given my interest in the ancients, that Sophoclean tragedies about war figure in my work. *The Philoctetes* and *Ajax* are brilliant, "safe" texts that remind us that the moral hazards of battle are age-old. Those plays once staged in giant amphitheaters in ancient Greece, written by the military general that Sophocles himself was, and performed for civilian and military alike, are homecoming plays. They are designed to show how the most decorated, valorous soldier can feel so dishonored that he takes his life (as Ajax does on stage at the tip of his spear); or how a sailor can struggle as a pariah after being marooned by his command, alone on an island in the Aegean for ten years (as Philoctetes was because of a fetid leg wound that made him a military liability at sea). These stories told onstage had impact then, and continue to do so, now. They serve as critical reminders that the humanities remain a way to help heal the warrior psyche, in part, by being brutally honest about the moral costs of war on all those caught in its web.

Moral Injury: In a Different Voice

A Deer in Hunting Season

In late 2005,* "Sally,"† then twenty-two, deployed to Iraq from an Air Force base in the Midwest. The walk into the chow hall each day was a routine reminder of her perilous state as an attractive woman in a predominantly

* Excerpt from chapter 5, "Rebuilding Trust," in Nancy Sherman, *Afterwar: Healing the Moral Injuries of Our Soldiers* (New York: Oxford University Press, 2015), 105–10. By permission of Oxford University Press, USA. I am deeply grateful to Katherine Ward for her assistance in formatting this excerpt for this volume. In this abbreviated version of the original piece, most endnotes and citations have been removed. Refer to *Afterwar* for complete notes and references.

† "Sally" is a pseudonym. The interviewee asked that her name not be disclosed. I interviewed this Air Force service member in June 2012.

male and fairly sexist military. "I would walk in and everybody would stare at me," she said. "I felt like a deer in hunting season." She felt guilty relief when another woman would come on base, and eyes were redirected. What particularly upset her was that officers led in the staring: "The first ones that I noticed ogling me were the commanders, the higher officers, and after two seconds, they would look down or look away. So they are feeling kind of ashamed, and they know that they all have simultaneously reached that point in ogling and feel like, 'I shouldn't be doing this.'"

Sally wasn't the only woman I interviewed who told me of the chow hall ordeal. "When I would go into the dining room, I mean *everybody* is looking at you. There will be tables of guys elbowing each other: 'Hey, check it out,'" a mid-level Air Force officer told me on a recent visit I made to give a talk at the Air Force Academy. The leering wore on her, though she was no stranger to that kind of gender-drenched environment. In 2003, she was a freshman cadet at the Academy when it was roiled by sexual harassment and assault scandals. She now teaches there and sees an all too familiar pattern of sexism persisting in many of her classes and pervading life on the base, in subtle and not so subtle ways.

In Sally's case, downrange, her officers' predatory leers inspired little confidence in their leadership: "When all else fails, they're who I should be able to go to with problems . . . but they're having a hard time, just struggling with my presence." Still, she felt conflicted throughout her deployment, and afterwards, about whether she was empathetic enough toward many of the males and took seriously enough their sense of sexual deprivation. She worried that she was putting her own fears before their needs. "We're sexual creatures, I understand this," she told me. "So, I'm sure in an all-male shop the sexual urge was a little bit more rampant and the frustration dealing with that built up . . . I think I always fought with whether I was compassionate enough for them . . . I always struggled with how much I could put up with, and how much I couldn't."

Two harassment incidents forced her to turn to her superiors for intervention. In the first, a unit member began to stalk her, spreading rumors that they were sleeping together. Given the daily chow-hall ogling, she was "already hypervigilant; then, on top of that, I had to look out of the corners of my eye all the time to see if someone was following me. It was really stressful." In a second incident, she noticed that her underwear went missing while she was doing her laundry one day. She had stepped outside the laundry area to take a break for a few minutes; when she returned to fold the dry clothes, her panties and bras had vanished. She felt embarrassed and exposed, and ashamed even to have to write to her mother to ask, without explanation, for a care package, not of goodies but of a new supply of underwear.

After the theft, she decided it was time to report what was going on to her immediate supervisor, a male NCO (noncommissioned officer). Though she was reluctant to burden him with her problems in the midst of a war, and especially embarrassed to have to expose the "weird" underwear theft, she felt threatened and needed help. It got to a point, she said, where "I just couldn't take it anymore." We might say that she took a stab at trust.

Trust and trustworthiness are irreducible elements in the fabric of military life. They are the glue of any good military and are key to the willingness of battle buddies to fight and die for each other. Ordinary trust is the confidence that people won't betray you or waylay you in an alley or fail to bring you your soup, if they're your waiters. The bar is obviously higher for battle buddies than for waiters and diners. And yet trust is constantly tested in war among those who are supposed to be one's archdefenders. Betrayal by command or peer or institution is all too common a theme in military life and a significant cause of moral injury. The residue of those betrayals is part of the long afterwar in need of repair, in part through the renewals of trust at home.

The issue can be especially acute for women in the services, at home and abroad. Overall, women make up about 14 percent of the active-duty force, and on some bases abroad during the recent conflicts, they have been only 2 percent of the personnel, or 1 in 50. Betrayals in war zones can leave women with a profound sense of isolation, unprotected on American bases in a foreign enemy's land. On ships, where battle can quickly turn internecine in the absence of an outer enemy, women often feel especially alone and at risk. Trust's call, so critical to a band of warriors— that one can count on a buddy to cover one's back—falls on deaf, and sometimes hostile, ears. The reasonable expectation that battle buddies will be trustworthy, motivated by goodwill, respect, or conscientious performance of duty—or more minimally, interest in reputation bound up with being regarded as trustworthy—is too often violated. Systemic biases underlying gender betrayal in the military, including sexual assault, harassment, unwanted contact, and inequities in prosecution, have been slow to be exposed, and only recently have made their way to the Senate floor, with proposals and responses of service chiefs. High-profile cases expose a broken judicial system and ill-thought-out responses to political pressures that can make worse the inequities.

It is not just *women* who are abused sexually inside the wire. In a recent report on sexual assault, the Pentagon estimated that 26,000 service members experienced unwanted sexual contact in 2012, up from 19,000 in 2010. Of those cases, 53 percent involved attacks on men, mostly by other men. This should not be surprising, given that men make up the bulk of the force and predatory sexual behavior has long been a form of bullying and entertainment in an all-male force. When I taught at the Naval Academy in the mid-1990s, the masculine entrenched environment made life for some of my women students desperately uncomfortable. A more recent high-profile sexual assault case at Annapolis, and campus-wide shunning of the female accuser, suggest that patterns of sexism have not changed much in twenty years and may even be more entrenched now than then. Given the difficulties for victims of sexual abuse, male and female, to come forward, the statistics likely underreport the incidences. Victims are left to suffer with shame and humiliation and trauma that are often overlooked in favor of more traditional combat exposure trauma.

But what the public debate presumes is that we all understand well enough what trust is and how to rebuild it. I don't share that presumption. Given how critical trust is within the military and to reentry at home, it warrants our careful scrutiny. In this essay, we listen to several female service members and the serious challenges to trust that they face. And we listen to an ancient Greek male warrior whose willingness to trust the Greeks after a massive betrayal gives general insight into the conditions necessary for trusting again.

Why Trust Others?

I conceive of trust as what philosophers call a "reactive attitude," which involves an implicit or explicit call to a person that you are holding him to account, with a normative expectation of an appropriate reply. Specifically, it is a summoning of another to recognize that you are in need or dependent in a specific way and require attention or assistance in that domain. In a most general sense, it is an exposure of vulnerability to another of one's finitude as a practical agent, with the expectation that the other will be responsive. Trust is as basic to the military as forming a cadre.

But why think you can trust another, especially when you lack strong beliefs that the other won't let you down? Why should a trustor trust a trustee to do something?

Consider Sally again. In coming forward, Sally might think, this man may be no more concerned about my well-being than my harassers. But in his role as supervisor, he is *constrained* to help me, and if he cares at all about compliance and conscientious fulfillment of his duties, then he should behave reasonably. In the philosophical literature, some have objected that this line of thought amounts more to *reliance* on another person than real trust (where reliance is a predictive notion that could be answered by the workings of a machine, stable patterns of nature, or a person's dependable psychological habits). Trust, in contrast, is a normative notion, an expectation based on a belief about how people *ought* to behave toward you, given your normative standing or status. Specifically, it is an expectation of another's genuine interest in your well-being or dignity. As one philosopher has argued in important early work on trust, trust is the expectation of another showing you goodwill. But while conscientiousness may be a thinner kind of moral (or normative) motive, it still seems to ground a kind of trustworthiness. Indeed, in Sally's case, knowing that her supervisor is motivated by conscientiousness in taking care of his troops might be enough for her to feel she can count on him. In this regard, conscientiousness as motivating trustworthiness works like goodwill. It is just part of my role as a conscientious teacher to be responsive in various ways to my students—and so, too, a doctor toward her patients and, similarly, a first-line supervisor toward his soldiers. His job just is to take care of those under his command.

The rub, of course, is that in practice, in the context at hand, an entrenched male military, what constitutes the ideal of a conscientious commander is often laced with deep-seated bias and built-in institutional prejudice that can harm and disadvantage women and other minority and marginalized groups. (The issues can range from sexual harassment and assault [of women and men alike] to gender "naiveté" with regard to hygiene requirements that can mean downrange port-a-potties that can't handle tampon disposal and stench.) The more general point is that social norms can compromise positive responsiveness to need, whether the responsiveness is in the form of goodwill (respect and benevolence) or a blander conscientious performance of duty. Each alike can be blind. On their own, they are abstract ideals that don't necessarily meet the needs and capabilities of real people in concrete cases.

Others have argued that the ground of trustworthiness has little to do with moral motives, thick or thin, and reduces simply to self-interest. To be regarded as trustworthy by others satisfies a person's basic need for self-esteem: We desire and take pleasure in each other's good opinions.

And being trusted is one such important opinion. The "cunning" of trust, as Philip Pettit puts it, is that it takes a motive that might be thought of as problematic and tames it for its social capital. In a parallel vein, another author argues that it is in a trustee's own self-interest to maintain a trust relationship and so in her interest to "encapsulate" the trustor's interests within her own. Trust banks on that confidence: "You can more confidently trust me if you know that my own interest will induce me to live up to your expectations. Your trust is your expectation that my interest encapsulates yours."

But while it may be useful at times to ground trust in another's self-interest, relationships built on mutual self-interest (such as utility, as Aristotle argued long ago in cataloguing different kinds of friendships) tend not to be all that stable: "The useful is not permanent but is always changing," he reminds us. Self-interest is a wobbly ground for friendship, in part because what's in one's interest doesn't always coincide, or coincide for long, with the interests and needs of another. Similarly, self-interest is too transient a ground to motivate stable trust. Self-advantage can pull apart from what others are counting on one to do. And when it does, and prevails, trust and trustworthiness give way.

This is the backdrop for thinking about Sally's narrative. Imagine for the moment what she was probably hoping: that her interaction with her supervisor would be trusting in the sense that he would show her some goodwill. In coming forward, she is hoping he responds to her with genuine interest in her well-being and with an acknowledgment that she has been mistreated and threatened. Her trust overture may well be tentative. It's as if she is asking her supervisor, implicitly, if she can trust him before she trusts him. We do this kind of thing all the time when we make general inquiries: "Can I ask you a question?" is sometimes the preface to asking a question. What we are trying to do is establish our listener's standing, or maybe "instate" it through some prep work. We roll out the substantive exchange slowly so that we can build confidence in a partnership. In *deciding* to come forward, Sally is doing some of this. She's setting up a meeting, asking her supervisor to make time, asking him, in a way, to warm to the idea of being interested in her well-being and her personal safety on base.

Once they meet, his goodwill toward her would be communicated in just that kind of responsiveness, adapted, of course, in the way that attitude always is, to our personalities or temperament and professional codes of conduct. But the point is that goodwill is normatively expected.

But so, too, is conscientious fulfillment of his office as a good supervisor, role modeling by example, and setting the right kind of nonsexist tone for the command climate within his unit. When she exposes her vulnerability, she in essence is saying, "I'm counting on you. I can't handle this one on my own." The interaction, ideally, puts in motion a reflective loop: he knows that she is counting on him, and she knows that he knows, and so on. As Aristotle might put it, building on a metaphor from the ancient Greek Stoic Chrysippus (280–207 BCE), and preserved by Seneca in his account of the mutual interaction in benefit and gratitude: Each "does not fail to notice" that the other "has properly thrown and caught [the ball] from one pair of hands to the other." That mutual acknowledgment ought to reinforce the supervisor's sense of being held accountable and of Sally's holding him accountable. But she might also think about his potential trustworthiness in more strategic terms, as we've said: that it's in his basic self-interest to care about her opinion of him, and that of other women on base who, if he responds well, may come to view him as a trustworthy advocate and good leader.

However, from my conversations with Sally, it's clear that she didn't ever develop that kind of trust toward her supervisor, or other senior officers, male or female, for that matter. (There were no female officers in her unit, and the one female officer outside her unit was well above her rank and outside what Sally viewed an appropriate reporting chain.) In short, Sally never got the sense that her supervisor was particularly responsive to her. In the case of the stalker incident, he did step in and mediate. But in the case of the underwear theft, he wasn't particularly empathetic or much interested in following up. He didn't seem to think it threatened her in any serious way or made her feel less safe in a war zone. In the end, she relied on her supervisor in only a perfunctory way; she never felt like she was being cared for in the way that noncommissioned officers are supposed to "take care" of their troops. The suspension of trust exposed an irony not lost on Sally: "I remember I did seek service with a chaplain . . . and he happened to be a captain. One of my complaints was that I didn't feel like I could trust any of the officers. It was an awkward moment, because I'm telling an officer I don't think I can trust officers!"

In the end, in the absence of trust, she became self-protective. She "androgenized" herself, she said—never wore makeup and cut down on her use of shampoo after receiving flirtatious comments on how nice her hair smelled. "You just don't want to look pretty. You want to be clean. But that's it." And she began carrying an unconcealed knife to meals, clipped to her wallet and slung around her body on a string.

TRUST AS REPARATIVE

Sally's bid at trust was not successful. Her resentment and fear on base went unabated. She never got the reassurance that what happened wouldn't be repeated. Her wariness toward many of the males around her triggered a backlash of defensive hostility and more reactive vigilance on her part. Her supervisor did little to improve the climate. A year or more after her deployment, she was still cautiously working out "trust issues" back home: The knife was "only an Iraq thing," she told me. "I now carry mace in my car. For the most part, civilians take care of their sexual needs. And I have good enough judgment to know how to keep myself away from the wrong people." By and large, she was amazed at how much more easily she could breathe on a large coed university campus that had near gender parity in its student population. Her sense of being routinely toyed with as a woman was beginning to lift.

Put all this into the language of expressed reactive attitudes, the manifest attitudes by which we hold each other accountable as members of a shared moral community: expressed resentment is moral address mediated through anger. We react with hurt and pain to something that has been done to us that violates due regard or a norm, and we sanction the transgressor through blame. Resentment demands recuperation of respect and goodwill in a negative way, through direct or second-personal reproach. Indignation is a third party's reproach toward those who have injured you. In one sense, it is moral protest *on your behalf* for an injury against *you*; in another sense, it is moral protest more globally for an affront against *one's shared humanity.* Either way, it involves the kind of intervention and empathy Sally hoped she would inspire in her supervisor, in even the faintest way, when she came forward.

But of course we hold each other to account in positive ways, too, as I have been arguing throughout, and we build partnerships and engagements through more reparative forms of moral (and normative) address. Resentment sometimes paves the way for it. In a formulation used earlier, the "preventive fantasy" in retributivist attitudes is the thought that the other *might have* acknowledged me. There was room and reason in another's deliberations for a different, more positive response and regard.

Trust makes good that fantasy. As another philosopher has put it well, "the sought-for 'answer' to being 'addressed' in the mode of resentment is 'be assured, trust again.'" This is to say that trust can be reparative. To loosely repurpose Nietzsche's idiom for *ressentiment,* trust is a *positive* "reactive pathos." It is a positive attitude of holding another accountable that may work to undo resentment.

While resentment looks primarily backwards, *reacting* to what another has done, trust along with hope looks primarily forward, imagining and *projecting.* Trust is anticipatory, and broadly speaking, takes the form of a confidence (albeit often mild or weak), or an expectation about a person that falls short of sure belief and that involves some exposure to vulnerability and risk-taking. When expressed and explicit, as we have said before, it signals to the other that one is counting on her to recognize and respond to one's dependency or entrustment in a certain domain. We are counting on her to be responsive to our trust and to mirror that trust through trustworthiness. Granted, as we've noted, there are often backward-looking (reactive) reasons that support one's forward-looking projection of trustworthiness in another, such as past evidence of goodwill or solidarity or conscientiousness. Still, in trusting, one takes a gamble. That is especially so for Sally. She comes forward hesitantly in a way that so many victims of sexual harassment and abuse do. She fears she won't be taken seriously or believed, and that talk of bras and panties will seem like girly patter. She's not playing along in the "bro" game. Still, Sally takes a chance in summoning help. It is clear that she is not asking for a moral bludgeoning against the stalker or underwear thief; reparative trust can be built on empathy. Empathy goes a long way—in this case, by the supervisor showing that he "gets it," understands why she might feel unsafe, inside the wire and not just outside. If she trusts, in part, it is in order to bootstrap trust with a trustee who hasn't yet fully earned it. Even if she fails, she reasons that she needs to take the risk—treat the supervisor *as if* he's trustworthy and responsive to her call. She doesn't begin by wearing the knife. That comes after.

"He Gave Me His Hand, but Took My Bow"

Let us now enter the realm of Greek mythology and take up another complex tale of testing trust. The trust trial comes in the aftermath of a massive betrayal by command, a festering resentment, and an entreaty to trust again by an emissary of the group who betrayed. The strange trust relationship I refer to is that between Philoctetes and Neoptolemus in Sophocles's tragedy *Philoctetes*. The case has little on its face to do with women in the military. But it has everything to do with betrayal and abandonment, and the bootstrapping of trust afterwards. And in this regard, it speaks to women and men in the services who may suffer betrayals by command, or by political leaders, or by public and private institutions of all sorts, or by civilians too ready to say to a service member, "I just can't imagine what you've been through" and so perpetuate the myth that the military are made of different stuff from the rest of humankind, and that their experiences and traumas are somehow unfathomable and unspeakable. That remark is part of an implicit call and response, antiphonal to a service member's own defensive retreat, "You wouldn't understand, you weren't there." From both sides, the remarks conspire to create a romantic view of the warrior class that too easily lets civilians off the hook and invites isolation and betrayal by distance.

Our tragic tale has to do with profound isolation and betrayal. But before recounting the story, it is important to remember that Sophocles (496–405 BCE) was himself a Greek general whose plays, like *Ajax* and *Philoctetes*, were public reentry rituals of sorts performed before returning veterans. They served as a public homecoming, or *nostos*. The audience would likely include top brass in the front rows, and hoplites, or foot soldiers, in the upper reaches, in an amphitheater that could hold some 15,000. The audience knew war all too well. Sophocles was writing in a century in which there were seven decades of war. The reenactment, or *mimēsis*, of betrayals by command, awful separations from family and home, abandonments due to war-incurred disfigurements, and psychological maladaptations were among the themes. But so, too, especially in *Philoctetes*, was the theme of repair through trust and hope. The audience learning from the suffering (and growth) onstage, through the cathartic and identificatory emotions of pity and fear, could, as Aristotle teaches in the *Poetics*, engage in their own healing from war.

The story will be familiar to some readers. Philoctetes is a Greek warrior marooned for ten years on the island of Lemnos, abandoned by his Greek commanders as they headed on to Troy. He was left behind because of a fetid foot wound he suffered as the result of a bite from a poisonous snake guarding the tomb of the goddess Chryse. Shunned by his command and by a fleet that couldn't tolerate the putrid smell of his mutilated foot or the constant shrieks of his anguished wailing, he was left to die with his "weeping disease." But ten years into his solitary confinement,

Philoctetes, or more properly his bow, becomes critically necessary for the victory of the Greeks against the Trojans. And so Odysseus, trickster and cunning speechifier, enlists a boy warrior, Neoptolemus, with the right credentials and ancestral lineage (he is son of the deceased and glorious Achilles), to do Odysseus's and the Greek army's bidding. The two arrive at the island, Odysseus keeping out of sight as he coaches Neoptolemus to capture the bow through a snare of trust: "You know I could never speak to him as you can / He will trust you, and you will stay safe."

Like a good military interrogator, Neoptolemus is to build trust in order to exploit it. Of course, it is not intelligence that he will gather, but the "unassailable weapon" itself. He is to say that he too has a grudge against the Greek commanders for not holding him worthy of inheriting Achilles's arms. And from that sense of shared *ressentiment,* Philoctetes will begin to make himself vulnerable to Neoptolemus's overtures. He will begin to trust.

The trusting at first seems odd. Why should Philoctetes trust this young stranger who has pulled in from Troy and arrived so mysteriously on his island? Moreover, is it trust or just desperation that disarms him of caution? For he is miserable and lonely, and above all else craves safe passage home. He longs for human contact, and after a decade of solitary confinement thirsts for any news a messenger can bring of the battlefront and the fate of his fellow soldiers. In light of all this, is he just too ready to gain a friend, as a possible meaning of his name suggests ("he who gains a friend")? Trust is an attitude born of dependency. But when the need is abject and the power others have over one is near total, trust is manipulated, not given. Indeed, as I said, Neoptolemus's narrative of betrayal by the Greek commanders might be seen as an ancient version of a rapport-building technique that a good interrogator uses. The good interrogator develops an intimate and empathic relationship with his subject, and may even sow the seeds for an erotic or idealizing "transference" onto himself that can then be exploited for further domination and advantage: Neoptolemus rehearses plausible grounds for rapport: "Abused and insulted, I am sailing for home / Deprived of what is rightfully mine / By that bastard son of bastards, Odysseus. / I hold the commanders accountable. / Philoctetes is moved, as planned. / We share a 'cargo of common grievances,' he says. / 'You and I sing the same song.'"

The trust is coerced by faked trustworthiness, or at least trustworthiness fashioned with bits and pieces of truth, designed to ensnare. That is the hoax, a kind of Trojan horse rolled onto this island, once again engineered by the wily Odysseus, with the "young warrior" Neoptolemus (which is just what his name means) being initiated by his side in the sorts of treachery often morally permissible in warfare, though typically not directed against one's own. But is there any genuine trust and trustworthiness displayed in this play? Is there trust and trustworthiness that is not part of an intelligence scheme? There is. But it has to be developed. And its manifestation is critical for Philoctetes's moral repair from the double moral betrayal he suffers by his command (the first in the original abandonment by his commanders, the second in this trumped-up trust hoax). The power of trust in this parable, and the fact that it comes into being in the very moment of a potential massive betrayal, is an object lesson, albeit an idealized one, of trust's generative capacities.

The pivotal moment comes when Philoctetes, persuaded to leave the island with Neoptolemus and set sail for what he believes is home, gathers his few belongings, including his famous bow. Eager to get his hands on the bow, Neoptolemus asks to see it. Without the slightest reluctance, Philoctetes begins to entrust Neoptolemus with the very bow that has kept him alive on this island, protected from predators and provided with food. "I will grant your wish. There's nothing I wouldn't do for you," obliges Philoctetes. Neoptolemus gently demurs: "Is it allowed [themis]? If not, I will relent." Philoctetes assures him that it is permissible, and more importantly, that he trusts him because he has shown him goodwill and kindness. In that, he says, he mirrors Philoctetes himself, who received the bow from Heracles as a gift for his own demonstration of kindness.

There are two wrinkles in this passage, and they mislead about what is most fundamental in the trust exchange. The first is the apparent worry about background norms, implied by the question of whether it is right or permitted to hold the bow. Can he, Neoptolemus, really hold this sacred bow? Will it offend the gods? Is it okay to touch it? Is Neoptolemus really concerned about acting in conformity with a divine norm, or is he just exhibiting fake decency in order to mask his intention to steal? I suspect it is the latter. But whatever the answer, the basic trust isn't grounded in Philoctetes's expectation of Neoptolemus's compliance with some external norm. Rather, I want to argue that it is essentially grounded in the interaction itself—in Philoctetes's calling out to Neoptolemus saying, "Look. I'm counting on you as competent here. I'm counting on the idea that you'll take seriously my dependency and be responsive to it in your own reasons for action." Moreover, that trust is projective. The trust is expressed here as a way of trying to elicit trustworthiness from Neoptolemus. It scaffolds trust, nurses it along, and helps it to grow through the expectation that he ought to be trustworthy. That is part of trust's cunning and perhaps why, at times, it can create not just trustees but also dependents, manipulated into collaboration.

The second wrinkle is that Philoctetes's own remarks bury this point. He suggests that his trust is based on his anticipation of Neoptolemus's continuing to show goodwill and compassion toward him in his suffering. Neoptolemus has become a "priceless friend," and friends act out of goodwill and benevolence. I can trust my bow with a friend, he thinks. He won't steal it. He won't "stab me in the back," as we would say. But even in this kind of case where trust imputes goodwill to the trustworthy, there is something more basic going on. Philoctetes is telling Neoptolemus that he is counting on him. And that expectation can itself, at times, motivate. So Philoctetes assures Neoptolemus, "Don't worry [*tharsei*, have confidence], the bow will be yours to hold / And then hand it back to the hand that gave it." He piles on additional reasons for his trust, namely friendship, goodwill, and compassion. And they too, no doubt, can incentivize and bring Neoptolemus around. But in a barer, more minimal way, Philoctetes is fostering trust simply by projection of his trust, implicitly saying, I'm counting on you to keep safe the bow and then give it back. Being responsive to another's dependency is the bare bones of trustworthiness.

Moreover, in this staged case of trustworthiness, though Philoctetes presumes Neoptolemus's goodness, we as audience have an ironic distance that Philoctetes does not yet possess (and will have only in retrospect). We know that despite the fact that he seems genuinely moved by the islander's suffering, Neoptolemus is still in the employ of Odysseus, and his goodness, even if native and genuine, may just be instrumentally deployed here. So we are suspicious, rightly, from our position of knowledge, that his antecedent goodness or good name is doing any work here other than that of ensnaring his prey.

But, despite this, it would be hard to come away from this scene without seeing a genuine spark of trust and trust responsiveness being kindled. What we see, and probably what Philoctetes also picks up in Neoptolemus's response, is that he is answering an address to be trusted and trustworthy. He is responsive to the address, "I am counting on you." And recognizing that he is being so addressed, and acknowledging it, however thinly, back to Philoctetes, adds a new level of being counted on by him. Put differently, Neoptolemus's "catching the ball" is the first step in the reciprocation. And that acknowledgment, that one is being counted on, is then thrown back and caught by the trustor in a way that reinforces the trust.

There is much more to say about trust and trustworthiness in this play. Neoptolemus insists repeatedly on his trustworthiness with respect to the safekeeping of the bow, and his sincerity seems to grow the more he is exposed to Philoctetes's excruciating suffering. Philoctetes's utter dependency on him makes it hard for Neoptolemus to carry through with the plot. And he opts to return the bow to Philoctetes rather than continue as Odysseus's lackey, despite the consequences for the mission. It takes a *deus ex machina,* in the form of Heracles, to resolve the plot and assure Philoctetes that his (and the bow's) return to Troy will bring both victory to the Greeks and the cure for his noxious wound.

So goes the plot. The take-home lesson is that in this story Philoctetes, though traumatized by betrayal, still reaches out through trust, and thereby elicits trustworthiness in a potential enemy bent on subjecting him to yet more betrayal. Part of the work is done by the cunning of trust and not just by Philoctetes's generous and resilient spirit or by Neoptolemus's potential compassion, pity, and remorse. These other factors no doubt play an important role in a richer trust relation that can be read into this play, but I don't want to over-moralize the story or lose sight of a ubiquitous, more easily available form of trust that is also part of this story. I am keen to show what a basic display of trust itself can sometimes do, by calling out that one is counting on another to do something (or be competent in a certain domain), and how the fact of dependency may become a compelling reason in that other's deliberations. Whether it is an overriding reason is another matter. And what Neoptolemus must do is to figure out precisely what Philoctetes is counting on him for and whether he can comply in a way that minimizes conflict with his other important standing obligations, including trust relations. But the general point is that expressing trust can bootstrap trustworthiness. It projects onto another a normative expectation that can have causal efficacy.

Trust from the Bottom Up

But trustors, of course, need to be wise and make their addresses to those who are plausibly competent to aid and assist in the domains that are relevant. And those who are competent also need to signal their competencies, and in some cases contribute not just interpersonally but also institutionally, through networks of support. In the case of returning veterans, there can be a familiar shutting out of civilians, even family members, as potential recipients of trust: those who don't put on the uniform don't know what war is like. The resentment toward a civilian "Thank you for your service" can carry just that thought. And the retreat of veterans to their own circle gives permission to too many civilians to withdraw or believe that it is meddlesome or presumptive to think one has something to offer in helping a soldier process war's effects. But that's a myth that needs to be debunked by both sides.

I myself may have once, in a significant way, been complicit in perpetuating the myth. And the insight speaks to a more general point about elicitations of trust responsiveness. As I have said in earlier remarks about my interest in writing about war, my dad was a World War II veteran (an Army medic) who died several years ago. I was left to clean up his effects in the hospital room. And in putting away his belongings, I found his key chain, with his dog tags (Army identifications) attached. They were well worn, and his name, "Seymour Sherman," was just visible. They had been touched and rubbed and fingered for some sixty-five years. My mother said he had carried them during their whole marriage. But I never noticed them before, and he never showed them to me. Perhaps it was a case of willful ignorance on my part, and willful concealment on his, a "don't ask, don't tell" policy of sorts. But his war experiences were by and large not something to be shared with his children. They were his private burdens, not ours. And we complied. Despite the remnants of World War II in our house—what I remember best was the pile of scratchy brown-green Army blankets that were spare bedding in our hall linen closet—we didn't talk about the war and how it could have affected my dad—or, for that matter, all my uncles who also served. It was taboo.

I mention this because many returning veterans do feel, as my dad did, that the inner landscape of war is for soldiers and not for the civilians to whom they return. Why spill out the gore or the doubts or ambivalence to one's innocent family? War is a moral maze about killing and being killed, about liability to lethal and nonlethal harming, about the boundaries of wartime and peacetime, and adapting to the fuzzy boundary crossing. The most resolute Marine may still wonder if he did enough to prevent harm to innocent civilians or avoided undue risk to his troops. Guilt, shame, and a sense of betraying others can easily commingle with adrenalized pride, bravado, and the overwhelming sense of purpose and meaning that participation in war, even an unjust or imprudent war, can offer. The psychological and philosophical mess is hard to untangle and

easy to wall up. And there is a certain comfort in thinking one is protecting others, innocent others, from one's toxins. But it comes with a
price—of alienation and isolation. In this regard, Philoctetes becomes
a bold metaphor for the anomie of a veteran, war-wounded, resentful,
still "at sea," alone. Philoctetes's homecoming (*nostos,* in Homeric idiom)
is all too uncertain—will he come home and in what condition? How
will he be seen? How will he reenter? We are now bringing home the
remaining service members from the longest war in American history. It
should not surprise us if many return with "nostalgia," meaning literally,
in this seventeenth-century, Greco-derived medical term—homecoming
pain (*nostos algos*).

And yet Philoctetes heals, or at least begins to. And so he is also a
remarkable symbol of the power of transformative trust and how it can
bootstrap trustworthiness in the right set of conditions. Trust embeds
hope, hope *in* others, that they may be responsive to one's need. Philoctetes pleads to Neoptolemus: "Have mercy, my son . . . Don't let it be said
in scorn that you tricked me . . . You're not a bad lad, but I think you've
been trained by bad men." He invests "parental" hope in the youth; Neoptolemus can overcome the bad influences. And even if his empathy is
a bit out of sync at times, misattuned, and subjecting Philoctetes to fresh
soul wounds and narcissistic injuries, even if there are many good reasons
for him not to risk more vulnerability, the price of that protection is high
and at the cost of connectivity with self and others.

Sometimes those who signal competence and interest may be representatives of important institutions responsible for key policy changes and
the behavior of scores of others. Neoptolemus symbolizes that, too: he
is an emissary of the Greeks. And his tender relationship with the needy
Philoctetes will change the view of those in power toward this forsaken
bowman.

This brings us to our own stage and a public campaign to make visible
to those in government the systemic sexual harassment and assault in
the armed forces. A few words are appropriate here, as the issue illus-
trates well how, as in the case of Philoctetes and Neoptolemus, counting
on another and being counted on can be a catalyst for change at high
levels of power. In the background to the advocacy is the documentary
The Invisible War (which premiered at the 2012 Sundance Film Festival
and was later broadcast on PBS), which features interviews with veterans of the different branches of the armed forces who recount the incidents that led to their assaults. The documentary is harrowing. I have

shown it to students—women and men, civilians, veterans, ROTC cadets, and active-duty officers, including one high-level Army Ranger battalion commander, married to an Army colonel and West Point sweetheart. What he saw struck a deep nerve. He had just returned from ten years of back-to-back commands in Afghanistan and Iraq. During one of his commands, one of his troops got an emergency call in the midst of a tense engagement: his wife, serving in country in a different unit, had just been assaulted and raped by a fellow soldier. He needed his commander's permission to leave his post immediately and go to her aid. My class froze in hearing the account. The vulnerability that the Ranger commander felt, himself in a dual-career Army marriage, was raw and in the room. All of a sudden my students were looking at a brawny, brainy, invincible-seeming soldier who was not so invincible.

There was another moment that brought the reality of inside-the-wire sexual assault close to home. The film culminates with the exposure of a horrific rape, perpetrated not far from the Georgetown campus, at the prestigious Washington, D.C., Marine Barracks, "the oldest post of the Corps," and home of "The President's Own" Marine Band that plays "Hail to the Chief" at parades and ceremonial missions. Barracks Row in Capitol Hill S.E. has itself become a trendy scene of bars and restaurants, with military pageantry punctuating one corner as Marine sentinels stand guard at the gated courtyard of the historic Barracks. But after watching the film, it would be hard to look at those gates without deep suspicion about what takes place inside.

I leave to the side the harrowing testimonies of the victims and their loved ones. I urge readers to watch the *Invisible War*. The deep misogyny depicted in the film will not come as a surprise to some. The history of U.S. servicemen's treatment of women in regions where they have served, whether in Normandy during the invasion in World War II or in Subic Bay in the Philippines during Vietnam, has not been pretty. Prostitution and objectification of women have gone hand in hand with U.S. military engagements. It may not be too cynical to say that what was turned against occupied women is now turned against those within. (I have my own stories here: My father, treating troops returning from Normandy on the *Queen Mary*, told me in one of the few conversations we did have about war that, in addition to amputations, what he was treating in his many trips was rampant syphilis and gonorrhea, amid the pleading of his soldiers to not tell the wives at home. And while I was teaching at the Naval Academy, a colleague and retired Marine colonel who commanded troops in Vietnam told ethics classes of how he ordered the bulldozing of prostitution sites his Marines were frequenting that put missions at risk and made light of the humanity of too many women.)

What is crucial to our narrative with regard to beginning to restore trust for today's women who serve is that several of the survivors featured in the film (in particular, Kori Cioca, beaten and raped by her supervisor in the U.S. Coast Guard; Ariana Klay, an Iraq War Marine who returned home to be raped by a senior officer and his friend, and then threatened with death; and Trina McDonald, who was drugged and raped by military policemen on a remote Naval station in Alaska) went on to tell their stories to senators on Capitol Hill, including two female senators, Senator Kirsten Gillibrand of New York and Senator Claire McCaskill of Missouri. Deeply disturbed by what they heard and by Department of Defense statistics that confirm an epidemic of sexual assault in the ranks, each proposed legislation to give victims greater power in the legal process. This is not the place to track legislative reform. Nor is it the place to track whether these milder reforms have enough muscle to do real work in fair adjudication for victims of sexual assault within the ranks.

What I do want to expose, though, is that these bills (and especially Gillibrand's) represent direct personal *and* institutional responses to the testimony heard and to the systemic fear victims describe of not coming forward because they won't be believed. It is an illustration of the call and response of vulnerability and the bid for trust ratcheted up to an institutional level through individual engagement—in this case, women listening to other women.

Building trust is a complicated matter for those who have been violated, whether the trust bond is with a producer making a documentary that might change a national conversation, or with a senator who tries to change adjudication procedures, or with a young warrior who shares your grievances, seems of noble cast, and promises you a way out of your desperation. There is risk, exposure, potential betrayal, and sometimes retraumatization. But significantly, even in the case of restoring trust in an institution or organization, the trust is typically built bottom up, in one-on-one interactions, as in these examples, in conversations with an empathic producer, in private hearings with a public official who seems to "get it," in an enigmatic relationship with an emissary who reaches out and recognizes anguish. The interaction moves both ways: there is exposure and vulnerability, on the one hand, and recognition of the dependency, on the other—there's empathy often, and an acknowledgment of the need to respond, in part precisely because one is being counted on. Trust even in institutions as lumbering and bureaucratic as Congress often begins in one-on-one engagements, where there is some sense of uptake, mirroring, and recognition of value. The reach of even that uptake, though, is limited. A senator may not convince enough fellow senators. Military court cases may still embed entrenched sexism by keeping the case within the chain of command. Test cases may founder because of bungled prosecutions and weak or inconsistent testimony from the plaintiffs. Still, getting some senators to take seriously the sexism in the military and begin to fix a broken system is a start.

"I'll Be on the Big White TV Screen"

We have been talking about trust among adults. But coming home from war is often coming home to children, the children a mother or father has left behind. And we would be naive to think that these trust bonds are not among the most fragile. We know from famous developmental research conducted by British psychoanalyst John Bowlby in the wake of World War II, and evacuations of children during the London Blitz, that attachment and trust go hand in hand, and that separations early in life can affect a child's sense of "secure base" that's critical for social and emotional growth.

Concern about the effect of separation on her children must have been in the background of a remarkable set of practices that Air Force Colonel Stephanie Wilson put in place as she prepared to deploy to Ul Adeid Air Base in Qatar for a yearlong senior deployment in the Air Force. I came to know Stephanie at the Woodrow Wilson Center in Washington, D.C., where we were both public policy scholars during the academic year 2011–12. Stephanie is an African American engineer with a master's degree in organizational management from George Washington University, who entered the Air Force through the ROTC program at Georgia Institute of Technology. By May of our year at the Wilson Center, Stephanie was preparing for her next mission, commanding some five to six thousand persons in logistical mission support for Iraq and Afghanistan. It would involve leaving behind her young children—her then five-year-old daughter, Mikalya, and her two-year-old son, Liam. It was her second long deployment in three years; the last overseas deployment was in Ramstein Air Base in Germany.

This time round, Skype would be the family glue, with her husband, Scott Wilson, a retired Air Force flyer working on a Ph.D., in charge of the home front and of rounding up the children daily for Skype time on the TV screen with Mom. The kids just had to be in the room, playing and chattering, with Mom in the background as part of their daily routine. True, she wouldn't be hugging them: "Skype hugs are not real hugs," as one Air Force colonel's wife once told me in describing the hug "good night" her son had each night from her husband. The touch, the smell, the feel, so crucial in early attachment, would not be there. But Stephanie would be there in voice and image on the screen, and in that sense, with them physically every day. The time difference was seven hours. The chat would take place in the morning for the kids: "I'll be on the big white TV screen while the kids are running around in the living room talking to me. So, they don't have to sit in one place. They can continue life, and Mom can just observe and be part of that life for half an hour every day. That's my goal; half an hour every day . . . During the previous deployment, the attachment bond got built in a different way: My daughter was one at the time, and I sat down before I left and read about thirty-five books on videotape—by video recorder—and my husband would play one a night for her. And so that's how she got to see who Mom was: I was the girl reading books at night. My daughter was at the age where she didn't need to see the book. She was just fascinated drinking her bottle, listening to her mom."

In this new deployment, roles would be reversed: her daughter would be reading a book to her once a week over Skype as part of the routine.

Not all parents, military or otherwise, are as creative or as conscientious as these two. I suspect the fact that Stephanie is a logistics expert and engineer by education and training explains how she tackles a problem. But also, not all parents have had to face the same trials. At age three, Mikayla was diagnosed with kidney cancer, and within days, Stephanie and Scott were able to change their career plans so that they could be based in Washington, with access to Walter Reed Hospital, where they would have the best fighting chance of beating the cancer. And they did. Mikayla has had a remarkable recovery after aggressive rounds of chemo and radiation. "I'm leaving her healthy, she's completely healthy," Stephanie tells me with enormous relief, when we spoke over lunch just days before her departure from Dulles. Anything is "a cakewalk," she laughed, compared to fighting your child's cancer.

Still, she knew the departure and separation for a year was its own trial. It would begin with two and a half long hours of waiting in the airport lounge. And then, in civilian clothes, she would step onto the plane and leave Scott and the children behind: "That's probably the hardest part—it was the last time I went—that first step on the plane. I've jumped off a plane before, out of a perfectly good airplane before. The first step is the hardest. Stepping into nothingness is the hardest. Stepping onto the plane is the hardest."

For Air Force Colonel Stephanie Wilson, stepping onto that plane was parachuting into the abyss. The metaphor absolutely paralyzed me. I imagined myself ejected into a black chute with no chance in hell of a soft landing. But for Stephanie, a wingman trained in parachuting, the metaphor had its comforts. And imaging it afforded her a "pre-rehearsal," as the Stoics would say, to anticipate perceived danger and detoxify some of the sting that comes with being unprepared. "That's how I think of it mentally. I'm mentally prepared to jump out of this perfectly fine airplane. So, mentally I have that. So how am I now going to take *this* first step? I am going to allow myself to cry. I'll have my box of tissues there. I'll have my pictures there. I've totally war-gamed this thing in my head. It's okay to cry."

Her Stoic pre-rehearsal had its own twist. She would "war-game" it so it was okay to cry. She could cry with advanced permission, and so with a kind of resolute control. The tears would flow—there would be no surprise there. The only issue, she joked, was whether she would have enough tissues.

A year is a highly abstract concept in the mind of a young child who can barely understand the passage of time. And so again, the logistics of counting a week was a problem to solve. There would be jar of goodies in the kitchen, and every Friday, each child would reach in and pick out a treat, "marking each week Mom is gone."

All this is a way of laying down the trust bond in advance, or at least its means. Colonel Stephanie Wilson is anticipating her responsiveness and the conduits that will have to be in place for mutual responsiveness to grow—the nursing story hour, the Skype half hour, the weekly count-down that brings a young family closer to real time together. Thousands of other military families, some strained by a decade of separation, have been enacting some version of this. It is an enactment to keep the trust exchanges alive.

Trust, Betrayal, Emotion, and Ache

Trust is a future-leaning, reactive attitude, directed toward others and also, by extension, toward oneself, self-reactively. It is a mental attitude that is an emotion, felt and often explicitly expressed. But in what sense is it really an emotion? In what sense is the soldier who, acting through and living with emotion, trusts civilians to understand, or supervisors to not betray her, or senators to acknowledge her defilement, or an emissary to take her home? Aristotle tells us that emotions are accompanied with pleasure or pain. But trust doesn't have a strong valence, a lot of zing, or wing, or heat. Even if it isn't a belief, in the sense that the reason we turn to trust is precisely because we lack the evidence that would ground former belief, still trust doesn't have that excitable feeling we associate with many emotions. Of course, many emotions have their own quietness, and we know well by now that an emotion's "feel," as the critics of William James on emotion long ago pointed out, is not a reliable indicator of either emotion in general (we could just be feeling edgy) or of an emotion in particular (resentment, for example, rather than shame).

But perhaps the better way to get at trust as an emotion is by what it does rather than how it *feels*. To trust someone is to organize one's attention in a certain way, to notice what another is signaling or open to, to block out some doubts or suspend suspicion and build up an "epistemic landscape." But trust doesn't just see someone in a certain light. It makes an investment in that person to do something with the thing or confidence that is entrusted. Trust digs us into vulnerability. And we expose that vulnerability—show it to another, in our face, or voice, or expectant or beholden tone. And we disclose that dependency to ourselves, often by externalizing it to others or by trying it out in a performance. But trust in another may not so much see or find value as help build it, elicit worthiness, as we've said, that isn't yet obvious or proven. And all that can motivate us to share burdens, entrust intimacies, seek succor, come out of a shell, and be less alone.

The bottom line is that trust, qua emotion, makes us vulnerable to others: to their help and hurt, to their power over us, and to our desire that they be responsive to us. Trust, as emotion, is a basic form of attachment. It is dependence writ large. And as important as trust is to a military corps, the idea of dependence is not something many soldiers, Marines, wingmen, or sailors want to embrace full on. To be self-reliant, stoic, to suck it up, and soldier on are the mantras. Trust may be basic to a cadre, but willful determination and control are how one survives. Or so goes the myth.

But even if there is ideological resistance to the deep dependency and vulnerability that goes with trust, the violations of trust make the fact of dependence all too emotionally clear. And that is what we have been detailing—the ache and agony of betrayal and the cautious resowing of seeds of trust in its aftermath.

TWIN TALES

Ancient stories, like that of *Philoctetes,* are our own stories through which to understand betrayal and the possibilities for trust's renewal. Other war stories are also ours.

A Civil War Philoctetes is perhaps Summerfield Hayes, fictional as well, nineteen years old and a Union soldier from Brooklyn, whose three days of battle take place in the opening campaign of the North against the South in the Battle of the Wilderness. Like Philoctetes, Summerfield is abandoned by his command, in his case as punishment for failing to rise from sleep at the bugle's reveille. He lost his hearing from an intense mortar attack the day before and slept through the call. His commander strips him of his rifle and identity papers, and blasts him with the humiliation that would leave him stunned and mute, "I have no time to be playing nursemaid." With that, Summerfield Hayes is deserted, left to make his way between enemy lines in the smoke-shrouded forests of northern Virginia, with no weapon, no buddies, and no name. He finds his way somehow to a Washington hospital, unable to utter his name, or his circumstances, framed by his command as a malingerer. One missionary nurse, named "Walt," with a gray beard, soft wrinkles under his eyes, a tattered haversack, and a fondness for verse, recognizes that Summerfield's invisible and silent wounds must tell a story as grave as those that can speak through gushing blood and sawed-off limbs. Summerfield keeps looking for his wounds; he must have them if he is so sick. Nothing else could cause him to waste away as he does. He strips down over and over. He knows they must be somewhere.

They are there, wounds of betrayal, distrust, and abandonment. And they ache intensely. It is a fictionalized Walt Whitman, a nursemaid of the soul, who trusts the realness and hardness of this nameless Union soldier's wounds and who helps him to find them, and recover them, in voice and memory. That overture of trust, an act of faithfulness, is the beginning of a long and arduous healing for Summerfield.

Summerfield has neither the agony nor the luxury of Philoctetes's fetid leg as tangible legitimation of a deeper moral hurt—indeed, he wants that validation desperately and often contemplates returning to the front to secure the badge that can prove his wound. It is only through the work of friendship and trust (of Walt) that he comes to accept that the hurt of being deserted by one's own troops is no less real than the hurt of losing an arm or a leg by enemy fire.

We shouldn't be glib here. Philoctetes's wounds are physical as well as psychological and moral. And presumably that festering, foul-smelling leg is the cause and putative justification of the moral betrayal: he must be cut off from the whole if the whole is to be saved; with a little utilitarian logic chop, the sacrifice of one soldier preserves the army of many. War always puts its human assets, and not just its matériel, at some risk. *Philoctetes* is just another case of balancing force protection against the exigencies of the mission.

But there is something insidious, haunting, cruel, and inhumane about Philoctetes's sacrifice, and it has to do with the trauma of isolation. Philoctetes has been a prisoner in solitary confinement for a full ten years. In his case, he has nature and the beasts as his companions. Not all are so lucky, especially those who have spent the past decade in the U.S. detention center at Guantanamo, set up as a part of the "global war on terror." Still, Philoctetes was put into solitary by his own side, by his own command, and that is perhaps the unkindest betrayal. And that's the reason his trust in Neoptolemus is so fascinating. Why should Philoctetes trust this emissary sent by his betrayers? And why should Neoptolemus be moved to renege on his plot? The moral address in this interaction, the signaling of dependency and the projection that it will be recognized and acknowledged as legitimate, are the components of this new trust bond. (And perhaps that was also so with Summerfield and his Walt.) Trust and trustworthiness are built here from the ground up, on the ashes of soul-shattered living. This is an ancient and abiding lesson for veterans coming home and for civilians to whom they return.

Ghusoon Mekhaber Al-Taiee

GHUSOON MEKHABER AL-TAIEE (Iraq) is a researcher, journalist, and women's activist who has written for several news agencies, among them Rafidain, Voice of the Arabs, and Anbar Media. In articles such as "Home and War," she argues for women's empowerment and exposes the obstacles that Iraqi women face when trying to complete their educations, especially in rural areas. She is the director of Hala Center for Training, Development and Consultation and has conducted research on women and violence at Al-Mustasiria University, in the Department of Political Science.

Why I Write about War

Many of us agonize over the word "war." This word conjures up a reality that societies have experienced throughout the ages. It brings to mind different kinds of wars—regional, national, international, and global. When the state becomes weak and unqualified people come into power, law no longer applies, and the system degenerates into chaos. The state becomes as fragile as a lamb. Armed groups of outlaws, antidemocratic groups that promote a particular ideology, emerge. They permit no diversity of thought. On the contrary, they abolish freedoms. They suppress opposing opinions using different methods of oppression, such as marginalization and assassinations. The tribe assumes power and rules in a way that protects its own rights. The leaders do what they want, and no one can stop them. The different kinds of wars that result from these developments affect individuals and communities. They leave in their wake psychological, moral, economic, political, and cultural damage. They weaken political and cultural foundations and form a corrosive environment for everyone: children, adolescents, men, and women. That's all that comes from war. Victory becomes everything, no matter what the cost or sacrifice. Those of us who have seen war know that what we really need is to build peace. We need quality leadership and laws that serve as a foundation for modern democratic systems.

Why do I write about war? When you read this essay, you will see the devastation caused by war, and you will understand.

The Dark Thoughts of Women

We were suddenly submerged in dark thoughts. No one knew when they started or how they grew. And no one knew how to get rid of them!

ISIS, as the Islamic State is known, is one of those forces that emerged during a weak regime whose leaders based their authority on a particular ideology. Secular governments, such as Al-Maliki's, depended on the support of clerics with ties to Iran, and they favored one sect over others. Eventually, their doctrines were challenged, creating political instability. It was a period of change and transition. The result was a political vacuum, which ISIS moved in to fill. Now dissenting opinions and ideas were no longer tolerated. Minorities were marginalized. Power was concentrated in the hands of a few, who used force against certain sects and rejected the policies of legitimate rulers. Those who felt neglected by the government supported these new outlaw forces. They had suffered from marginalization and repression in the past, and they believed that ISIS would be their savior, that ISIS would stand up to the existing government, whose agenda they saw as unjust and racist. But they would pay a high price.

Under the shadow of ISIS, the country sank into darkness. According to some agencies and researchers, up to 90 percent of women in ISIS-held territories were affected by the war in one way or another. In general, they fell into three groups. The first was comprised of women who simply surrendered to the new reality. These women suffered horrible psychological and physical damage. They were beaten and raped. Some were sold in the markets like animals. They felt they had no choice but to submit to their captors. Some were kidnapped and outfitted with explosives to be used in suicide bombings in different parts of Iraq and Syria. For them, death was their liberation and salvation.

The second category was made up of the women who resisted with all their power, and some of them escaped and survived. These women never surrendered to the men of ISIS, preferring death, even committing suicide. The results were dreadful. Many of them disappeared and are still missing, but a few fought against ISIS and lived to tell their stories.

The third category includes the defenders of ISIS, some of whom became active ISIS operatives or combatants. These women joined ISIS for many reasons. ISIS often used the cover of Islam to convince women of the validity of their ideas, and women who had never known anything but a simple life, limited by all kinds of restrictions, now saw the possibility of leading a new kind of life, one that would be purposeful and allow them to achieve their dreams of giving themselves completely to their faith. In other cases, women were brainwashed, often by other women who were close to the men of ISIS (their wives, daughters, sisters) and took those men as role models. Once these new recruits were in the circle of ISIS, they became completely submissive and obedient, doing as they were told without discussion, out of fear. Eventually, they realized that if they tried to escape, they would be killed, and so they had no other option but to cooperate. Better to work with ISIS, they thought, than to rebel and get killed, raped, or beaten.

The women of ISIS played different roles. With time, they were not just limited to fulfilling the demands of Jihadi marriage, instilling extremist thought in the minds of young people, as it had been during the first years. Instead, they performed myriad duties. Some joined the ranks of the combatants and took part in different operations. According to international reports, women make up one-third of ISIS, including about 690 European women. French intelligence has issued a report confirming the presence of more than 500 French female terrorists in Iraq and Syria. The study reveals that at least 35,000 women have had children in ISIS-controlled areas during the past five years, the result of ISIS's attempt to restructure the population. Furthermore, the study reports that children have been used for propaganda purposes more than three hundred times. ISIS often shows violence involving children in order to intimidate their parents into submission. Sometimes, for recruitment purposes, ISIS shows children images of boys playing with weapons or joking with soldiers. The idea is to convince the children that war is an adventure, a game.

ISIS gave a larger role to women after its recent losses in Syria and Iraq, establishing the Al-Khansaa battalion for women. Women have been instrumental in producing and disseminating propaganda and in raising money for Jihadist groups. Women under the age of thirty can carry the weapons left to them by men killed in battle. The task of the members of Al-Khansaa is to support the organization by recruiting women and scrutinizing women's behavior in the cities of Mosul and Raqqa. According to published reports, ISIS divides women into three groups. The first, consisting of female prisoners, attends to reproductive and domestic issues. The second deals with educational and health services for women. The third group of women is called "martyrs." They carry weapons and are of different Arab and non-Arab nationalities.

ISIS issued a document called "Women in the Islamic State" that details female roles and highlights the most prominent features of its thought on women. For example, under the pretext of religion, ISIS forces women to wear the hijab, to cover their faces and hands, and to pray regularly. This document, which ISIS uses for propaganda, argues that women are more intelligent and skilled than men and are therefore capable of serving its cause.

Women sometimes choose to join ISIS because they are convinced of its extremist ideology. An example is Asmaa Al-bukharie, who risked the lives of her children and her husband, fighting to the last bullet against the government security forces. Some women are drawn to ISIS by the promise of adventure and excitement. These women have a romantic perception of ISIS, as ISIS publicity responds to their desire for a life of freedom and dignity. Still others believe that ISIS will provide them with the money they need for their families, only to find that the Al-Khansaa women's battalion will pay them only $160 a month. Convinced by ISIS-generated media, they follow a mirage and then pay a heavy price for it.

The victims of war include refugees and displaced persons living in camps, women who lost their houses, their money, their husbands, children, and families. Sometimes women had to take more than one job to earn money for themselves and their children. They had to search for work when there was a dearth of employment, health services, and educational possibilities. Some women even had to sell their bodies to get money to survive.

In the absence of a strong government, there is no place for women. Women live in fear of an unknown future. The question is: What will be their fate? What can be their fate if they don't even have their IDs and other essential documents? And what about those survivors who are mothers of children they had by ISIS members? Will there be a new day filled with brightness for them?

The result of this war against ISIS is a lack of employment opportunities and high rates of poverty. At times, the unemployment rate reached 40 percent. The psychological, moral, and social deterioration has been terrible. Today we are trying to rise again. We are trying to be constructive. We want to rebuild our country for ourselves and our society. Let the next life be filled with hope!

I am still experiencing the terrible nightmare of ISIS occupation as I write this. I remember the nightmare of pain and destruction that the women of my village witnessed, my mother's tears, the howling of children during those last moments before they were torn away from their mothers. Once, everything around the village was beautiful—the orchards, the rivers, the palm trees. But when the darkness came, it shut out all daylight. Our neighbor, Om Yehya, lost her husband in the war. Then her only son joined the martyrs, and he was also killed. As a result, she experienced a sorrow so horrendous that she lost her mind.

The spirit of my village haunts me. In the village streets, when they carry out the coffins, the screams shatter my eardrums. The scene frightens me: the women fall in the muddy muck and tear their clothes as they grasp at the coffins, while the adult men carry their beloved sons to the cemetery, praying over them, taking slow, deliberate steps, racked with grief and pain for those who were lost. We see these scenes repeatedly. The village cemetery is covered with bunches of flowers and adorned with flags. My head is filled with questions, foremost among them, Why? And I can't find anyone who is able to give me an adequate answer. I ask, then I hesitate. Silence. It's the war. Days go by, and dreams vanish in the wind. Within us, something grows: darkness.

Many years have passed this way. The war is taking new forms. There are new styles of fighting, modern ways to express extremism and sectarianism, which means greater and greater losses. Women give birth so their sons can fuel this war. We were unaware of the power of violence and the fragility of peace. Every child born in the village today must cope with two conflicting forces, each struggling to triumph against the other: the desire for peace and the inevitability of war. Psychological studies show that these children have been severely damaged by images of war, experiences of violence, and/or loss of parents. They crave peace, and they are terrified of another catastrophe. They need a period of quiet, a period free from anxiety, to recover.

We did not realize war would remain with us for so many years, that it would enter our lives, rob us of hope, and devour everything. Birds carry off the souls of innocent people, people who once dreamed of living in peace. I have taken up my mother's legacy of tears. I pray for this storm to pass and for peace to come. A different kind of peace. Do you agree? But war has developed, progressed in its methods, and escalated. Killing people has become an art. Murder and rape are an art. We are caught between the reality of loss and the dream of hope. Our dead no longer

lie buried in graves. Dogs eat their bodies, defile their flesh. Soldiers rape
our women. They kill children and childhood. We waste our tomorrows
trying to scrape together enough money, while they come and take what
belongs to others. Our books have been burned. Our schools have been
destroyed. Smiles have departed from our lips. Our dreams have blown
away in the wind, like dust. Flowers no longer grow around our house.
Look at where we were then and how we are now. Even after thirty-five
years, I am still witnessing war, hunger, thirst, poverty, and disease. And
now, last and worst of all, we are witnessing ISIS.

I will tell you the stories of some women who were born into this world
where we must fight until death.

A colleague of mine is named Mohammed. Mohammed's mother says:
"We intended to leave this town and go to another place that was not
under ISIS control. We whispered together secretly, so that no one would
know when we were leaving and where we were going. We decided to go
at night, leaving behind our house, our luggage, our beautiful memories
of the sounds of laughter and the smiles. We knew we might never come
back, we might face death. We stayed in the desert for a week without any
food or water, waiting for the light of hope. Then a man appeared and
asked us each for two hundred dollars to take us to the city. We didn't have
much money, but we gave him what we had. In the city, the security forces
demanded fifty dollars to drive us to the camps.

All of the stories tell of different ways of escaping. Some of the women's
husbands took off and left them alone with their children in the middle
of nowhere.

Selma left with her husband and children and headed for Al-Qaim.
Some men took money from her, but they took only her old, sick husband
with them, so she had no choice but to go back to her family's house in
Heet. She started the trip home, but the security forces prevented her
from getting there. She was left alone with her children for three days,
until finally someone helped her to reach the camps.

As if these stories aren't hair-raising enough, things got worse—as, for
example, when ISIS captured the Eizidi women and sold them as slaves at
the Nakhasa Market.

Henya was a fifteen-year-old girl when she and her three sisters fell
into ISIS hands. Henya told us that she had been sold three times at the
market. The first was for $21,000 to a Syrian Kurd named Abu-Ayman. He
raped her, then sold her to a Libyan man for $10,000. In the meantime,
her sister Hanifa was searching for her. She finally found her and bought

her for $14,000. Henya had gotten pregnant, but she had an abortion because she didn't want a baby from ISIS. The sisters were finally reunited, but one of them is now in Germany getting treatment because she was beaten so badly in the head. Their father died of a stroke after his daughters were kidnapped.

Mohammed, my colleague from Mosul, tells a story that will tear you apart. A woman who had four children was running from the bombing toward the car that would take them to the camps. She held her baby in her arms and two other children with her other hand. Her fourth son, who was ten years old, was running behind her. Just as she was getting into the car, the bombing intensified, and one of the bombs fell on her ten-year-old son. She was screaming for him. She couldn't leave her two children in the car because it would take off with them inside, leaving her behind, but she couldn't leave her son lying on the ground. There is no mercy in this war! Where is peace?

The war has killed at least eight hundred thousand people and displaced 15 percent of the population since it began. It has produced five million displaced persons and refugees. More than five thousand children have been born without anyone knowing who their fathers are, and the fathers have no knowledge of the children's existence. The war has destroyed our infrastructure. The economy is failing. There is no more development. We live our lives day to day, without looking forward. We've become futureless.

And you ask why I write about war.

I'll let you think about the answer.

Carolin Emcke

CAROLIN EMCKE (Germany) is an award-winning journalist. From 1998 to 2006, she was a staff writer for *Der Spiegel*, reporting from Afghanistan, Pakistan, Lebanon, Colombia, and other trouble spots. From 2007 to 2014, she covered conflict areas such as Israel, the West Bank, Iraq, and Haiti for *Die Zeit*. Since then, she has worked as a freelance writer and columnist for the weekend edition of *Süddeutsche Zeitung*. She is author of several books, among them *Kollektive Identitäten* (Collective identities); *Stumme Gewalt: Nachdenken über die RAF* (Mute violence: Reflections on the RAF); and, most recently, *Gegen den Hass* (*Against Hatred*). Her books have been translated into numerous languages, including English, Spanish, French, Dutch, Slovenian, Japanese, and Finnish. Emcke has lectured widely on theories of violence and witness writing. She was a visiting lecturer in political theory at Yale University during the 2003–4 academic year. Emcke has won many prizes for her reporting, most recently, the Johann Heinrich Merck Preis from the German Academy for Language and Literature (2014) and the Peace Prize of the German Book Trade (2016). The following selections are from *Von den Kriegen: Briefe an Freunde* (*Echoes of Violence: Letters from a War Reporter*). The first selection, from the book's preface, serves to answer the question of why I write about war.

From Echoes of Violence

PREFACE

At first there was only speechlessness.

After spending a month and a half in Albania and Kosovo during the war, I returned to Berlin in the summer of 1999 and did not know what to tell my friends. How to convey my experiences in words that would not disturb them? How to describe this encounter with death and destruction? How to explain that war and violence inscribe themselves on your soul and continue to live with you?

My friends did not know how to ask, and I did not know how to re-spond.

In an effort to overcome my speechlessness, I wrote a letter that was sent to a circle of about twenty friends via email.

I did not know then that the longing to tell my friends about war and its victims would become a ritual: after each haunting journey I would write a letter. Nor did I know then that this writing would eventually become a cathartic task, not merely an intellectual one. More and more, these letters became a means to reflect on my experiences and help me return to my life in Berlin.

Not all of the letters describe war itself—some portray the destroyed interior and exterior landscapes that war leaves behind.

Two letters—on Nicaragua and on Romania—do not deal with wars in the narrow sense.

They discuss structural violence rather than immediate physical or military violence.

In the letters I tried to express something that is not found in tra-ditional news coverage. The genre of the letter allowed me to combine different forms of narration: personal passages are followed by essayistic reflections; political commentary is interspersed with travelogues. I could *not* have written for publication in this way.

I wrote for my friends: artists and intellectuals around the globe with different religious and cultural backgrounds, whom I had met over the previous fifteen years.

At first there were no markers to guide me. I simply told my friends about my journeys, about what haunted me. I tried to answer their un-spoken questions: What were my reasons for traveling to war zones? How neutral could I remain in such places?

Over the years certain themes and ideas became clearer: the war, its victims, and the witness. The letters give testimony about what I have seen, but also about me: the witness.

There were reasons not to censor my personal comments for publica-tion. Over and over again, friends who read these letters responded with outrage and surprise: this they hadn't imagined, they told me. They had *no idea,* they said. All my friends were well informed—and yet through these letters they seemed to learn something different about the death and destruction at the fringes of the world.

Why?

In her book *Regarding the Pain of Others,* Susan Sontag writes about a phenomenon that I found among my friends: viewers or readers who are confronted every day with images of horror from war regions see those pictures—but they cannot *situate* them in a meaningful context. They become numb after a while, and in the end they do not believe that these images really correspond to a violent reality.

Letters from a witness whom one can imagine, who becomes visible, who describes how one responds to violence, who wanders between different worlds and tries to translate between them—someone who also mentions what goes wrong, what embarrasses, what is unbearable—such letters can be credible testimony to the wars and their victims.

Kosovo 1 (July 1999): Death and Destruction

Since my return, people ask me: "How do you cope with what you witnessed?" "How do you digest all the experiences?" The answer is: you don't. There are certain impressions you cannot "digest." The sight of a seventeen-year-old girl in the hospital of Prizren in Kosovo. She had been shot by a sniper the day before the allied forces entered Kosovo. She had a brain injury and urgently needed to be transferred to the hospital in Prishtina. That night she had stayed in a room with five badly injured men: Serbs, Kosovo Liberation Army (KLA) fighters, and Albanians, the enemies of the war, crammed together into one overheated room. You could hear her breathe. She would probably die within the next five hours because the hospital could not transfer her to Prishtina—the Serbian troops had stolen the only ambulance for their flight at the end of the war. The sight of a charred back of a dead Catholic Albanian Kosovar between hundreds of books in his house in Koronica. The muscles in the shrunken body were still recognizable—it looked like one of those charts from biology class where all muscles of the human body are schematically displayed. Except the man in Koronica was brown-black; his burned flesh was porous and looked hairy like scratchy fur. Arms and legs were missing. Maybe they had been cut off, maybe they were burned completely, maybe it had been the dogs.

The Homeric heroes in *The Iliad* fear death less than the thought of being left unburied—outside the city walls—at the mercy of stray dogs. It always seemed rather strange to me that a living person would worry about his corpse being tattered by dogs. I could not imagine a world in which dogs would run around with human limbs in their mouths. It was the brother of the dead man who brought us to this package of withered flesh. He walked from one room to the other, in a destroyed house, and talked as if it were still intact, as if that bundle on the floor still had anything in common with the human being he grew up with. And one does not digest: the sight of corpses without heads, of cut-off body parts, contorted bodies that had been pulled behind a truck for miles (also reminiscent of Homer); the sight of bloated or burned corpses, some two months old, one week, one day. There is this one image I cannot forget: the foot of a male body that we found in a ravine on a field near Meja. I still remember those two inches between the black leather shoe on his right foot and the blue cotton trouser, a peasant uniform such as I would see so often in the following weeks when looking at dead civilians. The corpse had been lying there, apparently, since April. In the meantime it had rained, and it had been as hot as it can be in a Yugoslav summer. One particular part of the image haunts me, a small detail: those two inches between the tied shoe and the hem of the trouser. Without the clothes that proved that this had once been a man, there were only two inches of dead, living flesh. Nothing else.

And there was this sound, very quiet, first unnoticed, and then so penetrating in its repulsiveness that no taboo, no shame, could repress my hearing it: parasites were eating the rest of a human being. I cannot forget the ten-year-old girl in Gjakova who stood in front of the burned-out ruins of her former house and could not say two complete, intelligible sentences. She spoke without pause as if her speech were making sense, she did not stutter, did not hesitate; she formed one incoherent sentence after another. Finally, we understood that in this house her father, her brother, her aunt, and two cousins had been killed. Her uncle and her two other brothers had been arrested by Serbian units and deported the day before NATO troops—the Kosovo Force (KFOR)—arrived. She told us that her father had fallen off the roof celebrating the long-awaited NATO intervention. He had broken his leg and could not move when the Serbian soldiers arrived at their house. They had told the girl and her mother to leave the house—and killed everyone else in it. I cannot forget how she stood there in her pink shirt, in front of her former living room wall, slightly oblique because there was no flat floor anymore. And I cannot forget that she could not speak properly, and that she occasionally only stared at us and then continued to speak. And that she did not seem upset at all. She was quiet and calm and only every now and then did she seem irritated—when she realized that she did not know the trick anymore, that trick that someone had taught her, years ago, in another time: how to form sentences and make sense to others. Then she paused and suddenly felt like a stranger to herself, and then she seemed to tell herself that these words that came out of her mouth were unintelligible. We were disadvantaged in comparison to other journalists who witnessed these images of death and destruction. Many reporters arrived in Albania or Macedonia only when the peace agreement was signed. But we had already been acquainted with the terrible events. We had been writing since April on the refugees and their fate, we had been listening to them: how their sons and husbands had been killed, what they had done before the crisis began, where they used to live, how they were expelled, how many hours they had walked till they had reached the border, when they had last seen their brother, where they were standing when a Serbian officer pulled a woman out of the throng of refugees, how they had been hiding in a barn. At the end of the war, when we entered Kosovo, we knew exactly where to go and what to expect there. We had a map of killing in our minds—even before we arrived at the sites of the massacres. But that meant that we could not relate to those tormented bodies as neutral bystanders toward anonymous corpses. After weeks of interviewing survivors in the camps in Albania, photographer Sebastian Bolesch and I knew the story of many of the dead; we knew whether their wives or children had survived on the other side of the border. It also meant that we could imagine the corpses before us as fathers and brothers, as peasants or writers. We could imagine their previous lives, and sometimes we knew their relatives in Albania. Impossible to gain distance. But it was also conciliatory: to remember the real person, the living father or brother or cousin or neighbor; to ask for their story and narrate it; to re-create in writing a world that was supposed to be destroyed; to give each of these stinking, faceless bodies a name again and not to turn one's back.

Kosovo 2 (October 2000): No Forgetting/No Forgiveness

The raped wives from Velika Krusa and Krusa e Male demonstrate for their disappeared husbands. The fleeing Serbs had taken them hostage at the end of the war and they have disappeared since then: nobody knows if they are still vegetating in Serbian prisons or if they were hastily buried in mass graves. The widows until otherwise confirmed stand outside the government building of Prishtina, and passersby simply cast down their eyes to avoid seeing them. The women seem like people from the past, with their headscarves, their gray and brown coats—they do not fit anymore in this lively, glaring city with its dynamic, young people. They stand close to one another on the walkway, like a herd of scared sheep, seeking one another's protection, hugging one another's fears and sadness. Nobody pays attention to them, nobody sees them. The same politicians who are unwilling to talk to these poor women, however, do not hesitate to mention their fate when they can exploit it in their speeches about independence and the impossibility of settling differences with Serbian civilians. The history of these women is of general political importance—but the women themselves are not. The crime committed against them is useful, but the victims of the crime are overlooked. Nobody wants to be reminded of their pain. Their sight irritates the general desire for normalcy.

Only a kind activist takes care of the old women, who are terribly disappointed that nobody wants to listen. They had traveled for hours by bus from the south of Kosovo, and now nobody cares. They are too tired and frustrated to even lift up the signs they had prepared with their husbands' names and yellowed photos. The story of the hostages, of the Albanian prisoners in Serbia, is the thorn in the side of any reconciliation attempt. When in the fall Vojislav Kostunica finally released Flora Brovina, the most prominent prisoner, the Albanians only shrugged their shoulders, rejected the importance of the gesture that they had been demanding, and asked for all the other prisoners.

Being back in Kosovo is depressing.

Domnica Radulescu

DOMNICA RADULESCU (Romania) is the Edwin A. Morris Professor of Comparative Literature at Washington and Lee University. Her novels and plays explore the traumas of war, exile, and displacement. Radulescu received the 2011 Outstanding Faculty Award from the State Council of Higher Education for Virginia, and is twice a Fulbright scholar. She is the author of three critically and internationally acclaimed novels—*Country of Red Azaleas* (2016), *Black Sea Twilight* (2010), and *Train to Trieste* (2008)—and of several plays. *Train to Trieste* has been published in thirteen languages and is the winner of the 2009 Library of Virginia Fiction Award. Two of her plays, *The Town with Very Nice People* (2013) and *Exile Is My Home: A Sci-fi Immigrant Fairy Tale* (2014), were finalists in the Jane Chambers Playwriting Competition. The latter play was produced at the Theater for the New City in New York in April/May 2016. Her most recent novel, *Country of Red Azaleas,* is inspired by events of the Bosnian War of the 1990s.

Why I Write about War

I do not consider myself a war writer, but a politically engaged writer who, among other things, explores the ways in which war affects the personal lives of people and the survival strategies they develop in war situations. I have a mediated, or oblique relation to various wars, in particular World War II and the Bosnian War of the 1990s. As a creative artist, I have tried to construct what I call an aesthetic of trauma. As a scholar, I write about the aesthetic of trauma, of war and exile, in theater and narrative works.* I do not write about or describe battle scenes or military actions, but the ways in which civilians are affected by the violence of war in all aspects of their lives. The aesthetic I use in depicting these realities combines a lyr-

---

* I explore and outline an aesthetic of war and exile in my recent book *Theater of War and Exile: Twelve Playwrights, Directors and Performers from Eastern Europe and Israel* (2015).

ical element with fractured narrative lines, with dark humor, and, in my plays, with an element of the absurd and the fantastic that evokes violence and its effects on my characters' lives.

My interest in stories that take place in times of war was spurred from early childhood, as I grew up hearing my parents' accounts of their childhoods during World War II. There is a photograph in sepia of my maternal grandparents that has always haunted me. I carried it in my purse together with a handful of other family photographs when I escaped from Romania to Italy in 1983. My grandmother is wearing an elegant black dress, her hair is gathered in a chignon, and she has a corsage of white orchids; my grandfather is wearing a tuxedo, and his hair is combed back, exposing his smooth, high forehead. They are both smiling and look radiantly happy. My mother always said about that photograph: "They were dancing at a ball during the war." That was all. The date on the back of the picture is December 31, 1943. Indeed, World War II, a New Year's Eve party at the height of the war, crossing into the horrific year of 1944—Romania still fighting on the side of Germany, and American and Russian bombs falling like rain over our country in the middle of the Balkans. One of the American bombs hit my grandparents' house and split it in half in the summer of 1943. My mother's relatives were all lucky to have found themselves in the half of the house that remained standing.

Growing up under the absurd dictatorship of Nicolae Ceausescu and hearing many more stories about my parents' wartime childhood experiences, I often came back to those two facts: my grandparents went to a fancy ball looking beautiful and radiant, and their house was split in half by an American bomb half a year earlier. How could they be so happy, so radiant? How could they dance, and how could my grandmother choose a delicate white flower and carefully arrange it in a corsage, all while bombs were falling from the sky and splitting people's houses in half or obliterating them altogether?

I only started to grasp that contradiction decades later, as an immigrant in the United States, after I had experienced and survived some of my own wars of a different nature: leaving everyone and everything familiar behind, settling in the United States as a political refugee, and coping with the resulting sense of displacement, loss, and homesickness. The image of my grandparents offered me solace and strength throughout some of the hardest periods of my journey—if they could not only survive but even dance, I could survive and be happy, too. And I finally understood that having survived the American bomb was precisely a reason to dress up, dance at the New Year's Eve ball, and be happy for every moment of stolen life.

When war erupted in the early 1990s in the former Yugoslavia, it felt like the reopening of an ancestral wound. My grandparents' crushed house started taking shape in my imagination and acquiring a tragic kinship with the bombed houses of Sarajevo. I had never even been to Belgrade or to Sarajevo, but I had grown up hearing of our Yugoslav neighbors, who apparently lived under a milder and more liberal kind of communism. They could travel to the West, and their food stores weren't always empty like ours. And I knew that Romanians sometimes crossed the border into Yugoslavia and then escaped to Italy.

In the late 1990s, I began to learn about the unspeakable atrocities committed by Serbian officers against Muslim Bosnians. The news of the genocide and the rape camps became unbearable. These stories took my breath away. I thought of the wartime childhoods of my parents and the wartime youth of my grandparents and the postwar Stalinist terror, which they still talked about in whispers around the dinner table so many years later. Sometimes I took out the picture of my grandparents at the ball and wondered how the Bosnians survived the bombs and sniper shots, how they carried out their everyday lives. I was concerned especially with the particulars: the meals they cooked, how they got their water, whether they ever read, laughed, or even danced anymore? More than anything, the mass rapes and the executions in July 1995 kept me up at night when my young children didn't. I started noticing occasional refugees from Bosnia, mostly women wearing colored headscarves like the ones we used to call babushkas in Romania. I wondered whether they'd survived rape camps, if they had lost family members, sons, husbands to the genocide or to snipers in Sarajevo. I wondered what was hiding behind their polite smiles, what stories they carried, what memories gnawed at them as they cooked their Bosnian meals, spreading the fragrance of cumin and cinnamon all throughout the hallways of my mother's Chicago apartment building, where some of them lived.

Years later, Sarajevo beckoned me with an irresistible call. In the summer of 2011, I arrived in this glorious and magical city and felt as though I had been born there. It was the same summer that a newly discovered mass grave was exhumed, containing 660 bodies from the genocide. The war was still fresh. I took everything down in my notebook: how people lived for three years without water, gas, and electricity, how they ran amid sniper bullets to get water from the few sources in town, how they even wrote poetry and wore their best clothes just to feel normal and beautiful on some really ugly days. People told me their stories of survival and also stories of everyday life. I knew I would spend the next several years writing a story that started there in Sarajevo, during the same decade when I was living in my native Romania, and that it would be the story of two women who grow up during Tito's regime and were young adults at the time of the Bosnian War. I knew it would be the story of two empowered women who were connected for life, and whose love and friendship survived all the upheavals of history. Their story would be akin to that of my grandparents' photograph in sepia: a snapshot of irrepressible passion for life in the midst of ruin, framed by Sarajevo's red azaleas, in contrast with my grandmother's white orchid. This is how my novel *Country of Red Azaleas,** of which the following selection is an unpublished chapter, was born.

Poetry, Music, and Birth under Siege—Sarajevo, April 1994: Marija's Notes

At night I saw Sarajevo as if through a thin layer of ice punctured by a sharp needle from my mother's collection of sewing needles. Then it trembled like an upside-down image in the water. Everything was upside down and oozing and punctured in this new Sarajevo of mine. Amid the chaos and the bombs, there was always a glittering point of comfort somewhere: someone was writing a poem, someone else was saying a prayer, someone was making love or reading by flashlight. Life under siege had its exciting sides. Finding ways of doing important or unimportant things, pleasurable or necessary things under fire was always a challenge and therefore exciting. It pushed your imagination to the limit. Weirdly, at the worst of the siege, I had a yearning to have a baby, to hold something small, alive, and pure in my arms amid all the death and bloody mortar. I had a yearning to create beautiful art and write scintillating articles, to sing melodious songs and dance fiery dances.

With the help of a childhood friend who was a journalist, I got an actual job writing for the only newspaper in town that was still being produced out of a Communist-era bomb shelter. The Cold War paranoia

---

* *Country of Red Azaleas* (2016) is inspired by events during the Bosnian War of 1992–95. My first novel, *Train to Trieste* (2008), has also drawn some inspiration from family stories during World War II in the depiction of some of its characters.

had proven to be of some use after all. The director of the newspaper had a fanatic love of journalism, reporting, telling the truth, the whole media and newspaper thing. The actual newspaper building had been blown up by bombs and practically burned to the ground at the very beginning of the war, just like the National Library with all the books I had loved leafing through as a young girl thirsty for knowledge, fiction, ideas. But this gutsy journalist found a way to still produce the newspaper. That period of running for cover through flickering, swaying, upside-down Sarajevo under fire and beset by snipers, and getting news and articles to the group of people huddled in the bomb shelter to produce the daily paper, was one of the most exciting times of my life. I called Lara from the newspaper once a week telling her all about it. Sometimes she sounded far away, not just because of the distance and the war between us, but because of something else. Once she told me she wished she were with me under fire, reporting from the bomb shelter. Then she started crying. She told me she felt so terribly torn about Mark's marriage proposal. Her parents were urging her to go, and kept saying things would only get worse. But she just couldn't bring herself to leave them and her sister Biljlana. "And then there is you—out there in the middle of this awful war, when are we going to see each other again?"

I wanted to tell her to drop everything and join me in Sarajevo, where we could both work as journalists under fire, and that I would arrange a transport for her to get there. I knew that Lara loved danger and adventure and we would have made a fabulous team. But all I said was: "I think you should marry Mark, Lara, it's your chance to start over, to have a career in political science, maybe become a professor and leave this miserable primitive part of the world forever." I only heard the sound of her sobs for a long time. I just sat in the bomb shelter holding the phone and listening to her sobs almost without breathing. For some reason I found her sobs comforting, at least I knew she cared enough for me that a brilliant opportunity of marital happiness and professional fulfillment in the United States of America weighed in her mind as much as our friendship. Then she stopped crying and asked sort of childishly: "Are you sure? Do you promise we'll see each other before too long?" I said I promised but did not cry. We couldn't both be sitting with our phones, each in our native cities, howling over something we had little control of. And I wanted Lara to be happy. I knew she was tough and adventurous but also more fragile than me, and at some point she would get tired of the journalism under fire project and wish she had flown away with her American prince.

Then she said: "When? When are we going to see each other again?" I
felt a strong compulsion to lie. "If you get married in Belgrade, I'll do
my damnedest to come to the wedding." I had no idea how much worse
things were going to get and that there was no way I would be able to leave
the siege area for a long time.

There were always broken windows, sharp screams, and grenade
sounds, sniper sounds like peals of thunder gone wrong. As if nature had
been crushed under human violence. I nursed a dying pot of African vio-
lets in my parents' apartment for a long time. But it was a luxury to water
plants when we didn't have drinking water. Running along the dark corri-
dors of our building and hearing sounds of glass shattering was the worst.
It scratched your nerves to a degree that you wanted to run out into the
street and face the snipers directly. On some nights my parents and I slept
in the same bed like refugees in our own house. We all became refugees
in our own city.

I was focused on survival like everybody else. But I was also searching
for something else. I was focused on an idea of beauty and strength that
might emerge from the rubble. The library was bombed, alright, millions
of precious pages had gone up in flames. I watched it burn like a torch and
wanted to bring water from the river to put out the fire. I wondered why
the entire city didn't just go to the river filling pails of water to put out
the library fire. I made lists of all the weaponry used against my city and
found it stunning. There was so much warfare ingenuity, we must have
been an important target with our handful of mosques and our Muslim
Bosnian culture: artillery, mortars, tanks, anti-aircraft guns, heavy machine-guns, rocket launchers, rocket-launched aircraft bombs, and sniper
rifles all aimed at the citizens of a relatively small city nestled deep down
in the Balkans—the city where World War I had started. Now it sounded
like World War II, or World War III. To whom did we owe the "honor" of
all that artillery used against a peaceful city? We kept asking, "What have
we done?" I wanted to ask the Serbian snipers just that one simple question, "What have we done?" International news often referred to the siege
as "armed conflict." Armed conflict meant we had done something bad,
that all of us Sarajevans were guilty of something, that we were part of a
squabble, a political debate of sorts with our enemies the Serbians and thus
found ourselves in an "armed conflict" and were fighting for our lives just
like the soldiers on the other side were. Apparently many Serbs, including
the leader of the entire project of ethnic cleansing, Radovan Karadzic,
justified their acts and the war based on things that had happened during

World War II and the concentration camp of Jasenova. Serbs had been killed in those camps at the hands of Croats and of some Bosnians, and now finally the time for revenge had arrived. Bosnian children had to have their brains splattered against Sarajevo buildings by Serbian snipers as a righteous and justified gesture that finally avenged and made justice for the camps of Jasenova a half century earlier. Paying for the sins of our fathers was inscribed with gruesome literality in our flesh and skulls.

The sniper-rifles were the main instruments of terror, more than any of the other artillery. Sometimes the mortars too—they killed more people at once. But the snipers punctured our days and nights and every one of our steps in the streets of Sarajevo until we were like a sieve by the end of the day: everything poured through us, nothing held. I clung to the reporting job in the bomb shelter for dear life. I brought news of survivors mainly. I wanted to focus on the survivors: a little girl hidden under a car holding her doll, an old man in the Ferhat-Pasha Mosque in one of the small cloisters sitting calmly and praying, my friend Ferida writing a poem a day and becoming pregnant, stories like that. I drove my parents' car through intersections at 130 kilometers an hour, feeling like an airplane pilot. Once we had a party with sausage, cheese, and whiskey inside the bomb shelter. We even had chocolate. We even danced. We danced the twist, the tango, the swing to songs by Elvis Presley, Frank Sinatra, and Elton John. In all the misery and terror it was glorious. Having chocolate and whiskey in an atomic bomb shelter from where we produced a two-page newspaper every day was truly glorious. They were packages of UN humanitarian aid that our editor had saved for us. Everything seemed possible and wickedly exciting in those days before the exhaustion and the despair set in fully over the next couple of years. We were all sexually aroused that night in that bomb shelter dancing, eating chocolate and sausage all in the wrong order, drinking whiskey and sweating profusely. Andrea, the assistant editor, gave me a Chanel lipstick in exchange for one of my dark eyeliners. I put on coral lipstick and she put on dark eyeliner, and we both looked sort of wrong but funny sensuous, like actresses in a movie playing disturbed housewives who smear their faces with makeup. We were drunk from the whiskey and we thought our lipstick and eyeliner experiments were the funniest thing in the world, as we were hidden in the bomb shelter in the middle of a brutal war raging outside. We told Mujo and Suljo jokes such as the one in which Mujo shoots Suljo because when he looks through the rifle he sees a cross and takes the rifle site as Suljo's face thinking his brother had become a Christian. The worst and funniest of all though was the one that went: "What is the difference between Auschwitz and Sarajevo? There is no gas in Sarajevo." I was ashamed of that joke and of my playing with lipstick, but I couldn't stop laughing for hours that night in the atomic bomb shelter.

Later in the siege we almost forgot how to laugh. We became accustomed to the worst and many forgot the peace days. We couldn't remember what peace was like. Had we always been under siege, had we always lived like that, running from corner to corner like rats? It seemed like an eternity. I did not want to forget the days of peace. I wrote down memories of peace and normality from before the war to make up for the hideousness of that every day under fire: sitting around the table and talking about movies with my parents; walking arm in arm with Lara whenever she visited during the summer, in the old section and drinking coffee at my favorite café near the Ferhat-Pasha Mosque, sipping the coffee, dripping a little bit of honey in it, delighting in the conversation about ideas of goodness in philosophies of the world. Eating a piece of fruit and drinking a glass of water in peace. A glass of water seemed heavenly. Simple things like that became a fierce fantasy.

In mid-October of the first year of the war I called Lara from the newspaper headquarters in the bomb shelter and she told me she was getting married after all and her papers were in order for her to leave to the States with Mark. She told me to not even think of coming to the wedding under those conditions, she was so scared for me, was I going to be all right? Was I going to be all right, was I going to be all right, a question that seemed to linger on her mind and that had completely escaped mine. It almost irritated me that she would ask such a thing, who the hell knew if they were going to be all right and still breathe the next minute or not? But Lara always caught herself when she made a blunder. She said she was sorry, she said she didn't know what to say, it was hard to choose one way or another, but she didn't want to miss that chance. "Do you love the guy?" I asked her mercilessly. She waited a couple of seconds before she answered. "Yes, yes, of course I love him. A lot," she said, "I love him a lot." In the space of those two seconds I knew it was something a little bit short of a big love. But it didn't have to be a big love. Even just a little bit of love became huge when you added the component of moving all the way to the United States and starting all settled already in the nation's capital, since it turned out that Mark had a nice apartment in Washington DC and another one in Boston, where he stayed for part of the time as he was finishing up his doctoral dissertation at Harvard. "Be happy, my dear," I said from my heart. "Happy, happy, all right? Be happy for both of us. You have to." For some reason Lara put Mark on the phone, saying he really wanted to talk to me. Mark got on the phone and sounded like he had known me forever. "Hi Marija, Lara talks about you all the time, but I mean really nonstop. She almost didn't want to come to the States with me because she was so worried about you. Is there anything I . . . we could do?" I had to laugh. I said, "Yes, stop the war!" He laughed too and said, "No, seriously, anything at all?" And I said, "I wouldn't joke about something like that. I am very serious, stop the fucking war!" Then Mark took it seriously too and said he was going to write to his representatives, to the president, to the UN, he was going to try to do something, anything to stop the war. I gasped in amazement and thought the guy must have been bonkers. "What a nut Lara is marrying," I thought to myself. But then he didn't seem like a nut, nor did he seem like a fraud. Maybe he was earnest, maybe there were Americans like that, who actually tried to stop a war in a country that very few people could even find on the world map. Lara grabbed the phone and laughed: "Listen Marija, we'll see each other soon, before too long, I'm sure, all right?" Then she said she loved me. She loved me like her sister: "You are my sister after all, you know, what the hell!" I think she must have been slightly drunk because I wasn't sure if she laughed or cried at the end. I hung up and I knew it would be a long time before we would see each other again. A minute after I hung up, the phone rang, and we found out that one of our reporters had been shot at an intersection. He was shot as he was pulling a child who had been shot from the middle of the road. The child lived, the reporter died. I went outside and it was raining. I stood in the street not caring about snipers and artillery of any kind and opened my mouth wide to drink the rain. A glass of water, a drop of honey, a cup of coffee, an embrace, a poem written by candlelight—it all seemed heavenly.

A girl in white was shining at the end of a tunnel like a sun. She had been shot and yet she was the light at the end of this tunnel. A man jumped in flames into the river off of the Mostar Bridge. I couldn't write about any of that any longer. I was searching for something ineffable, for something that hadn't been touched by any of it, not by snipers, artillery, rocket launchers, something that escaped whole, hidden in some secret corner. Nothing did. There were no secret corners, everything had been uncovered and ravaged. I dreamt of it though. I dreamt of the girl shining like an angel with blinding light in a doorway that led to somewhere safe. I had beautiful dreams and I wanted to be pregnant. The man flying like a torch over the Mostar Bridge was stunning in my dream, burning bright in his flight like a meteor moving through cosmos. I missed Lara, I missed our childhood, our crazy college years. Lara had been so right to fly away to her American dream. I sometimes envied her safety, her American husband, her career, the white suite at her wedding. Mostly I would have given anything for an hour of her safety.

Then I heard one day that Mark did keep his word trying to do something to stop the war: he managed to bring the director of our newspaper to America on a special fellowship to Harvard. It was his way of trying to stop the war. We thought that with him gone from the paper and in America on an important fellowship talking to important Americans and even to President Clinton, news of our misery would reach out and move everybody into action. We thought that they would all mobilize over there and indeed stop the war. What was Lara thinking when she heard the chief editor of the newspaper I worked at was in America and had been brought over by no one else but her own Mark? Why hadn't she convinced Mark to bring me over there instead? What was she thinking? Why was I hanging on to that dying city?

My father played his music at all hours of the day and night and his flute sounded like a serenade to death. It was as if death was standing on a balcony like Juliet resting her head on the back of her palm and as if my father was Romeo serenading death who looked so alluring and enchanting. His flute sounded like soothing silence at times, it was amazing how he could play that instrument and make it sound like silence. It was silence serenading death: raw and sweet at the same time, alluring and terrifying, sexual and macabre. My mother sewed needlepoint tablecloths by candlelight. We had more embroidered tablecloths during the war than there were safe spots in Sarajevo. My mother sewed herself to safety, each stitch a moment of safety in the night of Sarajevo.

I loved my city during the war more than at any other time. I loved it most when it was all shelled and toothless with hyacinths shamelessly pushing forth from devastated gardens and alleys in the spring of 1993 and again in the spring of 1994 and again in the spring of 1995. We all lived in shelled, damaged, bombed buildings and sunk deep in our hopelessness with every month gone by. There was a raw and bitter beauty about our hopelessness. If Lara could have only seen us. No Hollywood movie ever recorded or illustrated anything like that. Still, I craved a Hollywood movie, craved that shiny, glossy illusion telling me it was all going to be all right in the end.

After the editor left I sort of took over the newspaper, not because I wanted to, but because I couldn't not do it. There wasn't much we could print or even paper we could print on. It had gotten to be a one-page newspaper and sometimes people purchased it instead of buying bread. We sometimes got bread in humanitarian packages at the newspaper headquarters: sliced bread in plastic wrappings and we ate it shamelessly, selfishly, in a hurry. Together with twenty-year-old cans that we also ate in a hurry, laughing. They got to be known as the "Vietnam care packages." Every week I begged my colleagues to let me publish a poem in the paper, a poem translated from English or French, a stanza by a French Romantic or by an American modernist. We argued for hours over it, and I always won in the end. I told them desperate people under siege needed something like a drop of honey, a clear note, something to lift them above the daily news, which was always the same: how many were killed by snipers, what building had been shelled, and even news of unlikely survivals. All the editions were starting to look alike. Some days, everything looked like everything else: the shoe of a woman lying in the middle of an intersection and her other shoe a few feet away on the sidewalk, the doll of a child, one of the one thousand children who had been killed in Sarajevo, a burning car, a man carrying water canisters from the fountain at the end of the city, a stray dog gnawing on a questionable bone. There were categories of scenes and situations and objects that kept recurring and even in their unusualness became ordinary: the pattern of random objects and photographs from people who had been killed, the pattern of people who crossed the street nonchalantly and survived sniper bullets, the pattern of bloody parts in unexpected corners, everything became a pattern. In the monotony of daily destruction, a poem by e.e. cummings was like a peal of laughter, like a clear drop of honey, and its only pattern was that of musically arranged vowels and consonants. We always laughed when we argued about the poems. These were the only times we laughed. This was my proof that it was important to place a poem at least once a week in our daily one-page newspaper.

I held on to the stick of coral Chanel lipstick forever, and when the last of my dark eyeliner ran out, I begged Andrea to let me borrow hers, the one I had given her in exchange for the lipstick. Those desperate attempts at coquettishness and vanity were the only drops of normality in our lives, and we clung to them as if they were more important than food. Which sometimes they were. Some of the women who were killed at intersections by snipers were wearing lipstick at the time. I saw the photographs.

I sometimes took their pictures for the paper myself. I became obsessed with small things like that, because the big things were too exhausting, too monotonous, and too jarring on my nerves. We wanted to be beautiful when we died in the middle of that orgy of violence. We wrote poems and made jokes, we wanted to be witty when we died in the middle of all that artillery fire. That's why my father serenaded death with his flute. Since death kept coming our way in an unstoppable gallop, we might as well deal with death in style, with flamboyant movements and feathery sounds. We might confuse death for a while longer.

I took the cans of condensed milk that we got from the humanitarian aid to Ferida, who was pregnant like a full moon. Ferida wrote love poems and attended to her round belly every day. We had been high-school friends during the time I went to school in Sarajevo, and her parents were neighbors of my grandparents, on the hillside across from the cemetery. Around that same time, during the fall of the second year of the war, I heard that Lara was pregnant. She hadn't wasted any time. I couldn't imagine Lara pregnant somehow. She was so small and so cerebral, so stringy and so focused on the life of the mind, on problem-solving, that a baby seemed slightly grotesque. On some days the idea of women being pregnant and bringing more wretched crying individuals into that bloody chaos seemed incongruous—almost like a cruel circus act where all the animals ate their trainers, the clowns were shot dead, the ballerinas fell from the trapeze and died in a pool of blood, and then, in the midst of all that, a chimpanzee gave birth to a baby chimpanzee. What was the point?

On some days the war seemed like life, and new life seemed like death. I became fascinated with the big explosions, the different kinds of reds that unfolded like immense apocalyptic flowers across the sky. And on those same days, Ferida's round belly seemed like a tomb. But then I still brought her the condensed milk cans and stroked her belly and listened to her new poems. And for a few excruciating moments, I desperately wanted to have a baby growing inside my own belly. Being with Ferida made me realize even more how much I missed Lara and how jealous I was of her farawayness in America and her transatlantic silence and distance and her incongruous pregnancy. Then I heard that Mark had managed to get Hassan, our newspaper's editor in chief, a long-term position at Harvard, and that he had met with President Clinton. That he wasn't coming back to Sarajevo anytime soon and that he had brought his wife over to the States too. I was happy for Hassan because he deserved it. He had been the one to get us into the bomb shelter and to continue publishing the paper despite the relentless destruction around us. And he was a charismatic man of integrity, who would impress even the president of the United States with his fierce stubbornness, his determination to uphold truth, justice, objectivity. Yet something still stung me deep in my heart about Lara's husband bringing Hassan to America for good and not someone else—someone like me, for example. Didn't Lara have any influence, any say in Mark's decisions, I wondered? At that point in my life, I would have dropped everything, whatever there was to drop in the daily hell we lived in, and swum to America and to Lara's Washington. I sometimes went to sleep with the sound of that phrase rolling in my head over and over again like an inescapable refrain: Lara's Washington, Lara's Washington, Lara's Washington.

On some days, I was high on war and those implausible multi-red explosions and Ferida's poems. On other days, I wanted to commit suicide and blend in with the rest of the corpses piling up in our city as though we were living the Black Plague in the Middle Ages all over again. Now I fantasized almost every day that Lara would bring me over to the States, and I would leave everybody and everything behind and fly on that enchanted horse to America. But my father's serenade to death kept me immobile, tied fast to my decaying city.

I had no love affairs during the war, even though I wanted to get pregnant and everybody around me seemed to be sleeping with everybody else in indiscriminate combinations. After all, a war was going on, and death was always around the corner. You never knew when it would hit you, so you might as well grab what the moment had to offer: care packages, a bar of chocolate on the black market, or casual sex. But I wanted some kind of an immaculate conception, in vitro fertilization, something pure and sanitized that did not involve regular sexual intercourse. I remembered Lara's speech in one of the taverns where we were doing our antiwar gigs in Belgrade, and how she went on about the connections between macho sexuality and wars of aggression, the sexual component of wars, and the components of nationalistic libido. Her words lit up in my mind at that time. News of the rape camps were starting to reach us and something in me froze and became fiercely chaste. One day, Andrea from the newspaper came in saying that in the little village of Semizovac, between Sarajevo and Srebrenica, where my father's parents lived, the hotel Chez Sonja had become a rape hotel for Serbian soldiers. They kept Bosnian Muslim women hostage and raped them on a regular basis. That was only one out of many such hotels and camps strewn across Republika

Srpska. I knew the village and the hotel, and I could visualize it. I couldn't process the news though. It was easier to process the bombings and the snipers. They were more straightforward and cleaner.

One morning, I woke up with the unnerving feeling that the worst was yet to come. I wanted to contact Lara and beg her to bring me to America somehow. I would have walked the tunnel to the airport. Instead, I went to the newspaper and brought them my assignment for that week. I wasn't doing news of unlikely survivor stories anymore. I was sick of them and had doubts whether surviving was even the best thing to do under those conditions. I was more intent on *how* people survived than on *if* they survived. And was survival everything? What mattered most? On the worst days, I thought in upside-down and arbitrary patterns. A poem mattered more than a building, three rations of our half kilogram of flour mattered more than the national library, the life of this sickly ten-year-old girl mattered more than the life of this twenty-year-old healthy woman. One was blonde, the other brunette. I had no idea why such hierarchical values emerged in my exhausted mind, but they roamed and buzzed through it with a frequency equal to that of the sniper shootings—as if they were trying to keep up with them and resist their reckless brutality.

I now wrote reviews of underground art exhibits, poetry readings, and performances. Ferida started a poetry circle in the basement of her house. Mirza, a sculptor friend of mine, made sculptures out of found metals that came from anywhere: destroyed cars, parts of handrails, unrecognizably smashed and coiled metallic pieces. Some had stains of blood on them. We decided to have a combined art exhibit in Ferida's basement with poetry readings, Mirza's metal sculptures, artwork by a few other artist friends we knew, and music played on different instruments. I begged my father to join us and play his flute. At first, he refused with some vehemence, but suddenly my mother lit up and told him to go. She was going, too, she said. My mother had sunk into a pool of brooding silence when her factory was destroyed and she could no longer go to work. She preferred facing the danger of running and crouching by the sides of buildings to get herself to work rather than staying home in the dark with her thoughts and sewing by candlelight. So surprised was my father by my mother's momentary liveliness that he decided to accompany her. We all dressed in our finest. My mother put on her brown velvet dress that went so well with her brown hair, and my father wore his best gray suit with a starched white shirt and a yellow tie. I put on my yellow silk dress with black polka dots that Lara used to rave about. It was April, three years since the war had started. We went along the tram rails in the direction of the Holiday Inn Hotel, where all the foreign journalists were lodged. As always, we ran some of the way, then walked crouching against buildings for another part of the way. Suddenly, I felt an insufferable sorrow, as I thought of the three of us walking happily in Sarajevo during peacetime. Our steps lightened. My memory catapulted us all the way to the street and building where Ferida lived. We didn't care about the snipers anymore, for we were no cellar people who hid in their cellars all day long. We walked and ran in the street like normal people in normal times. A gust of nostalgia lifted us off the ground, and we glided through air holding hands like we used to when Sarajevo was a happy city, and we were a happy family, and I was a fierce little girl hungry for the world.

When we got to Ferida's basement, the place was full of people. Ferida looked plump and rosy, and her belly was ready to burst open with a healthy child, as if we lived in peacetime. Mirza's sculptures were horrid and stunning at the same time. The many cuts and glints and coils of metal looked like sad monsters. There were musicians with violins and guitars. One of them brought a keyboard, while another one brought a tuba. Ferida had baked bread by putting together several rations of flour, and there were even vodka and eggs. Somebody must have paid big money on the black market for them. My father felt shy at first. His emaciated yet still beautiful face with the gray mustache wore a shadow of profound exhaustion. But when the other musicians invited him into their midst, and they started talking about what pieces to play, his face lit up with a long-absent smile. The place was decorated with colored paper and flowers, as if for a party. We attacked the vodka with more voracity than the food and told Muja and Sulja jokes, making fun of those Bosnians who had stayed and not found a way to escape—people like us, stupid Bosnians who hadn't run away as the smart ones had done. People who had stayed in Sarajevo during the war. Almost everybody read poems, original poems or works by known poets. After reading a couple of her own poems, Ferida chose to read a stanza from Wallace Stevens's "The Idea of Order at Key West." She enunciated each word like she was biting into a honeyed apple. "She sang beyond the genius of the sea . . ." Ferida swayed in the rhythm of the vowels and consonants which burned indelible marks on my brain. ". . . and yet its mimic motion made constant cry . . ." After she finished reading, she floated across the room holding her pregnant belly like a trophy.

Then the group of musicians conferred among themselves for a while and said they were preparing a surprise. They tuned their instruments and whispered to each other. Mirza's coiling sculptures waited in resignation. Then the ad-hoc band started playing waltzes. Of all the choices they could have made, they decided to offer a medley of the best-known waltzes: Strauss, Chopin, Tchaikovsky, Shostakovich. The odd combination of instruments made the medley sound funny at times and unbearably sweet at others. My father's flute always came in like an elegant whisper, the tuba contradicted everybody, the strings kept the harmony, and the keyboard gave it playfulness. People started dancing with each other like mad, as if their lives depended on making those waltz steps in the crammed, damp basement. At Shostakovich's "Second Waltz," a deep sob joined the music. It was Mirza, the sculptor, sobbing like a child. Everybody was crying and dancing. I danced with Ferida and we both cried and waltzed clumsily, we were much better at rock. ". . . and yet its mimic motion made constant cry." We laughed at our clumsy steps, while my mother glided like a dream in her velvet brown dress.

When they commenced "The Blue Danube," Ferida crouched over and stayed like that for a few seconds. When she straightened back up, her face was burning red. "I'm starting," she said. "What are you starting?" I asked, as clumsily as I waltzed. Oh! She was going into labor! *What a time and place to give birth,* I thought. My mother saw Ferida and came over. She asked her about her husband. He was a doctor and was nearly always gone. Once in the hospital, he stayed there for forty-eight-hour shifts to avoid moving through the streets and getting shot at. "Yes, but you are giving birth now," said my mother, determined. "How funny that my husband is a doctor and he cannot help with the birth of his own child." I was glad that Ferida saw the comic element in that situation, but I felt entirely void of humor at that time. The musicians played wildly. In some sort of delirium, they performed one piece after another—all the waltzes of the nineteenth-century European repertoire. There was such a confusion of instruments and metals and human moans that my mind felt clogged and incapable of thinking. In spite of myself, I went to the musicians and told them to please stop playing because Ferida was giving birth. They looked at me, smiled, and went on playing. I screamed at the top of my lungs to stop, that Ferida was giving birth. The music halted with a screech. The silence that followed lasted only a few seconds. It hung like a huge incandescent ball in the air. Then the men started moving and talking incoherently, arguing with each other about what to do. Who should take Ferida to the hospital, should she even be taken to the hospital, or should someone go get her husband from the hospital? It looked like a Charlie

Chaplin silent movie to me, as I tuned out the vociferations. I had no idea what anyone was saying. The men's gesturing and voiceless arguing looked pretty funny. Ferida was lying on the sofa breathing deeply. I asked her how she felt, and she said: "Like I'm going to have a baby come out of me." I couldn't help laughing. She laughed too and told me that up in the house there were instructions and materials for the birth, left by her husband. Could someone go get them? she asked. I transmitted the request to the screaming men, trying to yell above their ridiculous din, and all of them answered at once that they would. Such wonderful gentlemen were our Bosnian musicians. In the end I asked my father and gave him Ferida's instructions.

It was late afternoon. Everybody did everything during daytime. Once it got dark, we were all left in the lonely obscurity of our apartments and houses. Ferida's baby was kind and polite to choose daylight to be born, I thought. My father came back flushed and happy that he could be of some use. He handed me a long sheet of paper with written instructions, scissors, alcohol, sterilized sheets, and gauzes. "Now what?" I said to Ferida. "We follow the goddamn instructions," Ferida said, which was very unlike her, since she never lost her temper or cursed. But I guessed giving birth would make the saintliest woman in the world lose her temper.

Ferida had contractions for hours, and the baby wasn't coming. It got dark and some of the men produced candles out of their pockets and lit them. "Anything is possible in times of war," I remember someone at the newspaper saying. Yes, indeed, war was a time of all possibilities. You could even deliver a child following written instructions, as if baking a cake: "count contractions, check dilation, massage cervix, tell mother to push once head is crowning, help baby out with own hands once head is crowning, cut umbilical cord with sterilized scissors a few seconds after baby is lying on mother's stomach," so on and so forth. Who had this husband written these instructions for anyway? Was he kidding? He should have been there with his wife, delivering his own baby, not leaving it to a bunch of vodka-intoxicated artists in the basement of their house. Ferida wasn't screaming or crying, she was just moaning and groaning periodically. A few times she cursed, which in her mouth sounded funny. Around nine in the evening the baby started to crown. I was crouching between Ferida's legs with the sheet of instructions in one hand and the scissors in the other. A couple of the men were holding candles on each side. This was a birth from hell. Or maybe all births were from hell, and into an even worse hell: the world. My mother was next to me and asked me to give her the scissors. We told Ferida to push, but she wasn't pushing. "Push, damn it," I heard myself say. Ferida looked startled almost, as if she had fallen asleep, but then she followed the order and started pushing. Everything went terribly fast after that. Once the head came out, the whole thing slithered out like a fish. Ferida gave two loud screams: the first when the head emerged and the second when the whole baby emerged. Then came a bunch of stuff that looked like some of the questionable masses of blood and flesh we sometimes stumbled into in the street on our daily races between sniper bullets: raw and offensive to the eye, but sometimes you were so fascinated by it that you couldn't stop looking at it. You wondered what part of a body, what parts of organs exactly they represented. The mass of bloody flesh that came out of Ferida after the birth of her baby looked just as revolting.

The beginnings of life were rather unseemly. What a miracle that humans recovered from their own births and went on living at all. I felt like I was going to faint, but my mother caught the baby and placed it on Ferida's stomach. Ferida asked, "What is it?" She wanted to know the sex of the baby, but I thought that she was asking something else, something incomprehensible, like what was wrong, what happened, what was going on? A baby was going on. Then Mirza shrieked from the dark, "It's a girl." Ferida started crying, and then my mother started crying. Then my father played the flute. It was a happy tune this time, something folkloric and indigenous. A serenade to life for once. The next morning, I heard that Lara had her baby too: she had a girl, and she called her Natalia. It was April 5, the three-year anniversary of the war. I went to the newspaper that day and wrote the story of Ferida's baby being born in the middle of an art exhibition/concert/poetry reading in the basement of her house. Sarajevo was still alive: we were dancing the waltz and delivering baby girls.

Aminatta Forna

AMINATTA FORNA (Sierra Leone) is a novelist, memoirist, and essayist. Her novels are *Happiness* (2019), *The Hired Man* (2013), *The Memory of Love* (2010), and *Ancestor Stones* (2006). In 2002, she published a memoir of her dissident father in Sierra Leone, *The Devil That Danced on the Water*, and she is the author of a forthcoming book of essays, *The Window Seat*. She is winner of the Commonwealth Prize and a Windham Campbell Award from Yale University and has been a finalist for the Neustadt Prize and the Orange Prize. Aminatta Forna was made an OBE (Order of the British Empire) in the 2017 Queen's New Year's Honours. She is Director of the Lannan Center for Poetics and Social Practice at Georgetown University. The selection below is taken from *Ancestor Stones*.

Why I Write (about War)

There was a time when war was a man's business. Wars were fought by soldiers, and soldiers were men. Men gave their lives. So naturally men, male authors, took custody of the stories of other men and the wars they fought. Soldiers were the greatest casualties of war. And in the minds of many people this continues to be the case.

But the nature of war has changed. The battlefields of Europe during the Great War, in which armies faced each other dug into opposing trenches on either side of fields emptied of crops and livestock, belong to the past. Many if not most conflicts now are civil conflicts, they are fought in urban areas, and they are fought by rebel fighters, factions, militias, and self-styled armies. The fighters of today are very different from those of sixty years ago and so too are their victims. According to the UN International Children's Emergency Fund, "Civilian fatalities in wartime have climbed from 5 per cent at the turn of the century . . . to more than 90 per cent in the wars of the 1990s and today."

"Armed conflict kills and maims more children than soldiers," noted Graça Machel, during her time as "the Secretary-General's Special Representative for Children and Armed Conflict." And women, too, suffer disproportionately as victims in war. The world now finds itself at a place in which, perversely, the safest people in a war zone are likely to be the combatants. The phrase "women and children first" takes on a new and chilling meaning.

The change in the way wars are fought, upon whose bodies, has changed who writes about war and how they write. My own vivid memory as a young woman in the 1990s is of the reports by the British journalist Maggie O'Kane, one of the first, perhaps *the* first, to bring forth the stories of the horrors being inflicted upon the women of Bosnia during the Yugoslav conflict. Maggie O'Kane wasn't the first woman war correspondent; Margaret Bourke White and Martha Gellhorn matched male reporters for courage as they filed reports from the front line. Maggie O'Kane's reports, though, were different, filed typically many miles *away* from the front line. They offered readers of her newspaper, the *Observer,* a different perspective on the Yugoslav war. Maggie O'Kane didn't talk to generals and commanders; she talked to the civilians in towns and villages near where the fighting was taking place, and she began to hear stories of rape, of the existence of rape camps where Bosnian women were held and used for sport by Serbian army soldiers. Rape was used as a weapon of war in Sierra Leone and Darfur, and that practice continues in the Congo. War is not, if it ever was, the domain of men.

My first book was a memoir, the story of how a country loses its way, blundering from a place where people recognized some degree of moral certitude, step by blind step, into the dark space in which democracy gives way to dictatorship, and oppression eventually gives way to war. When I am asked why I write about war, the answer necessarily takes me to how I came to write fiction. The answer is that my road to becoming a novelist was a convoluted one. I did not set out to become a writer of fiction; I metamorphosed into one.

I began my working career as a journalist. I thought journalism was a way of writing about the things that mattered to me and getting paid, which was what I needed at that time. In my mid-twenties I became a television reporter with the BBC. A decade later I was done. I have often said the happiest two days of my career as a journalist were the day I first walked into the BBC and the day I walked out. I was never content as a reporter for a large organization. And Africa, it scarcely needs to be said, was not a priority. Once, in the 1990s, following a tip from a UN worker, I approached my editor with a story about atrocities being committed in Darfur. My editor looked upon me with weary kindliness before he replied, "Middle England is not interested in Africa."

I left the BBC in 1999, when the war in my father's country and mine was reaching its nadir. My stepmother had been forced to flee in 1997 and had spent more than a year as a refugee in our home in London. It is an eerie feeling, to watch your country implode on television, to see places you have known destroyed, to search for familiar faces among the crowds of civilians trying to reach safety. And then there was the misreporting, the simplifying, and the plain inaccuracy of many of the press stories. Impossible not to notice how a contemporaneous war—that in the former Yugoslavia—was reported with every political nuance, whereas ours was stripped of meaning, turned into mere spectacle. Our violence was rendered "senseless" in the truest meaning of the word.

I left the BBC to write a memoir, *The Devil That Danced on the Water,* the story of the life and death of my father, a political activist who was executed in 1975 by the regime he had opposed. In his final letter, written on paper given to him in order that he might beg the president to spare his life, and written with a pen given for the same purpose, he wrote instead an address to the nation and had it smuggled out of the prison. In his letter he traced the events of the past and predicted war as the final destination for a country already on the path to dictatorship. The political underpinnings of the war rendered "senseless" by the world's media had been foreseen decades before.

Soon after the memoir was published I began work on a novel set across a timespan of one hundred years and told entirely in the voices of five women. In researching my memoir I had become aware of how much of the war had been waged against civilians, women in particular, and yet their accounts were notably absent from public narratives. Inasmuch as they were interested in the war, it was the story of the boy soldiers that captured the attention of the world's media. I began my research by interviewing any woman who would agree to talk to me, beginning with my own family, and once word got out, I found myself with no shortage of women who wished to share their experiences. One woman, partially paralyzed by a stroke suffered at the birth of her daughter, described for me the rebel invasion of Magburaka. Unable to flee on account of her disability, she had climbed into a large wooden chest and hidden there for the entirety of the onslaught. In writing "The Box," one of the stories that appears in the resulting work, *Ancestor Stones,* I tried to imagine the hours of waiting and terror that experience must have entailed. *Ancestor Stones* is a work of fiction, but the true accounts of women who survived the war are the fabric from which the stories are woven.

"Nonfiction reveals the lies, but only metaphor can tell the truth." I've quoted it so many times during moments like this one that on the internet it is now ascribed to me, but I was not the originator. That may have been Nadine Gordimer. I'm afraid I heard it secondhand and now cannot recall where. But the reason I quote it so often is because I have found nothing truer to my writing life. Becoming a novelist for me was the result of the incremental process of realizing, through the process of writing, the specific powers of fiction.

I teach an undergraduate class called "Witness Literature." In the first week we read and discuss Nadine Gordimer's essay "Witness: The Inward Testimony." Gordimer first delivered the essay to the Swedish Academy in 2001, just a few months after 9/11. It begins with the words: "September 2001. A sunny day in New York. Many of us who are writers were at work on the transformations of life into a poem, story, a chapter of a novel, when terror pounced from the sky and we were made witness to it." To act as a witness to world events, to bestow upon those events understanding and meaning, was, in Gordimer's view, the greatest responsibility of a writer. To witness, as she bore witness, to the injustices of apartheid in South Africa, was to do more than document that injustice but, in her own words, to enable the "transformation of events, motives, reactions, from the immediacy into the enduring significance that is meaning." In other words, to see beyond the acts of violence to what is really going on.

For me, as a reader, growing up in Sierra Leone and in Britain in the 1970s and 1980s, everything I knew about apartheid South Africa I gleaned from reading the novels of Gordimer and her contemporaries. The books that reached us were mainly those written in English by white, South African writers, because these were the writers with access to international publishers. It was only one part of the whole story, I realized, but it was enough. As a schoolgirl I wept over *Cry, the Beloved Country*. At university I went to Trafalgar Square and joined the protests. The white, South African father of a friend of mine challenged my understanding of the situation, using an argument popular among conservatives at the time, that apartheid and its laws stood for nothing more than the separation of the races. But I knew different. I knew what was *"really going on."*

In a sense the decision to write about war was forced upon me, I felt it my duty as a writer, but it also seemed to me to be a privilege to find myself alive and writing at a time when my country was searching for important answers.

The late Ursula Le Guin told us in 2015, three years before her death, that the world now more than ever needed writers who "can remember freedom." These are her words: "Hard times are coming, when we'll be wanting the voices of writers who can see alternatives to how we live now, can see through our fear-stricken society and its obsessive technologies to other ways of being, and even imagine real grounds for hope. We'll need writers who can remember freedom—poets, visionaries—realists of a larger reality."

Too often everywhere in the world the press favors the spectacular over the catastrophic, preferring to report individual atrocities rather than document longer-term injustices. The obligation to look beyond the immediate, as Nadine Gordimer said, is increasingly the job of the writer, of those of us blessed with the "awesome responsibility of [our] endowment with the seventh sense of the imagination."

The year 2015, when Le Guin spoke those words, was also the thirtieth anniversary of *The Handmaid's Tale,* by Margaret Atwood. I first read that book when it came out and I was at university. My stepfather worked as a diplomat for the United Nations and had been posted to Tehran some years earlier. As a consequence, I spent much of 1979 in Iran, witnessing firsthand the people's revolution that resulted in the overthrow of the Shah, followed by the hijacking of that revolution by religious zealots. I was fourteen, and revolutionary Tehran was a very strange place to go through puberty. My newly arrived womanhood brought with it no gifts, only the realization that I had become something to be controlled and constrained, something lesser than my brothers. I saw and experienced rights being withdrawn from people, from women, from me.

Atwood saw it too. The dawn of a new religious fundamentalism in the Middle East inspired her to write *The Handmaid's Tale* in answer to the complacency of the West, to the belief that it could never happen here. Gilead, the fictional American state run by Christian fundamentalists in *The Handmaid's Tale,* is both the past and the future. Every one of the horrific punishments described in the novel had at some point been used somewhere in the world. When I reread the book in 2015 to write about it for the thirtieth anniversary of its publication, I was astonished at Atwood's prescience: "It was after the catastrophe," says the handmaiden Offred, "when they shot the president and machine-gunned the Congress and the army declared a state of emergency. They blamed it on the Islamic Fundamentalists."

"We'll need writers who can remember freedom," said Le Guin. It's no coincidence that Atwood, Le Guin, and Gordimer are near contemporaries. They can remember apartheid in South Africa, segregation in the US, the Cold War, the Berlin Wall, Mao's China, the Khmer Rouge in Cambodia, the ebb and flow of freedom around the world.

I remember freedom. I remember freedom being taken away. I grew up in Sierra Leone. In 1961, some years before I was born, Sierra Leone had attained independence from Britain. For several years the country was heady with freedom. Democracy was young, too young to know that freedom can be both given and taken away. In the 1970s we came under the rule of a despot, and one by one our freedoms were removed. My father was a political activist, and his freedom and then his life were taken away. When I wrote my memoir of his life and death, the question I asked myself was, How does a country implode? I tried to trace the steps back from the point where we left the path. It is a question that has preoccupied me for more than a decade and over three novels, imagining myself each time into a different character with a different set of choices. I encourage all readers to do the same—to imagine what it is like to be Hawa, whose son joins the rebel soldiers and brings her looted gifts, or Serah tasked with bringing in the ballot as soldiers try to drive voters from the polling station, or consider the choices made by the morally equivocating Elias Cole, who betrays his friend and arguably in so doing, a future generation. How can we free ourselves from repeatedly committing the mistakes of the past? In *The Hired Man* I considered the war in Croatia, the many similarities in how a country on a different continent and many thousands of miles away had come to suffer the same fate as ours.

There are many reasons why I write. I write better to understand the world. I write because I wish the world to be better. I write because it is the thing I do best that might make that happen. Every now and again in a writer's life something occurs that makes you remember why you do the thing you do.

In May 2014, I received an email from a woman I had met only once in the past. She asked if she might put me in touch with a friend of hers recently released from detention in Sudan. He had read my book, she said, and knowing she had spent time in Sierra Leone, he wondered if she knew me. Well, Sierra Leone is such a tiny country I often say that there exist, rather than the usual six, only two degrees of separation. In other words pretty much everyone knows everyone else or someone who does. I agreed to take a call from her friend, the former political detainee who was then living in Kenya. His name is Ezekiel, and this is the story he told me.

Along with three other men he had been arrested the previous December, accused of conspiring to overthrow the government and charged with multiple offenses including murder, terrorism, and treason. The men were not held at the state prison but at the National Security Headquarters, where on many days they heard rifles being fired in the yard and were never sure whether these were drills or prisoner executions.

One day the men were each given a copy of a book and ordered to read it. The title of the book was *The Devil That Danced on the Water,* the author a woman called Aminatta Forna. The men read the book because they were obliged to do so, but they also discussed it among themselves in the evenings. They saw the obvious parallels in their story and the story they were reading, and they concluded that the reason they had been given it, as with the gunfire outside their cell windows, was to intimidate them. "They were trying to tell us," said Ezekiel to me during our conversation, "that the same fate awaited us as had awaited your father." But reading the book didn't make the men despair; instead, he said, "it had the opposite effect." It invigorated them. It renewed their convictions. It made them remember freedom, their own and their country's. The four men promised that if they were ever released they would find the author of this book and tell her what it had meant to them. At their trial a few months later the government case against them collapsed and they were set free. Ezekiel did not forget his promise to find me.

To write is to enter the thoughts of people you may never meet. There is nothing like it, this meeting of minds. A story travels continents and decades to resonate with each new reader in different ways. Each reader brings something of their own to the story. It is the sharing of human consciousness. Ask me why I write, and if I told you nothing else, I would tell you the story of Ezekiel.

From Ancestor Stones

ASANA, 1998: THE BOX

Five months earlier I had woken to a dawn the color of steel. The curious light lasted through the morning and into the day as if the sun had never risen. The land glowed in silvery shades. Here and there pools of quivering light rested upon the side of a house, on the great leaves of the vine that climbed the wall around my yard. In the middle of the day I looked up at the sky expecting to see clouds; instead I saw the sun, a white disc.

A hawk dropped out of the sky and drank from a puddle of water. A superstitious person might have made something of it, otherwise nothing else remarkable happened. My granddaughter had baked black banana bread and she brought me a piece of it on a dish with a glass of water, staying to keep me company. My appetite had waned as I had grown older, and I covered the dish with a cloth, telling her I would enjoy it later. We spoke little, content in each other's company. I liked simply to watch her liquid movements: flicking a fly with the corner of her dress, fanning her face with her hand, twirling the end of a plait. She sat on the step with one leg stretched out in front of her, the other bent, her cheek resting upon the knee, facing away from me. In the half-light of that day I gazed at the back of her neck, the soft furrow that ran from the nape of her neck down between her shoulder blades; from behind, the curve of her waist belied the child she was carrying, just now beginning to show in the roundness of her stomach. With each passing week the birthmark above her navel widened and stretched.

Adama had been eleven years old when her great-grandmother died. Too young to really remember, old enough not to have forgotten. She had loved my mother fearlessly. In a way I had never been able to.

When she was three, ignoring Kadie, her own mother, she strode with tiny steps up to her great-grandmother and demanded loudly to be taken to the toilet. My mother threw up her hands and stared aghast, as though she had never cared for a child in her life. Kadie quickly led the child away. But my mother had been amused. The girl called her Ya Mama and sometimes Yammy, and my mother encouraged it.

I know, it's the oldest story in the world. The fresh spirit who frees one that has been bottled too long.

She had been away when Ya Mama died. And she had appeared to accept it as children do when they have yet to learn the meaning of forever. Years later she began a game, which she played obsessively for a while. I came to think of it as the "remember" game.

"Remember when that bird landed on Yammy's shoulder . . ."

"Remember when I made her coffee . . ." Mud and river water, mixed together in a tin cup. My mother had been fooled into taking a hearty swig. Later, in the mornings, real cups of coffee just as I had brought to my own grandmother a long time ago. Afternoons, they napped together on the four-poster bed that once belonged to my father.

"Remember Ya Mama's feet . . ." My mother took care of her feet, soles as smooth as paper, nails dipped weekly in henna. When she could no longer bend to reach them, Adama buffed the undersides with pumice.

We would sit for hours sharing memories: fleeting, brightly colored, sometimes surrounded by darkness, passing them back and forth until I was no longer certain whose were whose. She lent me her own memories of childhood with which to remember my mother.

We had played the game the day before for the first time in a long while. Sorting reminiscences the way we had baby clothes. Storing some and putting others aside for the new baby, creating space for new things. That afternoon, though, there was no game. We sat together in a sleepy silence; I watched her head sink, listened to her breathing come in slow sighs.

I stood up to fetch a cloth to fold under her head. On my way I reached for the plate of banana bread. Hali! The plate seemed suddenly as heavy as if it was made of iron. My arm dropped. The plate slipped from my fingers, clattered and spun on the stone floor. Adama, startled, leaped to her feet. The heaviness slid down the side of my body into my leg. I tried to take a step, but I couldn't pick my foot up off the floor. Falling, I felt myself falling. With my other hand I reached for the table and missed. Through the gathering darkness I saw Adama hurrying towards me as I toppled forward.

Later I realized it had been haunting me, stalking me all that day: the steel-grey light—I would forever see the world in shadowy twilight. A doctor was called, a quack who gave me headache pills. Then a proper doctor who had studied in China. And he told me I had had a stroke.

I still went to the store. Adama pushed me in a wheelbarrow. The roads were too rutted to allow a wheelchair to pass. Kadie wanted me to stay home and rest. But I missed the smell, the feel of the place. "When did you ever see a mother sleep while her child was crying?" I told her. There was always work to do. On days when Kadie went to visit our other shops, I worked the till with my one good hand while Adama climbed the step-ladder to bring down the cloths.

My sister Hawa came to see me. Looked at me with sad eyes and shook her head. "Nothing happens for nothing," she pronounced with hidden pleasure. I gave a wave of my good hand, dismissing her. There's a certain kind of person who can always find an explanation for things that happen. My sister was one of those. Something bad befalls somebody they don't like and they say that person must have brought it upon themselves. When precisely the same fate comes their own way, this time it's a spirit bringing bad luck. A person they envy prospers only because that person made a bargain with a powerful spirit. But when they lose their own business, is it because they didn't work hard enough or because they ate all the proceeds and failed to reinvest them? Of course not. It is a *moriman*'s curse, purchased by a rival!

The doctor had explained to me exactly how it happened. A blood clot stopped up one of my arteries so the blood couldn't reach my brain. Like a dam in a river. Even I could understand that. He wrapped a rubber tube around my arm and took my blood pressure, tested my pee for diabetes, wrote a prescription and ordered me to cook with less palm oil.

I took advantage of my state not to offer Hawa anything that might encourage her to stay. She only ever visited when there was something she needed. This time, though, she seemed to want to stay forever. I peered into her shadowed face.

When had this secret war between us begun? I wondered. Five months later, though, her words came back to me. Terrible things began to happen to all of us. It was as though the end of the world had come. The earth crumbled, the sky rained down, people fled for their lives. Nothing happens for nothing. I wanted to straighten my crooked body, I wanted to stamp the earth, raise both my fists and scream at the skies.

What in the world had we all done to deserve such a fate?

WHEN I THINK back now, we kept the knowledge a secret, even from ourselves.

Lorries travelling roads in the South were held up by gunmen who hauled the driver down from his cab, thieved the goods from the back of his vehicle and carried them away into the forest. They set fire to the lorry, sometimes roping the driver to the wheel. Other times slicing off his ears and stealing his shoes before leaving him to walk home. A band of miners were marched away from their workplace and not sighted until months later when they appeared on the other side of the country. Their kidnappers never said who they were or what it was they wanted. There were rumors of tattooed strangers who arrived in towns and moved among the people, members of a secret clan, whose mark was worn by the women under one breast and by the men on the buttock. They looked just like you or me, it was said; some spoke in languages nobody could understand. They disappeared as quickly as they came. There were stories of young men and women who slipped away to join them. The youths' families claimed their children had been stolen and scoured the countryside. Then there were other stories, ones that made your eyes stretch. Of beings that could become invisible, that could fly, leap over houses, that gathered to dine on the hearts of their victims from whence they derived their supernatural powers. There came a time when everybody had heard these stories; some had even claimed to have witnessed them with their own eyes.

Yet who the strangers were, nobody could say.

Members of the ancient clans, the leopard and the crocodile, outlawed for many decades but still continuing their fearful practices, said some. Others insisted such feats were beyond the power of mortal man. And others still said everybody else was talking nonsense, these deeds were the acts of the army, devious in their hunger for power.

On the radio a Government spokesman reassured us. Small groups of insurgents were at work in some parts of the country. The army was involved in a series of mopping-up operations, they said. He made it sound as harmless as spilled milk.

What an insurgent was, nobody knew. Then somebody said it was another word for rebel. Rebel!

People whose children had vanished hid their faces. People reporting fresh disappearances had their homes turned over, the roofs torched. People fell silent, dared not open their mouths to speak. There was a stillness in the air. From the outside it looked like calm, but beneath the surface were turbulent, invisible currents: fear, suspicion, confusion.

Still, life continued, for none of us had the luxury of pausing. For many years that was the way we lived. Finding scapegoats. Turning our faces from the truth.

A ROOSTER used to call false dawns all through the night. I remember because when I woke up his voice was the first sound I heard. By then I had begun to find myself more and more a stranger to sleep. I knew I'd be awake now until morning. It was age, of course, and an effect of my condition. I couldn't keep my eyes open after lunch, only to be awake in the early hours, lying on my back, alone and floating unhinged upon a tide of darkness. That particular morning I woke with a full bladder. Impossible to wait for morning and Adama to come and help me. I put out my hand, felt for my stick, knocking it to the floor. I groped, found it with my fingers and hauled myself up.

Outside the air was cool, damp. I made my way slowly, inching forward with my now sideways walk, like a crab across the ground. I didn't bother to go all the way to the latrine. I urinated out of doors, something I liked to do: the feel of the air on my thighs, the breeze murmuring in the trees, the smell of damp grass, the sound of the night birds interrupted by the hiss of steaming piss. I pulled up my lappa. It amused me to think I was doing something possible only under the disguise of the night. What, I sometimes wondered, would happen if I were to do the same thing in the middle of the day? They would think I had finally gone mad, but men do it all the time, don't they?

Ah, my eyes, my twilight eyes.

But for them I would have noticed sooner.

I urinated with my back to the house. I closed my eyes, savored the weakness that follows the release. Finished, I opened my eyes and squatted there, in no hurry to go back inside, slowly generating the energy to stand up. My eyes rested on the horizon. I blinked. I squinted. Looked again. Brilliant dancing lights of orange, green and gold in the east. Not the warm glow of a bush fire, these were flashing lights, more like Chinese fireworks. I looked up at the night sky and saw the moon still high above me. I stood up, watched the shifting hues of this unearthly display. For a long time I was still, not knowing what to do.

Inside the house I shook Adama's shoulder, we were alone, the two of us. I showed her what I'd seen. We did not sleep that night, we kept a vigil on the back verandah, watching the lights on the horizon.

Early prayers and the mosque was full; my neighbor stopped by with this news—for I had long given up going. Afterwards everybody wanted to talk about the omens in the night sky. At ten o' clock my nephew came and pushed me to town in my barrow. Those days, the effort was far too much for Adama. Twice we had thought her labor was beginning, twice the birth attendant had been summoned. Both times it turned out to be a false alarm. Still, Kadie and Ansuman had delayed travelling to Guinea. In the end, though, Adama had urged her parents to go. Even if the baby came, we would manage.

Adama walked alongside me. The streets were quiet as we made our slow progress through them. In the square I noted half a dozen empty stalls among the regulars. No charcoal. Now, that was interesting. Charcoal was delivered from out of town first thing in the morning. I noticed one other thing, though I mentioned none of it to Adama—all the traders had already sold out of bread.

We opened up the shop, customers were scarce. A little after eleven Mr. Wurie passed by with news of strangers sighted on the main road out of town. It was only a rumor, he told us quietly, but we ought to know. I thanked him for that and his offer to help us in any way he could.

At midday I closed up the shop. Other shop owners had already done the same. We spent a short time moving stock to the storeroom at the back. I took the money box and hid it under the stairs. Afterwards we pulled down the metal shutters and set off home.

Just two streets from the house, past the old railway station, there is a place where the wall of a house juts out and the road curves sharply

around it. We turned the corner. On the road ahead of us I spotted Kamanda, the madman. He was wearing an old fisherman's sweater and a
pair of trousers with the seat torn out. Around his neck hung a necklace
of bottle tops and crumpled drink cans. Kamanda's face was running with
sweat, he was babbling, spraying great gobs of spit. His calloused feet with
their long, grey toenails stamped the earth as he marched up and down,
up and down, swinging his arms.

"Kamanda! Kamanda!" I called. For he was a gentle soul. I had often
given him the offcuts from reams of fabric, which he wrapped around his
head or tucked into his belt like fluttering handkerchiefs. I had never seen
him like this. I tried to calm him with my voice, but there was no reason-
ing with him at the best of times. For a few moments he seemed to settle,
only to jump up, as if to attention, and begin striding up and down again.

At home I sent my nephew back to his house. "Hurry! No shillyshally-
ing," I urged him. Then I busied Adama, telling her to bring the washing
in, round up the chickens, and to light a fire.

While she was occupied I went around the house collecting up all my
jewelry and precious things. From the suitcase under my bed I fetched the
gifts I had bought for Adama's baby, a silver coin with a hole in the middle
and a gold chain to hang around the baby's waist. Along with my most
valuable pieces I tied them up in a cloth and dropped them into the water
jar at the back door; then I sank a large stone on the top. The lesser pieces
of jewelry I spread out on the table in the middle of the room.

Outside I loosened the tether of the goat and waved my stick at her un-
til she bolted into the bushes. Afterwards I went to the yard and ordered
Adama to bring the biggest of the cast iron pots and twelve cups of rice.
Adama exclaimed upon the quantity, but did as she was told.

A lot of rice. Yes, indeed. I intended to cook enough to feed an army.

THERE WAS a town I used to visit. I had been there many times before.
In that town was a factory which manufactured dyes and finishes. Every
once in a while the owners produced a new range of colors and invited
all their customers to view them. I always took the job of going to see
the new range myself. Before I had my stroke it was something I liked to
do. I liked the metallic tang in the air inside the main hall of the factory,
the wooden vats of color stirred by men with iron paddles, the smudges
of color on the walls. Mr. Bangura, the foreman, was a cheerful fellow.
A widower whose wife had died of cholera, he had never remarried. On
the third finger of his left hand he wore a ring. Not an ordinary wedding

band, but a heavy gold signet ring engraved with two sets of initials. We always conducted our business upstairs in his office across a table holding many jars of pigment and glass tubes of colors. When our business was concluded he would serve me a cold drink out of the fridge behind his chair while we chatted about many things. Once he had joked that with our occupations we would make a good pair. And though I replied in a teasing voice that I was past all that, it occurred to me there was once a time when the idea would have not seemed such a bad one.

My visits to the factory also gave me a chance to see Alpha, who worked nearby as a teacher's assistant in a boys' secondary school. He would cycle to meet me, carrying lunch for us both in aluminum pots wrapped up in cloths. We would share our meal, catch up on each other's news and, after I had rested a little and Alpha run whatever errands he had in town, we would set off to the factory, Alpha walking his bicycle, me alongside him.

The last time I visited, the heat had been dazzling, the sun directly overhead. The grass was pale yellow and bone dry, rustling in what little breeze there was. The great, black boulders scattered at the bottom of the hills glistened in the sun. The sky was hazy, streaked with clouds. It was too hot even for the birds, who hid from the heat in the branches of the trees. The factory was some small distance from the town. Despite the heat, Alpha and I walked without stopping, lost in the pleasure of each other's company.

There was no guard at the factory gate. We passed through, still chattering, and we walked on up the empty drive. Mr. Bangura didn't hurry down to welcome me or wave from his office window as he usually did. I noticed, yes. But did I think it so very strange? I don't know, perhaps I only think so now.

The big factory door stood open. We stepped through. Inside the main hall, silent pools of color. A paddle lying on the ground by my feet. Not a soul in sight.

For some reason we did not call out. We stood still and stared around us. Only a moment or two later did we open our ears and listen, and when we did we heard a sound that must have been there all along. A buzzing, like a faint whine, like an airplane engine high in the sky. We followed the sound across the factory floor towards the great double doors that led out to the back, where deliveries came and went. On the opposite side was the storeroom where the tubs of pigment were kept.

One thing nobody ever mentions afterwards is the smell. The indignity of it, I suppose. Such a commonplace smell. One to make your mouth water and your stomach rumble. For the rest of your life at a family gathering, a festival, it will serve to bring back the nausea, return you to the horror.

What is it? It is the smell of roasted meat.

The roof of the storeroom was mostly gone; what remained had collapsed into the building. The windows were ringed with black, shards of darkened glass like broken teeth stuck out of the frames. On the ground below one window lay a tub, partly melted, the spilled violet powder a shock of color. The door had turned to charcoal, and split apart as Alpha kicked it. The sound of buzzing soared. All around us briefly turned to black as we were engulfed by a great mass of flies. I covered my face and hit at them with my hands, and once the air cleared I saw what was inside.

They had been rounded up and herded inside at gunpoint. We know this because it happened later, to others. Those few who survived all told the same story. At first they imagine it is a robbery, they are being locked up to stop them from raising the alarm. From the window they watch carefully the movements of the armed men. Then they see the plastic containers, smell the petrol as it is splashed on the walls and roof of the store. Men with guns encircle the building. Those inside begin to shout and hammer at the door, frantic now. Somebody takes a tub of dye and throws it at the window, it smashes the glass. They scramble over one another to escape the stifling fume-filled air and the certainty of death. The first one to try to climb out is shot.

The screams of the men as they burned must have been terrible, must have filled the air, sent the birds and animals fleeing. And yet nobody hears them. Their killers are deaf to them. There is no one else for miles. And afterwards, when the gunmen are gone, have ransacked the office and made off with the vehicles, silence follows. A desperate, resilient, unbreakable silence.

Alpha and I uttered not a word, not even a gasp, except the grunt he gave at the effort of kicking in the door. We moved around the corpses, who stared up at us through melted eyes, reached out to us with charred and twisted limbs. Some lay alone. Others were fused together, so here a corpse which seemed to have too many limbs, there a pair in apparent embrace. Most of all I remember the hands, by which I tried for a short while to identify Mr. Bangura, searching for his ring. Brittle, blackened sticks reaching out. For what? Curled claws, trying to hold on. To what? To life itself, I can only imagine.

So you see, on that day I believed I knew what was coming. I sat outside on my old stool and positioned myself where I could best see the road.

I settled down to wait. Whatever was out there was on its way. On its way to us.

Adama sat next to me; I watched her hands as she unpicked the frayed edge of a basket and prepared to repair it. I saw how her usually nimble fingers stumbled over the repair, weaving and unpicking the same few inches over and over. At that moment she turned her unblinking gaze up at me.

"Let me fetch you something to eat." She was concerned for me, as I was for her. Each one pretending for the other's benefit. I had no appetite, my mouth was dry as sand.

"Yes, please. I'm a little hungry."

As she rose she pressed the heel of her hand into the small of her back and stood there for a moment. I watched her cross the yard and bend over the cooking pots. For a while she remained doubled over. When she straightened again I saw her features tremble with pain.

Dear God, I said to myself. Not now.

She saw me watching and tried to force her lips into a smile. "Another false alarm."

"With your mother it was just the same."

We sat and waited, the cooling feast spread out in front of us. We saw nobody. No visitor come to pay respects, no neighbor to exchange the news of the day. Not even a single passerby.

In the last part of the afternoon I sat up suddenly, cocked my head and listened. I could hear dogs barking. Not the snarling, yelping of a scrap. Nor the howling call and answer that went on through the night. Rather a relentless, monotonous barking that started and did not stop. I sat listening while I worked out where in the town it was coming from, tracing its progression through the streets towards us.

I stood up and went, quickly as I could manage, into the house, unlocked the storeroom and gathered up a few pieces of smoked fish, some dried cassava. I poured two cups of rice into a handkerchief and knotted it. I found a packet of matches, a little money and a tin cup, tied them all up in a lappa. By the time I had finished I was exhausted.

I thrust the bundle into Adama's hands. I told her what she must do. She shook her head: "No!" she said. The baby might be on its way, I told her. I knew the pains had been coming all afternoon. I had seen her turn away from me every time it happened. The poor child began to cry, and, Oh, how I wanted to cry too, to clutch her and weep, for this wasn't how we had imagined it would be when she came home for the birth. Instead I reached out and gave her shoulder a shake. In the distance came the sound of gunfire. Somebody ran past in the street shouting a warning. I still had my hand on her shoulder, now I pushed her as hard as I could towards the door, telling her to find the neighbors and join them.

She went. She did as she was told. I said I would follow as soon as I could. Maybe the baby would come today, maybe it would come tonight. Maybe it would come next week. But it would come. I could only pray I would be with her when it happened. I kept sight of her as she walked through the banana groves. My ears followed her progress long after she was no longer visible. For several minutes I stood and listened to the clicking of her fingers fading as she walked into the arms of the forest. Only then did I turn to go inside.

When my mother died she left me her possessions, among them the great chest in which she once stored her belongings. It was empty now. I went over to it, dragging my bad foot along the floor. I opened the lid, laid my stick inside. With all the strength left in my one good arm, I hoisted myself up on to the edge. I balanced there for a moment, then I leaned forward and let myself topple in. I lay there, a little winded. Then I reached up and pulled the lid down over me. I curled up in the darkness and went on waiting.

I COULD hear nothing save a few muffled sounds. And all I could see was the narrow beam of light that came from the space between the lid and the box. For the first time I began to feel afraid. For a while I did nothing, just listened to the sound of my own breathing. In the closed space my breaths seemed raucous, as though they had transformed into vapors, clamorous with life, swirling around, searching for a way out.

I tried to make myself comfortable. I should have put down some cloths or sacking to line the inside. Too late now. I was lying on top of my stick and I squirmed until I managed to ease it out from under me. I turned on to my back and lay there with my knees bent. The temperature inside the box was rising, it would soon be as hot as a furnace. I loosened my clothing as best I could. I pulled off my head-wrap, bunched it up and put it under my head as a makeshift pillow. The effort made me thirsty, but I had no water. I didn't dare risk climbing back out; I would have to manage without.

After a bit I began to explore my surroundings. This had been my favorite hiding place when I was a child. I'd lie on top of my mother's belongings, waiting for someone to come and find me, as scared of being discovered as of not being found at all. When the lid finally opened above me, I screamed and screamed. Still, I went back, over and over, to hide in the same place. I didn't think anyone would imagine I would be so stupid as to choose such an obvious place. My double bluff never worked. I prayed it would work this time.

I ran my fingertips around the sides of the box. It was well made, solid and strong. We were more or less the same age, and yet I was the one who'd begun to sag and creak. The box on the other hand had only grown more handsome with the years: the richness of the patina, the worn-smooth surface. I had become so used to it over the years, I'd stopped seeing it, but it was a very elegant box.

I came across a knot in the wood and explored it with my fingers. It was grainy, at odds with the feel of the rest. I scratched it with my fingernail and felt it crumble. I reached up and took a pin from my hair and began to dig at the place. The knot wasn't wood at all, but some sort of plaster, probably where the carpenter had plugged the place where a knot had fallen through. I scratched away like a mouse until I had made myself a spyhole. It was a little high, I had to push myself up on one elbow, but it was better than nothing.

There was more light now, a circular beam coming in through the spyhole. I followed the beam to the other side of the box where it revealed a series of markings: vertical cuts, where somebody had scored the wood with a knife. Two rows often, one above, one below. A carpenter's trademark? Perhaps the box had been made using wood from something else. I ran my thumbnail across the rows, backwards and forwards, making a vibrating sound like a musical instrument.

Now I remembered. As a young girl, watching my mother. Every year, on the day we ate the first rice of the new harvest, going to her room where the great chest stood. With a sharp knife she would score the wood in the same place every year. Every year for ten years. Ten anniversaries. Ten birthdays. Asana and Alusani. Then Alusani died and stole her happiness to take with him back to the other world.

Rofathane. I had fought so hard to leave all that behind. And yet. We had a herbalist, a carpenter, a blacksmith, a birth attendant and a boy who never grew old. Soothsayers prepared us for the unexpected. Teachers travelled to us, bringing the word from Futa Djallon. People who wanted to live in Rofathane had first to find a patron and then to ask permission to settle. There existed an order, an order in which everybody had their place. An imperfect order. An order we understood.

A lullaby came to me, one my mother used to sing:

Asana tey k' kulo,
I thonto, thonto,
K' m'ng dira.

Asana, don't you cry,
I'll rock you, rock you,
Until you sleep.

I hummed softly to myself, and as I did so I began to rock back and forth, growing sentimental, a wet-eyed, foolish old woman. I thought of my mother and father, sleeping safely in their graves. I thought of Osman, of Ngadie. I hoped Kadie and Ansuman were still in Guinea and that they would hear what was happening and not come back. I feared for Alpha.

Voices! Ugly, bold, challenging. They seemed to come from all directions. Voices and the sound of running feet. The feet were bare, I remember that because there was something oddly unthreatening in the way they patted the earth.

I put my eye to the spyhole, and looked left and right.

Two men and a woman came into view. Walking high on the balls of their feet. The woman and one of the men were carrying guns, resting them upright against their shoulders, fingers on the trigger. Just like they do in the cinema. The other man carried a machete and smoked a cigarette. They were looking this way and that, all around them, as they advanced.

Such strange garb, they were dressed like children who had found a dressing-up box. A pair of ladies' sunglasses. A military-style jacket with gold epaulettes. A red bra. Jeans. Camouflaged trousers. A T-shirt with the face of a dead American rapper. A necklace of bullets. Around their necks and wrists dangled charms on twisted strings. They were talking to others I couldn't see, but their talk was unintelligible to me. I thought at first it was some strange tongue, the kind we made up as children. But every now and again a fragment of the exchange occurred in my own language. Gradually I realized that I was listening to several languages being spoken at once.

I had left the back door to my house open. This was how I could see what was going on. I expected my neighbors had bolted theirs before they fled, and sure enough a moment later I heard the sound of wood splintering, of a door being broken from its hinges.

Beneath the cooking pot in the yard the embers of the fire throbbed faintly. One of the intruders raised the lid of the cooking pot. Good, I had wanted them to find the food. I saw him dip his fingers into the sauce, he made a joke to the others.

I pulled my eye back from the spyhole. The other man was wandering dangerously close to the house. I listened to his steps as he approached the door, heard him carefully cross the threshold, the click of his weapon. My heart thudded, my breaths came short and fast. Surely he could hear me, I thought. I cowered inside the box, waiting for the lid to open. They would kill me straightaway, of that I was certain. An old, crippled woman, there was not much sport to be had with me. Softly, the footsteps came closer, inches now from my head. I held my breath.

He stopped, swiveled, turned. He had spotted the jewelry on the table. The chink of metal as he turned over the pieces and began pocketing them. The sounds must have alerted the others, I heard them coming to see what he was doing. I listened in the dark as they began to squabble over my possessions.

Somewhere in the distance a voice shouted orders. The three looters snatched up the remainder of the jewelry and began to move off. I put my eye to the spyhole, watched their backs as they disappeared. I lay back and breathed out.

I slept. I woke. I slept again. A serpentine dream wove its way through my mind. Dreams of discovery. Dreams of death. I slipped in and out of consciousness and woke struggling for air. My tongue was stuck to the roof of my mouth. For a moment I had forgotten where I was. My body was damp, pools of sweat had gathered on the floor of the box. Something had woken me.

I could hear scattered gunfire. From outside came the smell of burning straw. I peeped out of my spyhole. Against the darkness, a halo of flickering light: fire from flaming houses. In the yard a stone ricocheted. A figure appeared carrying a burning brand. It lit up his features, turning his nostrils into black holes, his eyes into dark hollows. With silent steps he crossed the yard, making for my neighbor's house.

The hours passed. I must have lost track of time. The next I knew the three from before were back. I listened as they slit the throats of my chickens and roasted them over the fire. The contents of my cooking pots were passed around. More people came, bringing loot from the surrounding houses. Evidently they had broken into the bottle store. There was music and much rough laughter. Different smells drifted into the box: the sour smell of unwashed bodies, rum fumes and the scented smoke of marijuana.

Hamdillah, how I prayed. I don't deny it. Not at all. To the gods of Islam and Christianity, to every god in the skies plus any others I might not have thought of. Would they set fire to my house when they had taken what they wanted? Would I die of thirst trapped in my hiding place? Somewhere my fate was already cast in stones.

Have you ever wondered what it is that makes people do terrible things? I have. Since that day, I have set my mind to it many times. All the stories of supernatural beings and yet those men and women out there were not so different from me, only that something inside them had been unleashed. So, where does it come from, the fury? A thousand indignities, a thousand wrongs, like tiny knife wounds, shredding a person's humanity. In time only the tattered remnants are left. And in the end they ask themselves—what good is this to me? And they throw the last of it away.

At dawn, finally, they slept. I listened to the sound of their snoring. I didn't dare let myself fall asleep again in case I snored too, or cried out in my dreams. The sun was halfway up the sky and the temperature inside the box was rising rapidly by the time they had woken up. Through my circular window I watched them rouse themselves, collect up their weapons and as much of their stolen booty as they could carry, and stumble away like sleepwalkers.

I waited two hours more, then I opened the lid of the box and climbed out. I plunged my arm into the water jar and retrieved the bundle. I allowed myself a few sips of water before I picked my way across the yard, through the banana grove and into the trees. I kept on walking. I left the path. I crossed the boundary into the sacred forest. It was a forbidden place, but what did that matter now? Things had changed, perhaps forever. The old order had gone, those rules no longer applied. I had to find Adama, to help bring her baby into this world.

With me I carried my gifts for the baby. But what would I say to her? How would I explain that her great-grandmother, who had lived for longer than eighty years, had learned nothing at all, had no knowledge to give? That she had arrived in a world where suddenly we were all lost, as helpless as newborns.

Scholastique Mukasonga

SCHOLASTIQUE MUKASONGA (Rwanda) was born in 1956 and experienced from childhood the violence and humiliation of the ethnic conflicts that shook her country. In 1960, her family was displaced to the polluted and underdeveloped Bugesera district of Rwanda. Mukasonga was later forced to flee to Burundi. She settled in France in 1992, only two years before the brutal genocide of the Tutsi swept through Rwanda. In the aftermath, Mukasonga learned that thirty-seven of her family members had been massacred. Her first novel, *Our Lady of the Nile,* won the 2014 French Voices Award and was shortlisted for the 2016 International Dublin Literary Award. It was made into a film, which premiered in February 2020. In 2017, her memoir *Cockroaches* was a finalist for the LA Times Christopher Isherwood Prize for Autobiographical Prose. In 2019, her memoir *The Barefoot Woman* was a finalist for a National Book Award. In addition, she has won many prizes in France and elsewhere in Europe, among them the 2014 Prix Seligmann de la Chancellerie des Universités de Paris, which recognizes work against racism and intolerance, for *La femme aux pieds nus* (*The Barefoot Woman*); the 2010 Prix Renaissance de la nouvelle Louvain-la-neuve (Belgium) and the 2011 Prix Bourdarie de l'Académie des Sciences d'outre-mer for *L'Igifou, nouvelles rwandaises* (*Igifu*); the 2012 Prix Renaudot, the 2012 Prix Océan France Ô, the 2012 Prix Ahmadou Kourouma of the African Circle of Geneva, and the 2017 Prix des Ambassadeurs francophones, Copenhagen, for *Notre-Dame du Nil* (*Our Lady of the Nile*); and the 2015 Prix Bernheim of the Foundation for French Judaism for her complete works. She was also recognized with the Distinction of Knight of Arts and Letters, accorded to Kigali, the capital of Rwanda, by the ambassador of France in 2013. The selections below are taken from *Cockroaches* and *The Barefoot Woman.*

Why I Write about War

Who had ever heard of Rwanda before the months of April, May, and June 1994, when a million Tutsi were massacred under the most atrocious conditions? It's true that Rwanda is not easy to distinguish on a map of Africa. It's like a piece of confetti, only half the size of Switzerland. Even well-informed people had hardly heard of the Tutsi giants, volcanoes on the slopes on which the last of the gorillas lived. Some held it up as a model: a highly Christian country, a paradise for NGOs, a peaceful haven in contrast with its huge, turbulent neighbor, the Congo.

Most of the time they didn't realize that it was a heavily populated country (today, nearly twelve million inhabitants), with densities of more than three hundred inhabitants per square kilometer. Did they know that it had been colonized by Germans and then, after the Great War, placed under Belgian authority? Rwanda was not a colonial creation like so many other African states, with boundaries determined by European interests. Before the arrival of colonists, Rwanda was one nation. Its rich and abundant oral traditions go back to the seventeenth century, and its archaeological artifacts, to the first millennium.

The complexity of its society and the richness of its rituals concerning the sacred royals had amazed and fascinated the first Europeans—missionaries and colonial administrators—who spent time in the country. The population consisted of fifteen or so clans that played an essential political role. They were divided into three communities: the Hutu, who were farmers; the Tutsi, who were breeders; and the Twa, who were potters or hunters. These three groups were not separate ethnicities, and certainly not separate races. They all spoke the same language and lived side by side, sharing the same culture. Although the royalty was Tutsi, and certain clans claimed privileges and wealth in the form of livestock, most Tutsi were indistinguishable from the rest of the population. The political and economic elite was comprised of Hutu as well as Tutsi.

One of the greatest misfortunes to befall the Rwandans, and the Tutsi in particular, was to inhabit the area around the mouth of the Nile. Of course, before the arrival of the Europeans, they didn't realize this. They ignored the myths about this mysterious river that every year flooded Egypt, a land where no rain fell—myths that had been accumulating since Antiquity. At the end of the nineteenth century, Rwanda was the last holdout, the last white spot, on the map of an Africa already disillusioned with colonization. At the mouth of the Nile, you could find some unusual creatures that seemed to have emerged from a legend. And if not, you could invent them. As a matter of fact, the complexity of the Rwandan political-religious organization fascinated the first observers so much that they concluded that it couldn't be the work of Africans, whom they believed incapable of creating stable states and refined cultures. All of that had to have come from the outside, from invaders who imposed their civilization on "the niggers." And that's the role that was attributed to the Tutsi. They couldn't have been completely black, people thought, imagining the craziest origins for them: Ethiopia, Egypt, Caucasia, Tibet. Or, they were the descendants of one of the ten lost tribes of Israel, people said. A new race was even invented for them: they were Hamites, descendants of Cham, or Ham, one of the sons of Noah! So in spite of themselves, the Tutsi found themselves engaged in the scenario of racist ideologies that dominated anthropology until the mid-twentieth century. The Europeans at first considered them a superior race, fit to be governed, but after the Hutu takeover, they were considered nothing but foreigners, invaders, true colonizers who must be driven away and finally eradicated.

On the eve of independence, Belgium, the governing power, and the omnipotent Rwandan Catholic Church, overanxious to achieve immediate independence, abandoned the Tutsis. We were in the midst of a cold war, and the example of the neighboring Congo no doubt provoked that reversal. A Hutu elite, formed in seminaries, demanded reforms that might have been justified if they had not included the racist agendas with which this elite had been inculcated. On All Saint's Day 1959, the first pogroms against the Tutsi, certainly orchestrated, broke out. Thousands were massacred, and tens of thousands fled to neighboring countries.

Like many other Tutsis, in 1960, my family was deported to a region in the south of Rwanda, near the border with Burundi. At that time, Le Bugesera was an inhospitable savannah, unhealthy and depopulated by sleeping sickness, the domain of large animals: elephants, lions, water buffalo, etc. They were no doubt hoping that the "refugees from the interior" would die there. But my family survived. It was in Nyamata, one of those villages full of deportees, that I spent my childhood. The daily persecutions and repeated massacres were a reminder that nothing awaited us but genocide. At any moment, under the slightest pretext, they could annihilate us. Fear was a dark shadow that accompanied us night and day. But that fear sharpened our senses and permitted us to survive for thirty years. My mother used to say: "Admire the fly, which sees on all sides. Tell yourself that you are a fly."

For we were not resigned. We were determined to survive. Many sought exile. I myself, forced to leave social work school in Butare in 1973, took the path of exile to Burundi.

I was in France when the genocide took place. April, May, June 1994. One hundred days, one million deaths. As would any other human being, I sought to find out if, among those in my family who had stayed in Rwanda, there were any survivors. I had no illusions: in Nyamata, there were only Tutsis. And then, a letter from Rwanda arrived. It was the list of my relatives. The list of my dead relatives. Thirty-seven names. That's when the sense of guilt at having survived overwhelms you, as a character who always carries a list of her dead relatives says in one of my stories ("Le deuil, dans L'Igifu" [Mourning, in L'Igifu]): "those who died far away from her, without her, without her being able to do anything for them, not even die with them."

It took me ten years to return to Rwanda. I didn't find anything of my childhood home. The Bush had invaded everything. They'd wanted to eradicate every trace of my people. That's when I understood what the Dead expected of me. I was the only vestige of their existence, the only memory, and it was through me, thanks to my writing, that they would survive. The Genocide made me a writer.

Translated from the French by Bárbara Mujica

From The Barefoot Woman

Saving the Children

Maybe the Hutu authorities put in charge of the newly independent Rwanda by the Belgians and the church were hoping the Tutsis of Nyamata would gradually be wiped out by sleeping sickness and famine. In any case, the region they chose to send them to, the Bugesera, seemed inhospitable enough to make those internal exiles' survival more than unlikely. And yet they survived, for the most part. Their courage and solidarity let them face the hostile wilderness, farm a first little patch of land that didn't completely spare them from hunger but at least kept them alive. And little by little the displaced families' makeshift huts became villages— Gitwe, Gitagata, Cyohoha—where people struggled to recapture some semblance of everyday life, which of course did little to soften the crushing sorrow of exile.

But the Tutsis of Nyamata weren't slow to realize that the tenuous survival they seemed to have been granted was only a temporary reprieve.

The soldiers of the Gako camp, built between the villages and the nearby border with Burundi, were there to remind them that they were no longer exactly human beings but *inyenzi,* cockroaches, insects it was only right to persecute and eventually exterminate.

I can still picture the soldiers from Gako bursting into our house, a rifle butt crumpling the piece of sheet metal we used as a door. They claimed they were looking for a photo of King Kigeri or covert letters from exiles in Burundi or Uganda. All that, of course, was pure pretext. Long before, the displaced families of Nyamata had thrown out everything that might possibly incriminate them.

I don't know how many times the soldiers came to pillage our houses and terrorize the people inside. My memory has compressed all those acts of violence into one single scene. It's like a film playing over and over. The same images again and again, engraved in my mind by my little-girl fear, later to return in my nightmares.

The scene that unfolds before my memory is peaceful at first. The entire family is gathered in our one room, around the three stones of the hearth. It must be July or August, the dry season, summer vacation, because André and Alexia are there too, back from their school a long way from Nyamata. Night has fallen, but the moon isn't full, because we aren't sitting outside behind the house, enjoying its light. Everything seems strangely calm, as if the soldiers had yet to pay us their first sudden, brutal visit. Evidently Mama has taken none of the extraordinary precautions I'll talk about soon. I see everyone in their usual places. My mother Stefania is squatting on her mat against the outer wall. Alexia is close by the fire, maybe trying to read one of her schoolbooks by the flickering light of the flames, maybe only pretending. I can't make out my father in the dimness at the far end of the room; I can only hear the continual, monotonous clicks of the rosary he never stops fingering. Julienne, Jeanne, and I are pressed close together near the front door that opens onto the dirt road. Mama has just set down the family plate of sweet potatoes in front of us, but we haven't yet begun to eat. We hang on André's every word as he sits in our one chair at the little table built specially for him—the boy, the student, the hope of the family—by our older brother Antoine. André is telling stories from school, and for us they're like news from a distant world, an amazing, inaccessible world, and they make us laugh, laugh, laugh . . .

And then, all of a sudden, the clang of the sheet metal crashing down: I just have time to snatch up my little sister and roll with her off to one side, dodging the boot that grazes her face, the boot that tramples the sweet potatoes and buckles the metal plate like cardboard. I make myself as small as I can, I wish I could burrow into the ground, I hide Jeanne beneath a fold of my *pagne,* I stifle her sobs, and when I dare to look up again, I see three soldiers overturning our baskets and jugs, throwing the mats we'd hung from the ceiling out into the yard.

One of them has grabbed hold of André, and now he's dragging him toward the door (I think I can see my brother's struggling body go past, slowly, slowly, just beside my face) and my father races forward as if he could hold back the soldier, and I hear my mother and Alexia crying out. I squeeze my eyes shut as hard as I can so I won't have to see. Everything goes dark, I want to burrow deep underground . . .

The silence makes me open my eyes again. My father is helping a wincing André to his feet. My mother and Alexia are cleaning up the spilled beans. Now, from next door, comes the same sound of boots, the same shrieks, the same sobs, the same crash of breaking jugs . . .

My mother had only one thought in her head, one single project day in and day out, one sole reason to go on surviving: saving her children. For that she tried every possible tactic, devised every conceivable stratagem. We needed some way to flee, we needed someplace to hide. The best thing, obviously, was to take cover in the dense bramble thickets that bordered our field. But for that we'd need time. Mama was forever on guard, constantly listening for noises.

Ever since the day when they burned our house in Magi, when she first heard that dull roar of hatred, like a monstrous beehive's hum racing toward us, I think she'd developed a sixth sense, the sense of an animal forever on the lookout for predators. She could make out the faintest, most faraway sound of boots on the road. "Listen," she would say, "they're back." We listened intently. We heard only the familiar sounds of the neighbors, the usual rustles of the savannah. "They're back," my mother said again. "Quick, run and hide." Often she only had time to give us a sign. We scrambled under the bushes, and a moment later, peering out from our hiding place, we saw the patrol at the end of the road, and we trembled as we wondered if they'd break into our house, ravage and steal our meager belongings, our few baskets of sorghum or beans, the few ears of corn we'd been foolish enough to put by.

But we had to be ready for anything: sometimes the soldiers were too quick even for my mother's sharp ear. And so, for those times when we wouldn't be able to reach the brush, she left armloads of wild grass in the middle of the field, mounds just big enough for her three little girls to slip into when the alarm was sounded. She kept a mental catalog of what she thought would be the safest hiding places in the bush. She discovered the deep burrows dug by the anteaters. She was convinced we could slither into them, and so with Antoine's help she widened the tunnels and camouflaged the entrances under piles of grasses and branches. Jeanne made herself even tinier than she was to wriggle into the anteater's lair. Sometimes, despite all my mother's advice and encouragement, Jeanne couldn't quite make it. A little concerned, I asked Stefania what would happen when the anteater wanted to come home. I've forgotten her answer.

Mama left nothing to chance. Often, as night fell, she called a dress rehearsal. And so we knew exactly how to scurry into the brambles, how to dive under the dried grasses. Even in our panic at hearing the boots on the dirt road, we scurried straight for the thickets or burrows where Mama had taught us to lie low.

The displaced families' huts had only one door, which opened onto the road. To ease our escape, Mama cut a second way out, opening onto the field and the bush. But soon that back door, more or less concealed like the hiding places she'd made in the brambles, was of no use at all. Once (with helicopters to help them) they'd beaten back the ill-fated Inyenzi offensive launched from Burundi by Tutsi refugees, the soldiers of the Gako camp lost all fear of ambushes and attacks. No more did they keep to the dirt road they'd always carefully followed. Now their patrols tramped freely across country, all the way to the Burundi border. Now danger could just as well burst from the bush as come down the road; no more were our thorny hiding places the impregnable refuges my mother found so reassuring. And so she set about making hiding places inside the house itself. Against the mud walls she stacked big urns and baskets, almost as tall as grain bins, for Julienne and Jeanne to crawl behind if the soldiers burst in. I was already too big to squeeze into the shelter of the urns' black bellies or the baskets' elegant curves.

My only recourse was to dive under my parents' bed. Those hiding places were meant more to comfort us than anything else, because they never fooled anyone, least of all the soldiers, who flushed us out in no time with vigorous kicks, all the while calling us cockroaches or little snakes.

Mama was never satisfied with her survival strategies. She was forever coming up with improvements to her camouflage, forever finding new refuges for her children. But deep down she knew there was only one sanctuary, only one way we could ensure our survival: crossing the border, leaving for Burundi, as so many Tutsis already had. But she never once thought of taking that way out herself. Neither my father nor my mother ever considered going into exile. I think they'd made up their minds to die in Rwanda. They would wait there to be killed, they would let themselves be murdered, but the children had to survive. And so my mother worked out every detail of our escape to Burundi, in case of emergency. She went off alone into the bush, scouting for trails that might lead to the border. She marked out a path, and under her guidance, not quite understanding why, we played that strange game of follow-the-leader.

Everything at home sat ready for the big departure, which might be announced at any moment, set off by rumors of massacres going around Nyamata, rifle shots in the night, the local governor's threats, a neighbor's arrest . . . A few sweet potatoes, some bananas, a little calabash of sorghum beer were always left wrapped up in a piece of pagne. We girls were meant to take that bundle along when we slipped away and set out for Burundi. It would accompany us into exile. My sisters and I refused to look at it, because to us it was a dark omen of the miseries awaiting us.

But it was Alexia and André who most worried my mother. They weren't there with the rest of us. They were at school, and wouldn't be back until vacation. Mama imagined the worst: one day Alexia and André would come home and find no one there. The house would have been sacked and burned, she and Cosma would have been killed, and at least one of the three girls, or so she hoped, would have managed to escape from the killers and find her way to Burundi. But then what would become of Alexia and André? They'd have to find enough strength after their long walk from school to head straight for the border and face the many dangers they'd find on the way: patrols, elephants, buffalo . . . And so, in prearranged places, under a stone, near a stump, she buried provisions—beans, sweet potatoes. I helped her dig the holes, line them with fine grasses, make sure some air could get in. But of course we had to change the supplies regularly, and then we ate the slightly spoiled food buried by a mother's love.

You always had to be on your guard, so my mother took great pains to keep up with the goings-on in the area. Especially in Nyamata, home to the local government, the missionaries and their church, the marketplace. She interrogated anyone she saw coming back from Nyamata, trying to detect presages of a coming wave of arrests or murders. Had anyone heard tell of a meeting at the mayor's, had they seen a big car from Kigali in front of the town hall? Had anyone spotted army trucks crossing the iron bridge over the Nyabarongo? Were there huge crowds at the market, were there fistfights? What were people saying in the bars? And at Mass, in his sermon, did Father Canoni go on a little too long about loving your neighbor? And what was the teacher saying, the only one with a radio? Stefania carefully evaluated the information, decoded the rumors, divined the imminence or absence of a threat.

But you also had to stay abreast of the neighbors' doings. She suspected them of planning to flee to Burundi without telling her. "One fine morning," she sometimes sighed, "we're going to wake up and find ourselves all alone. Everyone will have left for Burundi without a word to us." Her suspicion was particularly focused on Pancrace, just next door, who she was sure was secretly making all sorts of plans to get out. "That Pancrace," she would say, "he's a devious one, I know he's found some way of saving his family, but he won't tell a soul." On the pretext of borrowing some fire (when in fact the first thing she did in the morning was to check that the coals were still glowing under the ash), or a little salt, or a handful of beans, she would hurry next door and discreetly look around for signs of an upcoming departure. Soon she decided that Pancrace was digging a tunnel out into the bush. With the help of Antoine, she set out to do the same, with the entrance under the big parental bed. At the end of the week, as soon he came back from his job as a gardener at the Agronomical Institute in Karama, not even giving him a moment to rest after his twenty-kilometer walk, she handed him the hoe. Crouched at the edge of the hole, she gave Antoine his instructions as he slowly disappeared into the depths. Fortunately for Antoine, Operation Tunnel soon proved unfeasible, and the work was promptly suspended. But Mama remained as sure as ever that wily Pancrace had come up with many other undisclosed plans to save his life and his family's.

My mother's watchfulness never waned. It grew doubly sharp in the evening, at dinnertime, since it was most often at nightfall, or sometimes at dawn, that the soldiers burst in to ransack the houses and terrorize their inhabitants. She had no intention of letting our shared plate of beans or bananas distract her, so Stefania never ate with us. Once we were served, she hurried to the far end of the field, at the edge of the savannah. For many long minutes she stared into the tangle of thorn trees, listening for the slightest unusual noise. If she spotted the camouflaged uniforms of the patrolling soldiers, she raced back to the house and told us, "*Twajwemo*— we're not alone."

With that we had to keep quiet, not move, be ready to bound into our hiding places, hoping we'd be spared for this evening at least. If she found everything normal, she would gaze on us for a long while in silence.

Nothing pleased her more than watching her children eat. She'd saved them from starvation, working for the Bagesera in exchange for a few sweet potatoes, carving farmland from the inhospitable bush by her tireless labor. Day after day she won out over the implacable destiny we'd been condemned to because we were Tutsis. Again today, her children were still alive at her side. She'd snatched them away from death's clutches. She looked at the three of us, Julienne, Jeanne, Scholastique. This evening we were alive. There might never be another evening.

"In Rwanda," Mama used to say, "women were proud to have children. Many children. Especially boys. But in Nyamata they tremble in terror when they give birth. Not for themselves, but for their children. Especially the boys. They know they'll be killed. They know that one day or another, soon or far in the future, they'll be killed. Look at Gaudenciana, across the way, she should be happy and proud. Every woman in the village should envy her. She has seven children. Seven sons. What more could a mother want? And still she looks at her sons with sadness and despair. She never lets them out of her sight. She wants them beside her at every moment. She wouldn't let them go to school. She doesn't even send them to fetch water. She's afraid they'll never come back from Lake Cyohoha. They've never been to the market in Nyamata. It's as if all they ever do is wait for death to come. And it's not just the boys. Women, girls, their turn will come. You know how they killed Merciana . . ."

Everyone in Nyamata had seen how they killed Merciana, everyone looked on as she was put to death, and the women understood that they wouldn't be spared either, no more than their children. It happened back when the exiles were still staying in that cramped little school in Nyamata. The families had built little huts in the schoolyard to escape the closeness of the classrooms. Merciana belonged to an important family from Magi. They'd been deported to Nyamata like everyone else, but the father, whose life had been threatened, had managed to flee to Burundi. Merciana was the real head of her family, an "evolved person," as people said back then. I don't know where she went to school, but she could read and write. Knowing how to write is a dangerous thing when you have a father in Burundi. You're automatically suspected of corresponding with the Tutsis plotting their return to Rwanda, of being a spy, of passing information to people on this side of the border who might try to lend a hand. Not to mention that you might be hiding weapons. The mayor's thugs were always coming and questioning Merciana, searching her shabby little hut. We could hear the sobs of Merciana's brothers and sisters, her mother's pleas.

And then one day they came with two soldiers. They grabbed Merciana. They dragged her out to the middle of the schoolyard, where everyone could see. They pulled her clothes off. They left her completely naked. The women shielded their children behind their pagnes. Slowly the two soldiers shouldered their rifles. "They didn't aim for her heart," Mama said again and again, "they aimed for her breasts, only her breasts. They wanted to tell us Tutsi women, 'Don't bear any children, because when you bring them into this world you're giving them death. You're not bearers of life anymore, you're bearers of death.'"

Translated from the French by Jordan Stump

From Cockroaches

THE 1960S: HUTU TERROR, BETWEEN THE MILITIAS AND THE SOLDIERS

Those peaceful days were a rare thing in Nyamata. The soldiers of Gako camp were always there to remind us what we were: snakes, Inyenzi, cockroaches. Nothing human about us. One day, we'd have to be got rid of. In the meantime, the terror was systematic and organized. On the pretext of training or security checks, the soldiers endlessly patrolled the road, between the houses, in the banana groves. The soldiers pointed their weapons from the trucks that drove back and forth over the dirt roads. Sometimes they fired.

From Gitagata to the school in Nyamata, the dirt road joined up with the highway that went on to the Burundi border. All the children were in a hurry to reach school before the drum sounded. But they had an even more pressing concern: they had to listen for engines. If they heard the tiniest sound, they had just time enough to dive under the coffee plants, leap into the bush, or take cover in the first house they could find. The road to Nyamata was also the road to Gako camp. Military trucks often went by, and the soldiers fired or threw grenades to terrorize any child foolish enough to walk by the side of the road. Nothing the soldiers did on the Nyamata road was a scandal, since no one ever walked it but Tutsis.

One day there were four of us on the way to school: Jacqueline, Kayisharaza, Candida, and me. A truck suddenly appeared behind us. We hadn't heard it coming. All we could do was dive into the coffee plants. Too late! The soldiers had seen us, and they'd thrown a grenade. Kayisharaza's leg was shredded. She had to give up on school. She couldn't drag her dead leg all the way to Nyamata. She was the oldest girl in her family, and she became a burden for them, for her brothers and sisters. I don't know how many schoolchildren were wounded like that on the road to Nyamata.

And so paths had to be cleared through the brush, making the walk much longer. But the risk of running into an elephant or a buffalo frightened us far less than the thought of coming across an army truck.

A house was no sanctuary either. The soldiers often burst in, especially just before dawn or after nightfall. The sheet metal door fell to the ground with a clatter, and three or four soldiers raced inside. They brutally shoved us out; anyone unlucky enough to be slow about it was struck with a rifle butt. They lined us up along the dirt road, and while one of them kept us at bay with his rifle, the others inside scattered the straw of the beds, over-turned the jugs, took the clean mats—our spare bedding—down from the walls to throw them into the mud or the dirt. They claimed to be looking for correspondence with the Inyenzi in Burundi, or photographs of Kigeri. Once they'd made sure Kayibanda's portrait was hanging in the place of honor, they went off into the night or early morning to bring terror to other houses.

Sometimes, on the contrary, they confined us inside our houses. No one knew why this curfew had been imposed, or how long it would last. Then they forbade us to farm. The children couldn't go to school. The soldiers methodically patrolled the village. Anyone careless enough to set foot outside was beaten. Life became hard if the curfew went on: there was no way to fetch water or wood. We couldn't dig sweet potatoes or cut bananas. Even the latrines, which were generally far from the houses, off in the banana grove, were off-limits. Closed up in our houses, we were paralyzed with fright. We didn't dare speak.

The only seemingly inviolable refuge was the church of the Nyamata mission. As soon as we sensed some threat coming, we knew we had to get to that one place of safety. There was something reassuring in what happened next, since we'd seen it many times before. It would happen on a Sunday: the Tutsis gathered for Mass would hear the roar of a hostile crowd coming from outside the church's front door. The mob had clearly been mustered up by the local authorities, who took great care to keep their hatred at a fever pitch and incite them to violence. Sometimes the howling crowd would try to get in. Then the priest saying Mass, a German named Father Canoni—that's what we called him, at least—stepped away from the altar, took off his chasuble, went into the sacristy for his rifle, and slowly advanced toward the assailants. They hesitated for a moment, then backed away and ran off as fast as they could.

In 1994 the Tutsis of Nyamata once again sought shelter in the church, but this time there was no Father Canoni to chase off the murderers: the UN soldiers had come to evacuate the white people, and the missionaries went with them, knowing they were leaving for dead more than five thousand men, women, and children who thought they'd found sanctuary in their church.

Today the Nyamata church has become a genocide memorial. The survivors had to fight hard to keep it from becoming a place of worship again, as the Catholic higher-ups insisted. In a crypt, the skulls are lined up in neat rows, the bones carefully stacked. The sheet metal roof is peppered with bright, shiny spots where it was struck by bullets or grenade shrapnel. Against the brick wall, to the left of the altar, the Virgin of Lourdes watches over the now-empty pews, her veil red with blood. That Virgin of Nyamata was lucky. She too escaped the carnage. In many other churches, the killers shattered the statues of the Virgin. They thought she'd been given a Tutsi face. They couldn't stand the sight of her straight little nose.

Things turned still worse in 1967. From the earliest days of that year, we could feel the tension rising, something dangerous coming. Among the Bagesera, the town councilors held mysterious meetings to which only Hutus were summoned. The rumor was that machetes were being handed out. Some were even distributed at the town hall, people said. Then sometime in April, maybe Easter Monday, all the adults over sixteen were called to the town hall.

I stayed home alone with my little sisters, Julienne and Jeanne. It was raining. One of those violent downpours typical of the long rainy season, transforming the dirt roads into muddy torrents. I was inside, watching over the few beans heating up in the kettle. My two little sisters were outside in spite of the rain: the corn field had to be guarded, or the monkeys would beat us to the brand-new ears. The only sound I could hear was the patter of the rain on the banana trees' huge leaves. Those banana trees grow faster because of the household waste we throw at their feet. But suddenly I made out another noise I knew well—shuwafu! shuwafu!—the sound of boots in the mud. I rushed outside and ran straight into two soldiers driving my two sisters along with blows from their rifle butts. The little girls collapsed at my feet. The soldiers walked into the house, ransacked it in the usual way, then disappeared.

Trembling in terror, the three of us held each other tight. I'd put the sheet metal back over the doorway, as if that might protect us.

And then came the sound of shouts and tramping feet from the road. Through the holes in the sheet metal, we saw something that left us petrified with fear: a huge crowd of soldiers heading toward Lake Cyohoha, dragging bodies that looked like broken marionettes, among which I recognized some neighbors of ours, Rwabukumba and his brother. They were young men, not yet twenty. The bodies being dragged along—not all of them corpses, some were still moving and groaning—belonged to young men, snakes, cockroaches, Inyenzi, who had to be eliminated before they could turn dangerous.

We spent the night waiting for our parents. They came back very early the next day. They never said a word. My mother always took such care to elegantly tie on her *pagne,* but now she had it draped over her head, like the Holy Virgin. She said nothing. Neither did the neighbors, when they reappeared. They took care not to cross each other's paths, they pretended they hadn't seen each other. My mother murmured a strange word, a word she didn't understand: the English word meeting. We weren't supposed to have meetings. And when three people greeted each other, someone murmured "meeting" and they all fled in different directions.

When we went back to school, there were bodies by the highway to Nyamata, in the ditches. Some had been thrown there, others had been swept along by the rushing rainwater. Among them we recognized Ngangure, the father of Protais, who was in my class at school. Their families had been forbidden to pick up the bodies.

No one wanted to fetch water. We didn't dare. We made do as best we could with our stored-up rainwater, but soon it ran out, and we had no choice but to head to the lake. Drawing water is traditionally the children's job, so I went off with Candida.

On the lakeshore, things had changed. There were people we hadn't seen before: very young men, adolescents, just kids in uniform. But not military uniforms: they were dressed in shorts and khaki shirts, a little like boy scouts. They didn't have rifles; they had big sticks or clubs, studded with sharp spikes. They were living in the buildings that had recently been put up by the lakeside. Until that day, we had no idea who they were meant for.

Many of those boys were posted along the shoreline, as if standing guard. When we walked into the water to fill our calabashes, we saw what they were guarding: the tied-up bodies of victims slowly dying in the shallows of the lake, little waves washing over them now and then. The newcomers were there to keep away the families who wanted to rescue their children or at least take home their bodies. For a long time we found little pieces of skin and rotting body parts in our calabashes when we fetched water.

Soon our new persecutors made themselves known: they were the revolutionary youth brigade of the single party, the MDR-Parme-hutu. In truth, they were hoodlums picked up in the streets of Kigali and trained for violence and murder. They were quick learners, and soon mastered the only lesson they were ever taught: how to humiliate and terrorize a defenseless population.

Every day toward mid-morning, the youth of the single party paraded in double time, their cudgels or clubs on their shoulders. They sang at the top of their lungs, and their songs seemed to be meant for our ears. They sang the praises of Kayibanda, the emancipator of the Hutus; they celebrated the people who would forever be the majority, the only real Rwandans, authentic and indigenous, the Hutus. The parade route was always the same: from their camp on Lake Cyohoha up to Rwabashi's hut, where the dirt road met the highway from Nyamata to the Burundi border. The first half of the parade was fairly orderly, but not the return trip. Once they reached the highway and turned around, the young people of the party broke ranks and spread out along the path back to camp, turning into a violent, pillaging mob. Woe unto any careless passerby who hadn't had time to take shelter: he would be punched, thrown to the ground, beaten. The women who sold peanuts and sometimes bananas in front of their houses hurried to bundle up their wares before they could be trampled and looted. Sometimes the thugs invaded the houses, simply for the pleasure of wreaking havoc. And we heard their laughter, mingled with insults, as they boasted of their exploits.

From then on, going for water from Lake Cyohoha meant exposing yourself to all sorts of torments, because you had to pass by their camp. Coming back from the lake with our calabashes on our heads, we found our persecutors waiting. Now we were at the mercy of their sadistic whims. And they had plenty of imagination. For a little fun, they emptied our calabashes so we'd have to go back for water, then broke them when we came by again. They laughed and laughed. Or else they would line us up along the path, spit in our faces, and stomp on our feet with their big army shoes. And they laughed at the tears of the little snakes, the cockroaches, the Inyenzi. Sometimes it was more serious, their eyes were red, they weren't laughing, they beat up the boys and dragged a girl into the undergrowth behind their camp to be raped. That was why we took to fetching water only in the fierce heat of the early afternoon, while they were taking their siesta, doing our very best not to make a sound.

Of course, it was the girls that interested the young revolutionaries the most. On the way home from their parade, they would come after any girl who hadn't had time to hide. Rapes were not rare. A few poor girls became their playthings, just as young Tutsi women and girls would be during the genocide. At least there was no AIDS in those days.

The hunt for girls was especially intense after dark. At that time, I was spending the nights with my cousin Mukantwari, who might have been twenty years old. It's a custom in Rwanda for girls to share the bed of young women of marriageable age. This is especially common among cousins: they spend the night telling stories, posing riddles, making fun of boys, and laughing without end.

My cousin lived with her grandmother Bureriya, a bent-over old woman she kept company. Her parents lived across the way. Her father Ngoboka was a very strong man, afraid of no one. He had an axe that kept away anyone who might mean him harm.

More than once, the Parmehutu youth tried to get their hands on Mukantwari. As soon as we heard them coming, Mukantwari and I would dive under her grandmother's bed while the old lady brandished her little stick and shouted, as loud as she could: "Go away! Go away!" She snatched up a burning branch from the hearth and waved it in the assailants' faces.

Hearing her shouts, Ngoboka—whose name means nothing other than "He-who-comes-when-he-is-needed-most"—came running and drove off the would-be abductors, whose bravery did not extend to confronting a colossus and his terrible axe appearing all at once in the night.

The Tutsi girls fascinated the Hutus. Their leaders set the example: marrying a Tutsi was one of the privileges of the victors. They came to Nyamata to take their pick.

In Nyamata, then called the municipality of Kanzenze, the mayor was the first one to do so. He was a Hutu, "from Rwanda," as we said. No one educated enough for that post had been found among the Bagesera. The mayor was an old bachelor. No one knew why he'd never married. But in Nyamata it wasn't hard to find a wife. He set his sights on Banayija, a very beautiful girl whose impoverished mother supported herself and her four daughters by selling loose cigarettes and sorghum or banana beer. When the mayor came for her daughter, he didn't ask Banayija's opinion, or her mother's. "The Tutsis and their daughters have lost the right to be proud," he liked to say. And he went off with Banayija.

Many others came to help themselves in Nyamata. Any girl whose beauty put her in danger was hidden away. Often, though, the parents felt so threatened that they didn't dare refuse. Besides, handing a daughter over to the persecutors might mean saving the family.

Translated from the French by Jordon Stump

Florinda Ruiz

Florinda Ruiz (Spain) is an award-winning photographer, translator, poet, professor, and director of the Writing Program at Washington and Lee University. She has received a State Council for Higher Education in Virginia award, a U.S. Department of Education Title VIA Grant in collaboration with Roanoke College's Modern Languages Department, and an All-College Exemplary Teaching Award at Roanoke College, among other recognitions. Her scholarship and artistic work encompass a wide range of topics, from the transmission of the classical world in Europe, Spanish Islam, and migration studies. Her scholarly articles have appeared in Brill's *Explorations in Renaissance Culture,* the *Sixteenth Century Journal,* and *Renaissance Studies,* among others. As a translator, she worked in the United Arab Emirates (UAE) and published *Primeras memorias,* the memoirs of the sheikh of the Emirate of Sharjah and minister of culture in the UAE. Her chapter "Islamic Spain after the Thirteenth Century" appeared in *Arabic Heritage in the Post-Abbasid Period* (2019). Her latest essay "Iberian Metaarte" is forthcoming in *Crear entre mundos: Nuevas tendencias en la metaficción española.* A longer version of this essay appears in *Voices on the Move* (2020), edited by Domnica Radulescu and Roxana Cazan.

Why I Write about War

> Sing, goddess, the rage of Pelias' son Achilles,
> its devastation, that gave the Achaeans endless pain
> and hurled many brave souls of heroes to Hades—
> while it made their bodies a delicate feast for dogs
> and all birds, as Zeus' will was fulfilled.
>
> —*The Iliad,* 1–5

The Iliad's first lines speak of a conflict that spans beyond Greeks and Trojans to all civilizations, centuries, and continents. The endless warring of humankind and horrific loss of life repeats itself as a permanent failure of humanity—or is it a universal trait of humanity itself? I see war as an inherited and flawed gene, transmitted by the very DNA of human experience, which has dictated the fate of civilizations, nations, and individuals.

I come from Iberia—an invaded land, a land of invaders, a nation of conquerors and conquered peoples, a site of dictatorships and revolutions, a mix of peoples who have defended their particular beliefs, yet fought to impose them on others. I write of a bellicose land at the crossroads of oceans and seas, continents and races, empires and republics, dictators and monarchs, conquistadors and revolutionaries, fascists and communists, dream-catchers and dream-smashers. From Hannibal's North African campaigns onto Hispania in 237 BC and the Roman siege of Numantia in 133 BC to the current deadly risks undertaken by African immigrants escaping wars to enter Spain, Iberia has been linked to constant struggles both in its peninsular territories and overseas. Some of my ancestors' last names, *Rabal, Moro,* or *Medina,* echo the losers' tragic lot in the clash between Christian and Islamic cultures and the Moors' final expulsion in 1609, when Philip III banished the Moriscos. Already in 1267, the Andalusi poet Abū al-Baqā' ar-Rundī recorded in his famous elegy the profound despair for and sorrowful resignation to the looming destiny of the fallen Muslim cities after the first expulsions:

> Ask Valencia what became of Murcia,
> And where is Játiva, or where is Jaén?
> Where is Córdoba, the seat of great learning,
> And how many scholars of high repute remain there?
> And where is Seville, the home of mirthful gatherings
> On its great river, cooling and brimful with water?
> These cities were the pillars of the country:
> Can a building remain when the pillars are missing?
> The white wells of ablution are weeping with sorrow,
> As a lover does when torn from his beloved:
> They weep over the remains of dwellings devoid of Muslims,
> Despoiled of Islam, now peopled by infidels!
> Those mosques have now been changed into churches,
> Where the bells are ringing and crosses are standing.
> Even the mihrabs weep, though made of cold stone,
> Even the minbars sing dirges, though made of wood!
> Oh heedless one, this is fate's warning to you:
> If you slumber, Fate always stays awake.

The so-called Spanish Golden Age saw the expansion of a vast empire and the human devastation that its military power brought to indigenous populations in transatlantic colonies whose gold, silver, and raw physical labor it exploited. However, my school history books during Franco's time hid those stories and spoke only of "discovery" and "salvation." After more loss of life in successful wars of independence throughout the Americas, the collapse of the empire signified the birth of new forms of warfare as revolutionary responses to threatening forces of power. The start of the Spanish Civil War in 1936 served both as a rehearsal for and a preamble to imminent military horrors inside and outside of the peninsula. The initial romantic euphoria and spontaneity of Spanish fighting militias and the limited international help that Spain received was not enough to triumph in modern warfare and defeat a fascist enemy who used, for the first time in Guernica, air raids against civilian populations. The Republican side of the civil war was supported by international writers from Hemingway to Malraux to Day Lewis to Laurie Lee. The last of these understood his participation as a volunteer in the war as a "grand and uncomplicated gesture of personal sacrifice and faith, which might never occur again . . . [F]ew of us yet knew that we had come to a war of antique muskets and jamming machine-guns, to be led by brave but bewildered amateurs. But for the moment there were no half-truths and hesitations, we had found a new freedom, almost a new morality, and discovered a new Satan—fascism."

I write of battles whose burdens were carried upon the shoulders of nameless people, my ancestors, jailed and killed grandparents—as my great-grandmother called them, *carne de cañón* (cannon fodder)—targets of religious persecution, bastions of resistance, expelled to unknown territories, executed by firing squads, killed in transatlantic conflicts, often simply lost and forgotten. The echoes of their suffering bounce from the hinges and joints of altered history schoolbooks, to ignored corners of our museums' greatest paintings and treasures. As testimonies of ethnic, religious, and political cleansings, their memories, in search of a voice, peek at us from dusty family photographs and treasured jail letters, from torn posters of civil war propaganda and quiet voices of unrecorded family conversations, from service records of military archives and black-and-white TV images of a dying dictatorship, from the proud symbols of a strong new democracy and images of anonymous frail migrant faces in daily newspapers.

Obscured as victims often are by the mythology and manipulation of the victors' corpulent regimes, my poems ensure a posthumous remembrance of the lives and sentiments of the inaudible fallen. War is not simply the backdrop of each poem, but the active center stage that manifests the human tragedy of actors and victims, their fears, hopes, or endurance. I bear witness to lost and silent voices, to words that were burnt or hidden even when they were written, to their shattered lives or limitless resilience. As a photographer and an artist, my poetic creation is the mechanism that helps me bridge a gap of thought and silence between the visual and the verbal. It is a tool to share the emotional experience of an object, subject, place, or event with qualities that go beyond the physical aspects of an initial image; a way to step into the conflicts of my culture and inhabit subjects that surround me. This blend of images and words gives me the exhilarating chance to engage with the idea that exists behind a visual representation of reality. An image could be worth a thousand words, but my poems are the result of a thousand images. They are verbal collages inserted in "multiple-exposure" verses: reconstruction of shattered souls, poetic reflections on the background, associations, outside forces, and profound emotions that shape and ground the appearance or construction of images, the subjects, and the very viewing act.

The overwhelming personal and cultural significance of these conflicts has always been present in my life, my family, and in Iberia. So, as a direct or indirect witness to an event or as a member of its surrounding culture, I strive to engage responsibly, aesthetically, and ethically with the suffering of others, stretching the canvas, the lens, the language, to evoke and converse with the saddened spirit of the pictorial. I can thus hint at necessary or avoided questions, forgotten or ignored realities, and underlying or unspoken truths. The final goal: the chance to offer the possibility of a breakthrough for a productive negotiation between the consequences and reality of war and poetry.

Moriscos, 1609

Forbidden faith.
Banned language.
        Hands of henna, outlawed.
Our names, dropped.
Our rituals, banished.
        Abolished identity.
Forced were our baptisms.

Obliged to recite by heart
someone else's prayers.
   Conversos, Marranos, Moriscos. We.
Nothing was quite enough
to erase our difference.

Our blood, one-drop,
an insubordinate aberration,
the stubborn otherness of birth.
Barred from our homes,
scattered through Iberia
as felons for mere being.

Suspicions, trials, and murders spiraled.
   Hunted
strangers in our torn-apart world,
once the backbone of a country's wealth,
now vulnerable and helpless.
   Cursed.

Not a danger to the crown's empire,
nor a threat to the monolith of its faith.
Prey to the zeal of purging.
   Limpieza de sangre.

A secret fleet of Spanish galleons
awaited, hidden, just for us.
   "Heretics, apostates, and traitors,"
read the Royal Decree of expulsion.
Three days' notice to removal,
Three days' notice to departure,
Three days' notice to a last farewell,
Three days' notice to forsake our children,
Three days' notice to never return to our land.

Dumped on African shores,
robbed, raped, ravaged.
Surviving on hopes of returning

to our abandoned *mihrabs,*
living on broken vestiges
of Andalusian memories.

Our blood still dwells
        in altered Spanish names.
Our worth remains
        in each city's bricks and pillars.
Our treasures are buried
        in the mosaic walls of a country's consciousness.

Sing now the richness of our souls,
a memory to all victims of history.
        Spanish Muslim exiles, *Andalusíes.*

Milicianas, 1937 (Militiawomen)

The civil war hinted at a chance to grasp freedom,
illusory images of new hopes and roles.

Flag-waving,
    torch-bearing,
        pants-wearing,
            rifle-carrying,
                uniformed women,
fleeting dreamers
of justice for all.

"Look at them, comrades," men said,
"brave female warriors
facing the enemy, joining our ranks.
Where is your manhood?
your militant virility?
Mobilize! Enlist! Combat!"

We thought we were breaking
the walls of our gender.
We dreamed we were building
our equal new world.

Some died in harsh battles
while fighting together
against the same foe.

Men's praises soon turned into scorn and derision.
We came to be targets of ridicule and jokes,
short-lived war-like symbols,
first war-bait, then, whores
accused of inciting the soldiers' sex urges,
forced by our army to abandon all fronts.
Men to the trenches, women at home.

And so, we were sent back
            to farms and to factories,
                    to dirty street corners,
                            to kitchens and wards,
away from all fire lines,
dispatched to the rearguard.

The orders were sanctions
            to take on the pitchforks,
                    to feed the battalions,
                            or mend uniforms
as nameless brave women
in domestic home-fronts.

Our cause was thus killed
before the war was all lost,
our dreams were soon jailed
for decades to come,
or exiled, or in hiding, or asleep . . .
. . . not all gone.

New versions of us have emerged through the ages,
glowing, awaken,
souls always reborn,
a female mythology of blaring endurance,
a fearless spirit alive in the world.

Guernica's Manger

No angel of the Lord came into sight
to guide good shepherds to Guernica.
Instead,
a harbinger host of infernal winged beings
appeared one April through Iberian blue skies,
a modern blitz of deadly air raids,
a blanket deluge of black white grey waste.

The electric new star with its evil-eye blaze
blew out the peace-glow of a hidden old dove,
a nativity showered with torpedoes and bolts,
flaming torn buildings and towers of smoke.

A mother's loud howling, her baby now lifeless,
his dead body-weight falling down from her bosom.
A father dismembered, his tarnished sword shattered,
his hands vainly clutching a star scar and a flower.

The barn had no ox nor donkey for warmth,
just anguishing neighs of a death-wounded horse
and the stare of a brazen bull standing firm over all
with the wrath of sharp horns at his brutal command.

Like shepherds, the women were gathered around,
staggering, wounded, by the bulb's bursting jolts,
screaming and burning entrapped by the fire,
or holding a lamp with sterile dreams' glimmer.

Three tyrants,
        no myrrh,
        no incense,
        no gold,
just aerial death angels to spread through the world.

A Post-Franco Christmas Dinner, 1975

A month ago I saw the dictator's dead body
lying without flowers on a coffin-tray,
his image filling TV screens and magazines,
feeding the panic that gnaws in our air.
I'm anxious for my village's Christmas
away from the city's uniformed tentacles,
far from the fear of vigilant machine guns.

All eager for grandma's great cake,
we bump in the kitchen to inhale its sweet scent.
The music of laughter and mismatching chairs,
the ten conversations in flat unison,
herald the solace I seek for my soul.
Grandma and grandpa at one end,
mom and dad at the other,
aunts, uncles, and children in the middle,
space only for the warmth of each other's arms.

A dead piglet arrives without any cauliflowers,
bringing the fated 'dead' word on its tray,
and all conversations become 'the one.'
In the middle, younger aunts and uncles,
born after the civil war,
trade theories for our country's future,
invent images of unknown plots,
swap 'what ifs' with 'maybes.'

I see war memories rising in grandpa's gaze,
images of jail, treason, and severance,
gunshots still lurking in his old ears,
cold hugs of jail bars instead of grandma's arms,
his silence now swelling by my side at his table's end.

At the other end across the room, watching me,
I see a shadow of dad's six-year-old's fright
peeking out from his grown-up orphaned eyes,
boyhood visions of his murdered father,

The roasted pig. (Photo by Florinda Ruiz)

live nightmares of shelterless air raids.
But, hiding the pang of his childhood lost,
he blinks a smile at my teen probing eyes,
eager to trust that what he lived
will not repeat again.

Only grandma knows the fixing trick:
with the edge of a plate, she cuts the pig's head,
and a joint applause returns us to Christmas
with carols in honor of her grand magic feat.

Perhaps we'll be OK, but this time
I passed on the dead piglet on a tray
and, after kissing grandpa's bald head,
I skipped directly to grandma's cake.

Maritime Massacre

Dreams of food, water, survival,
a mother pushing him northwards.
She pressed, she prodded,

"no militias, no lynchings, my boy."
A crossing hope away from their inferno.

She imagined for him the colors of our side.
"Flee!"
And her only son took the northbound trail.
A journey of countless humans,
a tall order of endurance and discovery:
the exploits of a black conquistador,

Into the deep wide trench. (Photo by Florinda Ruiz)

black pilgrim, black cowboy, black astronaut,
the defiance of a black Herakles' heart.

The yoke of smugglers.
The toll of debt-bondage.
The threat of slave-markets.
The ramshackle prison camps.
The perilous sea crossing.
The final maritime choke point.
Worthy trials for a black young man's formidable labors.

A dinghy stuffed, 130 crowded hopes,
a squalid unseaworthy vessel,
bearing the wary spirits of waterless lands
scarred by the onslaught of starvation,
launching to fight dragons in our moat's waters.
He braved his fears into the monsters' deep wide trench,
our fluid deterrence to his human dare of crossing.

The news: "Another ravaged boat
has washed up on a European coast."

His infinite silence haunts her now
with tears attached to an everyday naming him.
She cannot know . . .

if his bold dreams capsized in the liquid cemetery,
if his hands held someone as the fosse welcomed them,
if his tears blended with the sea or dried in the sand,
if his shirt's wet wrinkles lie forgotten on some shore,

or maybe a rescuer found a living minute

to ask his name and touch him,
to hear a final sound from his breathless world,
to save a glimpse of the rhythms of his land,
to watch a wave erase the last footprint of his heroic intent.

V. V. Ganeshananthan

V. V. GANESHANANTHAN (USA/Sri Lanka) is an American writer of Sri Lankan Tamil descent. She writes primarily about Sri Lankan history and politics, especially the impact of Sri Lanka's quarter-century-long civil war on minority communities, women, and children. Her first novel, *Love Marriage*, is set in Sri Lanka and some of its diasporas. The book was longlisted for the Orange Prize and named one of *Washington Post Book World*'s "Best of 2008." She is at work on a second novel, excerpts of which have appeared in *Granta, Ploughshares,* and *Best American Nonrequired Reading 2014*. Her journalism has appeared in the *New York Times, Washington Post, Columbia Journalism Review,* and *Himal Southasian,* and she is a recent recipient of fellowships from the Radcliffe Institute for Advanced Study, the American Academy in Berlin, and the National Endowment for the Arts. She grew up in Maryland and teaches in the MFA program at the University of Minnesota. The selection below is taken from *Love Marriage*.

Why I Write about War

A dozen years ago, in the spring of 2008, I published my first novel, *Love Marriage*, which is about a young American Tamil woman learning about the history of her Sri Lankan and diasporic family. The book focuses on the Sri Lankan civil war, which began in 1983. The fight between the militant separatist Tamil Tigers and Sri Lankan security forces came to a brutal finish in 2009, about a year after the novel came out.

During the war's final year, as I traveled around the world doing events in support of the book, I encountered readers who were curious, readers who were moved, readers who thought they knew nothing about Sri Lanka, and readers who thought they knew everything about Sri Lanka. The last audience was made up primarily of people who had grown up in Sri Lanka. Like me, some of them were experiencing intense, alienating anguish; as the war swept to its violent finish, tens of thousands of Tamil civilians were dying, trapped between the security forces and the Tigers, and Sri Lankans around the world, especially Tamils, knew it. The Tigers said the civilians were with them by choice; numerous accounts show otherwise. Tiger cadres shot some who tried to escape as security forces bore down, while others found themselves conscripted into the Tigers' desperate ranks. The government, for its part, directed civilians to a no-fire zone but subsequently shelled the same areas—and denied it. The ghost of that knowledge was at every event I did, especially in the spring of 2009, when the vicious final battles were raging. I was reading to these audiences from a novel written by a person who had thought the war would never be finished, but I was no longer that person. And neither my readers nor I had imagined this horrific ending.

After the war ended with the defeat of the Tamil Tigers, certain sections of the novel became stranger in the rereading. The following excerpt of the novel commences by addressing the kinds of storytelling the narrator, Yalini, discovers in her family, and among other Lankans. "When the conflict begins must depend, like everything else, on the memory you acquire," she says, and recounts hearing different versions of the war's origin story. Indeed, in the years since the war, when the conflict *ends* has also depended on the memory you acquire. Sri Lanka may be postwar, but it is not yet postconflict, and women and children have endured the brunt of that conflict, while men have taken over its narratives. After the war, Sri Lanka's minority-dominated North and East had an estimated ninety thousand women-headed households, and high rates of poverty; the majority Sinhalese-dominated military continues to maintain a sizable presence in those provinces, citing security concerns. Still, a majority of government officials insist everything is fine: conditions are improving, and the country's minority communities have no legitimate political grievances. "None of the stories will be absolutely complete, but their tellers will be absolutely certain. This is how we make war," Yalini writes. This has also become how people talk about the war's conclusion and its contested aftermath.

The excerpt concludes with the narrator's aunt, Kalyani, talking about her experience of the 1983 anti-Tamil riots in Colombo. "I did not leave the house, and I did not allow my husband or my children to leave the house," she says. At this most dangerous moment, she wills her family to stay together, in the home that she has built with them. Later, racist government-aligned thugs destroy that cherished place, but Kalyani picks herself up and goes on; she manages to keep her children safe, to send them to school, and to build new homes in different places. She does this work over and over again; her life unravels, but "her eyes are on the sari blouse, the needle and thread moving in and out of the silk." This is the work many Tamil civilian women did during the war—protecting their families, remaking their households, and resisting the effects of militarization on their communities and children. Even now, this work and these stories continue.

From Love Marriage

And yet, Vani did not choose to leave Sri Lanka forever. She chose not to go back. It is not the same thing. But in a way, her reasons were the same as my father's. When the conflict begins must depend, like everything else, on the memory you acquire.

First: Who are you asking? To read the story in the press is to read a story that has never gone far enough. Ask one relative and this is how the story begins: the international Tamil conference came to Sri Lanka, and the government wanted it to be held in Colombo, which was the capital of the country. The Tamil organizers wanted it to be held in Jaffna, the northern city, which was their capital, and so they declined to move it. At the opening of the conference some government soldiers came and shot some young Tamil men. Almost all of them died, and this was what sparked the beginning of the actual violent rebellion: this blatant killing. Whereas before there had been quieter violence or discrimination. Those who attended the conference were mostly young men, young aspiring politicians who grew into old men with old memories of their friends who were killed. If you ask someone else, they will tell you a different story, say that the Tamils were making it all up, that there was no discrimination, that the island was an island of three languages and cultures, and that those cultures were equal before the Tigers began killing people, including their own. Ask another, and another. None of the stories will be absolutely complete, but their tellers will be absolutely certain. This is how we make war.

But there are some things that are indisputable: even now, it is the young men who disappear. The odd foreign journalist, here and there, but mostly the young Tamil men. Fathers fret anxiously over the whereabouts of their sons. Every night, mothers set places at meals for their boys. And every night, in many houses, some of those places go unfilled. There are people whose job it is to collect the names of the absent and to set them down, record them, send them to as many people as possible, humanitarian and political organizations. This hardly ever accomplishes anything. Years later, when children in other countries ask their parents about going home, their parents say no, that's not a good idea, not this year, it will be too expensive.

What they do not say: it is too expensive because the country runs on bribes, because you have to pay the police and the army and probably a professional escort to navigate for you, because the four-star hotels are the ones with the most security, not the greatest amenities, because you can only go home again if they promise not to bomb the airport.

And so, halfway around the world, here I am. Telling you about my mother's family. My mother herself would tell you that it began when she was ten. In the anti-Tamil riots of 1958, when she was visiting Colombo. They were on a road of Tamils, in Wellawatte. But one Sinhalese family lived there too. When they heard the mob coming, they shut their Tamil friends in their house, to wait in the quiet and the cool and the dark for the end. Vani, the little girl who grew up to be the nursery school teacher, Murali's wife, and later my mother, hid under a table. The Sinhalese family passed food through the cracks in the doors and the windows, and the Tamils waited and watched, knowing that it would be over and that it would start again.

I HAVE LEARNED that one way to get my mother to talk about herself is to ask her about other people, other things. It is a trick, really, nothing more. She is someone who is faithful to history and so she cannot help but include herself in the narrative as an innocent bystander, a silent guest. In this manner you can extract her character, piece by piece, because even the most self-effacing person can only remain an innocent bystander for so long before conceding to the power of her own past presence.

When Vani was at the convent school in Kandy, studying to be a teacher and beginning to be beautiful, she would often spend her weekends at Logan's tea estate in Nuwara Eliya, which was nearby. She was horribly homesick, and visiting her uncle Logan and aunt Kala made her feel closer to Urelu. Late in her childhood, her uncle had become the superintendent of three tea estates, which made him someone of considerable importance. She remembered his house having a formidable formality. He was a *dorai,* and this meant that he was a man of stature, someone important. A man in charge. His wife, Kala, who was the *doraisāmi,* was similarly intimidating. Logan ran the business of the plantation, and she ran the sizable house. They were both jobs that traditionally required homage to ceremony and to manners. It was not until much later, after both my mother and her uncle had emigrated, that her stories of him managed, finally, to permeate the shield of colonial formality that had been imposed on their lives in that place.

Logan resembled his late father, Vairavan, in many ways, except that the sternness in his face was a bit more sharply drawn. He had a lowering brow and a pronounced jaw. Only the rare and broad smile transformed that imposing face. He was a busy man, and he made time especially for his nieces and nephews when they arrived at his estate on holidays. They arrived by train, and it was a long ride, so when they arrived, they were always very hungry. They were not very old, but they had been taught how to behave, and so no one ever mentioned being hungry until they reached the house and were asked in to dinner. They were met at the station by the *dorai*'s man, who picked them up in a big, broad, black car that belonged to the estate and was at their disposal for the holiday. They clambered into it, always holding hands, brother helping sisters up into the high coach, suitcases rumbling in the back. Sometimes when they arrived it was raining, and then the ride to the estate was bumpier than usual and slightly unpleasant. They shivered from the wet and thought of what waited for them: the *doraisāmi*, smiling one of her smiles-with-teeth (which were reserved for people whom she loved specially), holding for them cups of hot tea with sugar (which is how they all drank it; although my mother does not have a sweet tooth, she would never dream of taking her tea *without* sugar—that was sacrilege).

At the gate, Kala took their umbrellas from them and ushered them into the house. The driver followed with their bags, and she brought them into the palatial front room, where they removed their shoes. They always brought her gifts: cans of fruit from their mother; fresh onions and toma- toes; special homemade sweets. After drinking their cups of tea (which always seemed to them deeper and bigger and more adult than those they had at home) they were ushered from the palatial front parlor into the even more palatial dining room, where they waited for their uncle, then ate their dinner, which had always been especially prepared for the first night of their visit.

They waited at the long, high table for Logan. Each place had a glit- tering set of dinnerware, but they did not touch anything. They always waited in polite silence until the door creaked and he came in, with his long, swinging gait. He always looked impeccable. How did he look so untroubled by an entire day's work on the hot plantations? He twinkled at them, and they forgot to wonder. He had looked very slightly tired when he walked in, but when he saw them, these children, his whole face lit up. During these years his own children were in England, studying, and his sister's children always made him happy. They greeted him and sat down, and then he rang for the cook.

Logan did not have a cook because he was rich; he had a cook because he was a *dorai* and it was one of the amenities to which a *dorai* was entitled. Even now, when my mother recalls these meals, there is a sound of amazement in her voice. That there could be such food, and so much of it! But even the food was not the best part of this house. They were most fascinated by the wire that ran from the kitchen to the wall to the table, under the table, under where Logan's hand rested as he ate. There was a small button there, and if he pushed it, it called the chef back into the room. The children loved this bell, the extra air of command it gave an already commanding man. As though it were proof that so many people listened to him. Which they did.

LIKE ALMOST every member of his family, my great-uncle eventually left Sri Lanka. There was nothing else to do, and I think that my mother likes to remember that bell under the dinner table, my great-uncle ringing for his servant, although that makes it sound like it was an imperious thing to do rather than merely the observation of custom. I think that my mother likes to remember this and then to think about how her uncle crossed the ocean, how he left, because the juxtaposition of the two memories proves to my mother that Logan is a brave man. This was what her family did: leave Sri Lanka, one by one, piece by piece. Although they left it until it was nearly too late, it was not something that was hard to do, finally— leaving. It was something they achieved, with that toughness that they had hoarded among themselves. My mother's family turned anger at their situation into a way out of the island.

My great-uncle Logan, still an almost-young man then, left the country after the riots in 1983, that great spate of ethnic violence in which Tamils were more often than not the victims. Young men in particular went missing or were beaten on the streets. He had left his position as a *dorai* when the violence began, and as he looked out his window and saw it beginning to escalate, he began to make phone calls. He called everyone he had known in what he was beginning to think of as his former life. The friends of the *dorai* he had been. He had never abused his position.

He had never treated anyone unkindly or unfairly. He hoped now that people would remember this. He hoped now that he would be able to secure what he needed from these friends to leave, and to take his family with him.

Someone called back: Two berths to India, uncle? This was luck, he thought; this truly was luck because these berths were beginning to be almost impossible to get, the ships crowded with the hard quick hurried breath of those escaping. Everyone he had ever known was leaving. He and Kala went over the sea on a ship to India, surrounded by men for whom he had worked and who had worked for him his entire life. They took almost nothing with them: a suitcase apiece. Everything else they left behind. Kala could not even bear to pack up the house. They left it untouched, with the two tall oil lamps from the tea estate shrine still guarding the front door. As though these symbols of prosperity could keep it inside the place in which they had once conducted their lives.

I THINK that my mother was proud to remember what Logan had been like, and that he was able to leave all of this grandeur for a far simpler life. This was what their family did: left Sri Lanka. This was something he did many years later, when my mother was already gone. Later, in Canada, he worked as a security guard for a time. In his adopted country, which was unsafe in new and different ways, it was a job that paid well. This was a profession that many Sri Lankan men took up after leaving their country. At home they might have been bankers, engineers, accountants, *dorais*. In the West, they looked after others, as they had once been looked after themselves.

This is how they left: they took the boat to India, and from there spent most of their money buying plane tickets to England. After a few months in England, they decided to try for Canada, which was taking Sri Lankan refugees. They bought tickets to New York. They did not have any money left for tickets back, and this was a calculation that worked perfectly. They landed in New York, and an acquaintance picked them up and drove them to the Canadian border. There, he left them with nothing. This was not abandonment; this was planned. To show, formally, that you were in need. To demonstrate that you were seeking refuge. And this is something that can still be done with honor.

Leaving: this is how it is done. Logan, who had once been a *dorai* of a tea estate in Sri Lanka and who was now just another Tamil refugee, walked toward the officials at the borders, his hands spread wide and open to show that he had nothing. Like a soldier surrendering, revealing that he is unarmed.

THE OTHERS, too, all found their way out, one by one, each one proving to my mother that she had been right to marry my father, and that she would be right not to go back. More than anyone else, my aunt Kalyani, my mother's older sister, is a labyrinth of information about these leavings. She keeps within herself the tiniest memories about the lives of those around her. She had once wanted to be a doctor, but when she failed the university entrance exams she became a teacher, and then a mother. She was such a spectacular success at both that almost no one remembers now that she wanted to go into medicine. That she used to sing on All-Ceylon Radio.

Twenty-five years after Vani hid under the table in the 1958 riots, there were riots again in Colombo, where Kalyani had moved. In the riots of 1983 the soldiers burned Kalyani's house. The choreography of her life at that time was very simple.

Kalyani is sewing now as she tells the story, patient and calloused fingers working at the pattern on a sari blouse. Her voice is matter-of-fact.

It all started like this, you know. There are the Tamil Tigers who want to separate the north. The boys in Jaffna set up a land mine, right, which killed thirteen Sri Lankan army officers in Jaffna, *ceriyā? Do you have that?* They were passing in a truck, and the land mine was set off and about thirteen officers died on the spot. They were all Sinhalese. That sparked the riots. It was July 23, 1983. A very hot day. The riots began the next morning. They started burning and looting. Houses were burned down, people were killed. The whole of Colombo was burning.

The twenty-fourth night, a curfew was declared by the government for the next three or four days, but the looting and burning continued. I did not leave the house, and I did not allow my husband or my children to leave the house. Then, on the twenty-fifth night, some thugs brought torches to set our house on fire.

When Kalyani saw the thugs coming down the road, she went to tell her husband, who was in the garden. Together they went to find their children, Haran and Krisha. The four of them jumped over the low wall into the neighboring garden and stayed hidden in that house. The man who owned the house was an atheist from northern India who had kept himself apart from the conflict surrounding him. From her hiding place

Kalyani could hear him talking with his caretakers about his business and the weather. As though there were not a war going on outside. She could not really believe it. There were the sounds of the men pacing back and forth and conversing, and under that, a steady sound of crackling and falling: the sounds of her house burning. She closed her eyes and listened to glass breaking and men yelling, the very calm and even voice of the Indian man speaking to his servants. She thought to herself, *A funny type of man, to argue that there is no God.* Perhaps the gods thought it an amusing jest, to have someone who did not believe in them be the person who saved Kalyani's life. When the riots died down they crept back into their house to see what was left, and found there was nothing but a shell of where they had lived.

When the riots died down, they all went to Haran's school and slept there for weeks, surrounded by other Tamil refugees in a makeshift camp. It was very hot and very crowded and they lay body to body on the floor of the school. Even in their sleep they dreamed of one another's sweat. In August, they were sent to Jaffna, crammed into a cargo ship. All the time, people were so close together that it was easy for government officials to forget individual names. This is how people become indistinct, lose each other. You become part of a crowd. Haran was only one of many young men, and to a stranger's eye, maybe a Westerner's eye, they all looked alike. Kalyani wanted to send him somewhere different, a place where his body would not be blurred into so many others. She did not want him to be one of the young Tamil men who disappeared under suspicion of being a Tiger.

A short while later, Kalyani managed to send Haran to the United States to live with Vani. He was just the right age to join the Tamil militancy, and there was no way he could stay in the country into which he had been born. The following year, Kalyani's husband went to work in the Middle East, and it was just Kalyani and Krisha. Haran never saw his father again; he died in the Middle East. Kalyani herself left Sri Lanka long ago and floats between countries and relatives, a nomad. She is not a permanent part of anyone's life. It is cold here in the United States, too cold for her. It is winter here and it is snowing.

I want to go back to Colombo and live there. I would be on my own. The weather here is not agreeing with me, she says to me now and looks out the window.

Once out of Sri Lanka and into the West, no one goes back. This is unsaid. It would be insanity. Her voice rarely betrays anything selfish, but I am struck by what I recognize in it. *Homesick.* There is nothing to go back to there. Her house was torched. She lived in that house for a decade. My mother has always mourned the burned family photographs, but now I realize how much more was there than just the pictures. My aunt is almost too quiet to hear.

Not only the pictures, she says. Everything. House and property, everything. Nothing left, nothing left.

In a moment, her voice is her own again, matter-of-fact. Her eyes are on the sari blouse, the needle and thread moving in and out of the silk.

Carolina Rivera Escamilla

Carolina Rivera Escamilla (El Salvador) is a writer, actor, and film-maker who lives in Los Angeles, California. She is a Fellow in the American PEN West USA Rosenthal Foundation's Emerging Voices Program. She is author of a book of short stories, . . . *after* . . . (2015).

Why I Write about War

I write about war because for years it surrounded me.

I write about war because it has marked me since I was a child, when I witnessed teachers being taken away.

I write about war to unsoil stained memories of violence and repression.

I have known people who got killed or disappeared in a civil war, some of whom were friends, neighbors, family.

I know suffering mothers who still search for their disappeared children.

I know fathers who dropped their children at the border Mexico shares with Guatemala.

I write about war so war may not reoccur.

I write about war because I belong to a place where protest and feeling alive meet.

Memory of war feels like disarray, a cyclone of sounds in the head, which have no parallel in the present circumstances I live in.

In Canada, and later in Los Angeles, the streets meant nothing to me because my body was still in the place I had left, where I once felt normal, where living in a warring place had become normal. I write about war because that was the crib into which I was born. I write about war because we should not forget what wars do. I know that writing about war actually opens up a second consciousness in me, as a writer and as a human being.

The following is an abbreviated version of a longer piece.

Alma at about Four-thirty in the Afternoon

I meet my friend Alma at the Art School in San Salvador at about 4:30. She hands me a package. "Be careful. They really need it."

I immediately slide it into my shoulder bag.

"What does he look like?" I notice a small opaque gray moth has landed on her right foot. It stands out against the black of her shoe. I remember what my mother says about moths, but I dismiss her superstitions.

"He's wearing a beige cotton shirt, faded jeans. He has wavy, relaxed dark hair, olive-colored skin, and John Lennon–style glasses. He's about twenty-five years old. He's handsome, by the way."

"How will he recognize me?"

"I told him you'll be wearing a typical Guatemalan blouse, since you're the only one with that style . . . very original." She almost breaks into a smile, but then leaves through the gate ahead of me, her face as gloomy as a cemetery. Her parting words: "Be brave." And from a distance: "Take it easy."

THE FEW times Alma came to my home, she always brought a bag full of vegetables. Once she showed up with fresh corn from her mother's *milpa*. Sitting at the table, eating lunch with my family, she talked with Mamá about her family and ended up massaging my mother's neck and shoulders. Before going back to art classes, Alma and I would climb the mango tree to gather green mangos. We would cut them into thin pieces and eat them with salt and *chile*. My younger brothers once bet a soda that no one could eat a sour mango with *chile* without making a face. Alma was sweet with them, always letting them win. She was the champion of making faces when eating the sourest mango.

I WAIT FOR Alma to be out of sight before I leave with the package. As I catch the bus downtown, I think of the one time I met Alma's mother at the Art School.

The nearly forty-year-old woman is standing at the entry gate, carrying a bag in her right hand. She comes inside dressed in an apron with huge pockets in which she carries all her documents and money, like my Aunt Tona. She is taller than Alma and her skin is lighter, but she has the same long black hair and wide clear brown eyes. She seems lost. She shifts position as she takes in the strangeness of boys with long hair—some smoking cigarettes—and girls with jean shorts and sandals, or '70s-style Kicker shoes. Alma and many of my friends have not been in school for the three days since the students took over the cathedral.

They look so much alike that I'm sure she's Alma's mother, but I don't approach her until my chemistry teacher, knowing that Alma and I are friends, asks me to.

"Hi, my name is Dalia. Are you Alma's mother? Alma and I are friends."

"Ay, yes, Alma has talked about you. Are you the one who has a lot of brothers and sisters?" She extends her right hand, after placing her bag on the ground.

"Yes."

"Where's my daughter? Tell me, please, because someone has told me that she is involved in bad things; that she is with these bad men who are giving trouble to the government." Her eyes are wide. "Alma is a good girl. I didn't want to send her here to the capital. This school is crazy. She wants to study music. I want her to get married to a captain in our town, but she doesn't listen to me. She wants to play her violin and be part of the symphony someday." She takes out a white handkerchief and presses it to her wide, wet eyes.

"Come, let's go in," I say. I sit down on the cement ledge at the base of the mural inside the courtyard at the school's entrance. I face the open sky in the direction of the cathedral. She sits next to me as we watch students go by, her body tensing. "I blame her grandfather for insisting she play the violin. He made a violin for her when she was very young, only five years old. They spent hours practicing. She's a good girl. She should have stayed home and married the captain, just as her father said, before he left us to go work in the city." She blows her nose into her handkerchief. Alma never mentioned the captain to me. Marrying captains, soldiers, and generals is what many parents dream for their daughters, especially in the countryside. My mother and father are not like Alma's parents. They don't even ask if I have a boyfriend.

"Alma is not here, but I'll tell her that you came."

"Where is she? Are you a good girl?

"She's . . ." I sigh and look away.

Am I a good girl? What a question to ask. I think of all the cigarettes I smoked with Alma, when I visited her at the occupied cathedral. I think of the two times I smoked pot, the many times I missed school to go to the beach with a painter, a boy older than me. I took off my shirt so he could draw my breasts, and then we ended up on the sand kissing. Is that what she's asking me? Or does she want to know if I'm also involved in politics?

"Are you a good girl?"

"Yes," I say smiling.

"Where's my daughter? Why isn't she in school? Why don't the teachers punish her for being absent? Why didn't they send me a letter to tell me that she is misbehaving? I can't read, but my younger daughter could read it for me."

I bite my lower lip and pat her on the shoulder. I want to tell her that nobody cares these days about who is present or absent at school. Some teachers are also at the cathedral with Alma. They believe this is part of our education.

"Tell me where my daughter is. I have to give her this bag. I brought her a new pair of underwear I made for her . . . and a blouse . . . some cheese and cream. She doesn't come home on weekends anymore like before." She pats the left side of my lap.

"Alma went to the cathedral on Sunday to pray," I explain. "While she was there, students took over the building to protest the bad education we're getting. She couldn't get out, but the government will sign the students' petition very soon, and she will be released." She says nothing, so I ask, "Who told you that Alma is involved in bad things?"

"Guadalupe . . . she goes to this school, too. She is studying music like Alma. She plays the piano. She lives next to our house in Concepción."

"Yes, I know her. Don't believe everything she tells you about Alma. She's jealous because Alma has a lot of friends. Everyone likes Alma," I say firmly. Alma's mother is quiet for a moment before asking, "Can you take me to the cathedral?"

"No, no, no one can go there. It's surrounded by soldiers, but she'll be fine. She'll come out tomorrow and you'll see her then. You can sleep at my house tonight."

"No, I have to go home today. The last bus leaves at 3:00 p.m. The bandits stop the buses to rob us as soon as it gets dark. Besides, I can't leave my young children alone. Yesterday my neighbor was killed, and these bandits raped his daughter and wife. People are saying they are *guerrilleros* fighting against the government, but I'm not sure they're right. I don't know what is happening anymore, because suddenly we are seeing these *bandidos,* but we are also seeing men we know are good people, who also are covering their faces and heads." She puts her hands inside her apron pockets.

"It's better for you to return to the terminal to catch your bus. I'll tell Alma to go home this weekend. She'll be happy to know that you came to see her. Let's go. I'll walk you to the bus stop." I'm already on my feet heading toward the gate. I look up at the sky and notice that clouds are accumulating, turning it dark gray.

"Please give my daughter this bag. Take care of her. She told me you're a good friend to her, and she knows your family. Don't let my daughter get involved in bad things. Tell her to come home, but not after dark because the bandits are killing people, no matter who they are." She puts her handkerchief inside one of the wide apron pockets, hands me the bag, and shakes my hand to say goodbye.

In her, I see my mother and the constant worry in this country for the security of daughters and sons. I think the mothers of the poor suffer most because their children have been the first to join the struggle against the government for improvements in their lives and those of future generations. "I'll take care of her. I'll come with Alma to visit you this weekend." I wave goodbye to her at the bus stop. She waves to me from the bus.

I never went to visit Alma's mother, and Alma never went back home. It was too dangerous for her after Guadalupe's family found out about her involvement with the guerrillas. Guadalupe married the captain who was supposed to marry Alma.

Alma's mother tells the entire village that bandits killed her daughter when she was coming home to see her.

ALMA DID see her mother once more. They met secretly at the village church. Alma came disguised as a city woman in a wavy brunette wig. She wore heavy makeup, a stylish dress, and high-heeled shoes. Later she told me that it was almost impossible to walk in those shoes. Nobody recognized her, not even her mother, not until she sat down next to her, pinched her elbow, and smiled. They went to the rear of the church. Alma tells her mother that it's good she told the neighbors that bandits had killed her. "You'll be safer now, and my little sisters, too." They hug, they cry, and too soon the Mass is finished. Alma causes her mother to miss Mass.

I LEAVE the school and walk along the boulevard to the bus stop. There are soldiers everywhere. Some of the soldiers stop people and ask for their documents. Mostly, they stop young students like me. The package is heavy. I feel my right shoulder dropping lower and starting to go numb. I try to focus straight ahead on the street, but my lips and eyes will not stay still, as I stare in the direction of the arriving bus.

Shit. God, whoever you are, and wherever you are, under the earth or above the clouds, listen to me now. I'm sorry I've denied you so many times, just as your disciple Pedro did, but you have got to understand that with all the misery and killing going on here, it's easier to befriend the devil than you. Look, even priests have been killed, but today, do me this favor, make me invisible, or make the package in my bag light and . . . Shit. How can I ask you this now, if I have never been a believer? I know that if the soldiers stop me now, if they open the package, it will be over. Yes, my life, my little life will be over. On Bus 22, I hold the heavy shoulder bag with the package on my lap, on my way downtown.

ALMA AND I entered Art School the same year. We had both just turned sixteen, fresh young students starting high school. As I got close to the school, on my first day there, my breathing ran fast and heavy like a river after a big storm. I had gone through the auditions two weeks earlier, and I felt so proud of being accepted into El Centro Nacional de Artes. My oldest brother was delighted.

Mamá and Papá were not quite convinced I should study theater. "You should go to sewing school," my mother told me. "Look, Milagro is already working in the factory and sews at home for many people in the *colonia*." She was seated at the kitchen table, a pile of my brothers' and father's pants at her feet, mending them one by one. I guess she said that in case I should want encouragement or permission to change my mind about theater. I slipped through the curtain into my room, pretending to look for something to write with. Then, I returned to the main room of the house.

My father said, "Well, you're going to be an actress now. Next thing you know, we'll see you in Mexican soap operas."

"No, that's a load of crap," I said, sounding very much like him. "I hope one day I can go to Russia to study theater and the methods of Stanislavsky and Bertolt Brecht."

In fact, I don't know anything about these big names. At school, I heard that some new teachers who have been to Russia are coming to teach us the methods of Brecht and Stanislavsky.

"What did you say?" Papá slicked back his hair with Vaseline with the same black comb he sometimes uses as a harmonica.

"Ah, nothing," I answered.

"Russia!" he yelled.

I run into my room. I want to put on my only pair of Levi jeans and sandals to go out. He pushes aside the brown polyurethane curtain that serves as the door between the bedroom I share with my two sisters and the living room. Holding his comb in his hand, punctuating his words, he says, "Be careful what you say. Right now, you could be killed in this country just for mentioning that place." I laugh nervously. He leaves murmuring, "She wants to be a Communist. Well, at least she's thinking about things . . . she's growing up."

As I leave to go to school, I say, "Bye, see you at supper," and my father hands me two *colones*. "Thank you," I whisper.

ON THAT first day, walking through the entrance of the Art School, I see Alma, leaning against the huge Dalí-esque mural just inside the main gate. Over the center of the mural, someone has painted the figure of a camouflaged soldier with an M-3 rifle. Alma leans against the wall right where the point of the rifle barrel ends. It's still early, so I wait, leaning against the mural too.

Her arms are crossed. It occurs to me that people with their arms folded don't want to be bothered by anyone. I keep observing her. Perhaps she's just shy. When Alma isn't looking, I scrutinize her from toe to head. I suspect she is doing the same thing to me, but when I glance toward her face, she is looking at my feet. I like her very long straight black hair. She starts playing with it, rolling it around her finger. I've always wanted long hair, but my mother complains that my hair gets full of lice, so she never lets me grow it.

Alma moves closer to me, still looking at my feet. I finally figure out why. My sandals and hers are exactly the same. Brown leather, with straps and thick soles cut from old tires. I move closer to her, too.

"Where did you buy your sandals?" I ask. "Are you new here? What's your name?"

She's right in front of me, smiling with child-like eyes, pointing at my feet. "My father makes them," she says. "You must have bought yours at Mercado Cuartel. That's the only place that sells them."

"Yes, you're right," I say, and that's all it takes to start our friendship.

We walk along the corridor and discover we have the same morning classes. I sit next to her, and she tells me she passed the audition for music. She has her violin with her. At noon I invite her to eat lunch at my house, but she says she brought food with her and prefers to stay at the school. She has mentioned she's from the country, and I sense the city is new for her. I stay with her, waiting for our afternoon classes. I don't want to go home.

In sixteen years, I've never missed lunch at home. I picture all my brothers and sisters in line waiting for Mamá to fill their plates. Nobody eats twice at my house, so Mamá will save my plate of food for later. I hope she doesn't come to look for me at school.

We sit under a mango tree behind the classroom, the thin dark green leaves adorning the brown branches. Alma opens a plastic bag and brings out a hard square of cheese, a small French roll, and a container of cooked red beans. "Let's eat," she says. I like the cheese.

For a few months during the two free hours we have every day before afternoon classes start, Alma plays her violin, while I dance around the mango tree. We laugh so hard whenever she dances while I try to play her violin. Together, Alma and I are magic, and our magic helps us to forget the daily routine. "Do you think we'll always stay close friends?" we ask each other.

"I want to take you to the green hills, near where I live," she says, showing me a book of stories she has written about the hills of Amatepec, just outside San Salvador, where during the week she rents a room in a house.

"When? Tomorrow? Let's not go to school!" I'm eager to escape the daily torment of soldiers trying to intimidate our teachers and interrogate us at school. "Anyway, we don't even have classes really," I add to convince myself more than Alma.

"Let's do it! We'll meet tomorrow at Parque Libertad." Alma nods her head and grins. She heads toward her music class humming Beethoven's Fifth Symphony.

"I'll read you the monologue I'm working on," I yell to her, but I regret my words as soon as they leave my mouth. My monologue is stupid. It is about all kinds of insects living in peace in a community. The protagonist is a frog that talks to ants and a butterfly. I'll have to explain to her that it's an analogy assignment for my drama class. Otherwise, I would not be writing about bugs. At any rate, my handwriting is terrible, like a hen with ink on her beak trying to scribble on the ground. Alma writes beautifully, but she puts Vs for Bs and vice versa, and disregards accent marks. We're the same that way. I'll read her the monologue and hope she doesn't laugh.

I arrive at Parque Libertad at nine in the morning. Alma is buying a bag of sliced mangos with chili from a vendor in the park. I walk slowly behind her, stick my index finger into her back like a gun, and say, "Documents out, young woman."

"Hey, you scared me." She turns around to face me. "I was imagining some illiterate soldier demanding my papers."

The woman with the basket of mangos offers a nervous but friendly smile, and sells me another bag of mangos.

"There's the bus!" She points to the opposite corner of the Parque. We jump on the bus and off we go.

The place is only about twenty minutes away from downtown. The road is still paved where we get off the bus, and Alma leads me up the dirt road that begins a few steps away. After a few hundred meters, we head into the bushes. Alma pushes aside some bamboo branches. "Over there, can you see the tall trees and the green of the hills?" The hills are a faraway wall that meets the infinite blue sky. The ripe yellow sun dissolves into the green grass. There are a few short guava trees in the middle of the grassy area, and bamboo takes over its edges. There are no birds singing here, only Alma and I, who run downward in a sloping spiral into the infinite green hills.

"Let's go there." I point to a spot in the distance. "I want to lie down on the little patch of green grass." I smile at Alma. We find a spring. I jump over it, turn quickly, and splash Alma in the face, just as she bends down close to the creek to splash water at me.

"Let's see who is the thirstier one here!" She comes at me with water cupped in her hands.

"See if you can rain on me. I am the earth," I yell and act out the role of the earth, arms uplifted in a graceful but silly pose.

"I am the rain. I will soak you, Earth! Rain, rain, drop your rain over her face," she sings, as she sprinkles water all over herself, and on me, too. We kneel again with arms uplifted to the sky. I imagine a great audience watching me from above.

"Let's act out the monologue you need to practice for your exam." She sits down on the grass.

"I forgot to bring it. I play an animal, a frog that talks to ants and butterflies. It's stupid!" Alma jumps around the grass like a frog. She hides behind a bush. I extend my arms and pretend to be a butterfly floating up and down the hill. The frog comes to me and says, "Butterfly, butterfly, let's go catch bugs to feed the poor." I laugh. We laugh. I fall to the ground laughing and hold my stomach, I am laughing so hard. Alma falls onto her back laughing, too.

I run to the other side of the knoll and lie down to let the sun dry me. Alma follows me. With her face to the sun, she spins in circles yelling, "I feel free, free!" and ends up at my side, still laughing. I read some of her stories. She allows me to keep them "forever, if you want." The thin copy-book with a cheap cover is like the ones my mother buys for my brothers, who are in elementary school.

"Is your stomach making noises?" I ask her.

"Yeah, I am hungry." She looks down and hears another growl. "Listen to my crying belly!"

We return downtown around three in the afternoon, wet, hungry, and still laughing.

AFTER EIGHT months at the Art School, things have changed. The soldiers sack the school, searching for weapons that aren't there. They smash all the art supplies. They smear and spill paint everywhere in the theater rooms and ask why there is so much red paint at this school. They smash the mirrors in the makeup room. They break the furniture. They detain students, who then disappear, their bodies never found. Some students get away and flee north. The chemistry teacher is killed at a teachers' protest. Thousands of students fill the streets in daily protests. They shout for better education and justice for the poor. They take over the cathedral. The police and military trucks circle the church, shooting wildly. Once in a while, students throw bags of food from passing buses, quickly pulling their arms back inside. People become scared when they see soldiers motioning with rifles and walk nervously.

I KNOW THE plan: I have to get off bus number 22 at the cathedral. Then, I will walk to Parque Libertad to catch bus number 27 to the university. There is always something going on at the cathedral. If there's no Mass, a protest will be taking place. Also, the Teatro Nacional is close by. I don't want to see anyone I know.

When I see the Teatro Nacional and the cathedral, I know it's time for me to get off Bus 22. The indigenous faces of soldiers, boys my age from the country or the *rancherías* near the capital, are stationed at the corners around the cathedral. The huge red Coca-Cola billboard next to the cathedral steps reminds me who really controls our country. I walk the two blocks to Parque Libertad at a normal pace, then board bus number 27 to the university.

ONCE ALMA and I worked a bus together. "Hurry up! Let's get on the bus for Soyapango!" I get a seat in the front; she finds a seat toward the middle. I open up a newspaper and read loudly: "Yesterday the guerrillas attacked two military headquarters."

From the middle of the crowded bus, Alma calls, "Which ones?"

"El Zapote and Santa Ana." I answer like a news anchor on television.

"How many were killed?"

"Let me see . . ." I scan the newspaper . . . "forty-one government soldiers killed by the guerrillas." As I read this aloud, something strange happens to my voice. It comes out hollow and bitter like a sad memory stuck in knots between my throat and my chest. I think about Dora surrounded by soldiers and shot to death in Parque Cuscatlán—and of Trompita, the musician, his body burned and eaten away by chemicals, a tactic favored by the military to horrify the people. His green eyes are all I can remember, the only part of his body found on the road. Then that dark night when Carlos and his girlfriend were abducted from their homes, and we never saw them again. I remember stories that circulated about the peasants killed in the mountains by the military forces. But the moment passes and calls me back to my task, which is to spread the word that the guerrillas are alive and fighting in the mountains. Although the front page of the newspaper says that more civilians and *guerrilleros* have been killed than military, I only tell the people about the military deaths.

We stand up and distribute propaganda to the passengers. We know these people would never see it otherwise. We keep our eyes on the windows, making sure there are no soldiers in the distance. All day long, going from bus to bus, we get out the message.

As we step off the bus, Alma's left fist shoots into the air as she shouts, *"¡Patria, o muerte, venceremos!"*

Another day we try this routine close to the Art School. We are dressed for work, she in khaki MacArthur pants, a plaid, four-buttoned boy's shirt, and a hat on her head; I, the same, only my pants are faded Levis. It's about three o'clock in the afternoon, and we're on our way back with some *compañeros* from a *MERS* protest in front of the American Embassy. Alma and I spray some graffiti on a neighborhood wall. It reads: *MERS: Movimiento Estudiantil Revolucionario de Secundaria is alive and present in the struggle!* Alma steps back from the long brick wall to appreciate our work. I am still squatting with the can in my hand finishing the last words, but I can sense her behind me.

I get up, and we cross the street in the direction of the Art School. Once inside, we'll drop off the spray cans and discuss the protest.

Suddenly, we hear an explosion. A ball of smoke rises from the area of the school. We rush to the corner and see a firebombed truck. "It's better if we stay away," I suggest.

The sweet smoky stench of burnt Coca Cola stays with us all the way to the bus stop. We decide to walk to Parque Libertad.

SOON I WILL be at the university. Bus 27 is passing by El Estado Mayor, the Military School, where the green-painted buildings, trucks and uniforms have given me goose bumps ever since I walked through this neighborhood with Mamá when I was little.

THE LAST time Alma and I worked together was probably more than six months ago. It began at a meeting where some *compañeros* informed us about the new American buses arriving in the country. The buses were being sensationalized on the radio and television news. "The American President Ronald Reagan is helping our society by sending new technology," our newscasters told us in their most soothing voices. They said, "the new buses have both radio and television . . . they are very nice."

Alma stands up. "Reagan is taking us for idiots. He's trying to be funny by sending the buses as a cover for the military weaponry he is secretly providing."

The next day, when the buses go into service, almost all of them are firebombed. After Alma and I empty all the passengers out of one bus, Alma poses like an eagle ready to fly, and, facing north with a grenade in her hand, she yells angrily, "Reagan, American Imperialists, we shit on your brains and stick your dreams of technological superiority up your asses! Don't you remember Vietnam?"

While she screams, I go back to gather up any forgotten bags or belongings to reunite them with the passengers outside. We warn them to run away. As we set fire to the last bus of the day, we hear, and then see, tanks approaching in the distance.

Alma makes sure I am out of the bus. Then she pulls the pin of a grenade and lets it fly through the open door. We run in different directions, disappearing into the crowds. That was the last time I was with her before receiving this package from her today.

I FINALLY arrive at the Universidad José Simeón Cañas at about a quarter to six. I meet my contact in the social sciences department, on the shady corner that has an exit from the campus, at the exact place Alma described. I find the man in the beige cotton shirt and faded jeans, just as she said I would. We've just met when the shockwave and heat of an explosion whips us both involuntarily in the direction of a chaotic crowd about a block away. We see students running, trying to escape as soldiers bolt through the smoke, striking with clubs, shooting their guns.

The young man tears the shoulder bag from my arm, squats, pulls the package from the bag, rips it open, and hands me a .38-caliber pistol. He scoops up all the other weapons for himself, telling me to move.

"Do you know how to use it?" He wipes the sweat from his forehead.

Suddenly, I once again feel intense heat. He looks around for an exit. I want to say, "It's hot," but instead, I say, "Yes, I've had some lessons."

He removes his glasses and I look at his eyes. They are hazel, set in a heart-shaped face. He wipes his glasses with the corner of his shirt. I want to tell him to clean the sweat from around his eyes, but I just watch him move. I squat, pressing my back into the wall to be at his level. He seems to appreciate this and draws close to my face. He whispers that the operation in El Zapote hasn't gone well.

"They surrounded the *compañeros* before they could attack. Alma was the leader of the mission. They killed everyone."

I run out of the university, sobbing, tucking the weapon inside my jeans. Which of these filthy fucking soldiers killed Alma? I ask myself. Why did she have to die, and why should I have to kill?

I slow down. I try to look calm as I walk through the long, messy traffic-filled Calle Panamericana. I have to act normally, so nobody suspects my pain. Keep going, I tell myself. Don't show what you feel.

I imagine my mother smiling. Is she smiling? Yes, she is, and her smile helps me to keep going. I cross to the other side of the street without noticing the traffic signal. Soldiers stare at me. It's starting to rain. I can feel the drops on my face, and I see the windshield wipers on the cars and buses flipping back and forth. Then everything blurs.

It's is 9:00 p.m., and I'm finally home. I go to the bedroom. My sisters are sleeping. Everyone is sleeping, except Mamá. She doesn't ask me anything. I've already put the pistol under the mattress. I listen to my sisters' breathing—dolls full of dreams. I cannot sleep. I'm afraid someone may have followed me. I look at the corrugated metal wall. Soldiers sometimes pass through the property along the other side and scrape the metal wall with their rifles. I hate that sound.

I can't tell anyone that Alma is dead. Above all, I can't tell Mamá. I worry that someone in the *colonia* saw me at the university today. This *colonia* has many *orejas*.

Nata, the owner of the local store, calls everyone in the *colonia* to say that the French rolls have arrived and are still warm. It's 6:00 in the morning. I haven't slept. I go outside to get water from the cement laundry sink. I scoop it up with my hands and splash it on my face. It's cold and smells like spring water. The coldness of the water reminds me of the time I played with Alma in the hills. I look up at the long green mango leaves dangling and moving in the wind. The sun's rays peek through the tree branches to the wet ground where I stand. They shine on the trunk of the mango tree. A tiny salamander looks for its way up the tree.

"What are you looking at there, wasting your time? You should have started the fire for the coffee on the woodstove an hour ago." It's my mother's voice.

"There's a baby salamander on the tree." I do not face my mother.

"Ah, I know, your father found the mother and its babies on the avocado tree and put them there. I think they were just born a few days ago."

I wish she hadn't told me the story of the salamanders. I want to think that it's Alma entering the world in a new form. Alma told me once that when she died, she wanted to be reborn as an animal. I told her I wanted to be a spider to weave the world the way I wanted it. By the time I'm ready to leave for school, Mamá is waiting for me at the table. There's a plastic cup of coffee, accompanied by a French roll. I come to sit with her.

"What's wrong? Why are you so quiet this morning? What's the matter with your eyes?"

"Nothing." I turn away from her.

"Did you hear that El Zapote was attacked? Many *muchachos* were killed."

"Yes," I whisper. "And a girl, too."

Trudy Mercadal

TRUDY MERCADAL (USA/Guatemala) is a journalist, researcher, interpreter, and translator who has worked for a variety of news media outlets (Al Jazeera, NPR, CBC [Canada]) and several independent film companies. She has done investigative reporting for the *New York Times* and translated for Global Sisters. Her research interests fall within the fields of social history and cultural studies, with a focus on race, gender, intercultural relations, and legal issues. Most recently, she has worked as a community organizer, an interpreter specializing in vulnerable populations and human rights, and a coordinator for international cooperation projects in Guatemala. She writes about popular culture, cultural history, and literature for publications in the United States and Latin America.

Why I Write about War

The reasons I write about war are a clear reflection of how the personal becomes political.

First of all, I am an American citizen, born in New Orleans. In the 1970s, my mother moved us to Guatemala, in the midst of the thirty-six-year civil war, where we lived during the peak years of massacres, violence, and dirty war tactics enacted by the entrenched military regimes of the era (1972–85). The perpetrators of the rural massacres that ravaged the country, which affected mostly the Mayan population, would later be tried and sentenced in war crime tribunals for genocide. For the children from the middle to upper classes living in the urban centers, the internal armed conflict, as the war would later be called, was largely an abstraction.

As the state became more overt, brutal, and indiscriminate in its repression, the bombings, kidnappings, forced disappearances, and targeted assassinations became common in the urban centers, and yet the children of the privileged—i.e., white, upper middle class, and attending private schools—were mostly shielded from the violence. Silence was maintained in part by censuring the press and proscribing any sort of literature that did not appear seamlessly aligned with the official discourse. This made it easier for the middle classes to ignore and deny, in the postwar years, the atrocities committed during the conflict. The official, dominant rhetoric was omnipresent and unrelenting: the military and economic elites were fighting the evils of communism; those who were killed or disappeared surely were involved in something nefarious.

My family was proud to be among the founders of the National Liberation Movement (MLN for its initials in Spanish), the extreme right-wing political party self-described by its leader, Mario Sandoval Alarcón, as the "party of organized violence." The MLN was known to control much of the paramilitary violence then sanctioned by the military regimes and conservative economic elites. Paramilitary violence was aimed at union leaders, indigenous and student organizations, and any other person or group that might be considered, accurately or not, as an "internal enemy" of the state.

Private schools did nothing but echo the prevailing rhetoric, and history lessons were best described as mythology and propaganda. Even today, most private schools avoid teaching the history of the internal armed conflict. For some of us, fractures in the discourse allowed the penetration of some disquietude, feeble as it may have been. In my case, my mother had grown up in the United States during the civil rights era and the surge of feminism. Although she was more progressive than the Guatemalan side of her family, her disgust with their views was muted. It is fair to say, then, that I was little exposed to any views contrary to those of the regime, even though there was ample opportunity to become aware of them: massive protests, publications, and ever more coverage by the international press, which could no longer be suppressed or denied. In that sense, I was just another product of the ideological machine meant to obliterate any kind of dissent among the population.

I would have to leave Guatemala and study abroad as a young adult to understand the extent of the violence and harm done to Guatemala society by the regime. Gradually, I became aware of the effects of the suppression of knowledge and information. It took me decades of research and study to grasp the structural roots of the violence.

Another reason why I write about war is rooted in the public sphere. My work as a writer and an interpreter/translator specializing in vulnerable populations and human rights reflects my academic formation—the years it took for me to understand the material and structural underpinnings of injustice. My interpreting—which is done mostly for journalists, filmmakers, and international aid workers—is also political, the praxis of my ideological stance.

The Peace Accords that were signed in Guatemala in 1996 heralded a new era of democracy and justice. The 1990s were a decade in which testimonial, political, and historical writing about the war years flourished not only in Guatemala but also the rest of Central America. However, the voices of women were largely absent from these Central American narratives, which is hardly surprising given that, historically, women's voices have been almost entirely absent from war narratives. War writing has been dominated by male voices and by documentary or archival evidence. Yet there was, in the 1990s, a growing sense that victim testimonials were important. Also important were the voices of women who had fought in the civil wars that beset the region.

The turnaround was fueled by the postwar spread of transitional justice systems, which advocated the use of courts and tribunals for redressing wrongs perpetrated against the victims, whose testimonies became crucial to postconflict investigations. Thus, postwar national and international justice systems opened spaces for victims to be heard.

Women's suffering differed significantly from that of men, as women were tortured and victimized in gendered ways. That is, their bodies and condition as women were subjected to specific forms of harm, such as rape or sexual enslavement in military camps. As a writer, I strive to give voice to women war victims. As an interpreter, I must often deal with the psychological and ethical connotations of victims' stories. Sharing their stories is an act of healing and hope but can lead to exploitation if the material is misused. Most of the women I speak with—whether civilians, militants, or guerrillas—suffer from post-traumatic stress and other forms of trauma, even now, decades after the end of the war. Many say that retelling their stories proves therapeutic, a phenomenon borne out by a wide variety of studies.

The Sepur Zarco trial marked a watershed in women's fight for justice, not only in Guatemala but worldwide. Fifteen indigenous women survivors of systematic rape and enslavement fought for years in the highest court of Guatemala. The case culminated in the conviction of former military officers for crimes against humanity. The court granted reparations, which were used to help fight the great poverty in the community by providing healthcare, education, and access to land. As the Sepur Zarco trial demonstrates, women's voices are of crucial importance to justice, as well as to the historical memory and survival of their communities.

While the case would not have reached the courts without the persistence of courageous women, it also required the participation and support of civil society and community workers, including that of interpreters for the Maya-speaking women. War writing helps us learn about our story as a society. We must face the long and well-documented role of the United States and other powerful nations in supporting the military violence in Central America during the dirty wars. The conflict in Guatemala can be traced back to the 1954 coup enacted by the U.S. government against the democratically elected president of Guatemala. We must accept our responsibility to redress the harm inflicted by our country.

I am conscious that, like many others of my socioeconomic group, my family in Guatemala was complicit in the wrongs perpetrated against the victims of the internal armed conflict, which produced an estimated two hundred thousand dead and disappeared, even if they did not participate directly. This knowledge impinges on my identity as an American citizen, which, in turn, makes me feels implicated, albeit unwillingly, in the conflicts that were fueled, and continue to be fueled, by American corporate and expansionist interests. For me, writing about war is a political act as well as an act of hope by which I work toward peace, transitional justice, and reparations.

Guatemalan society cannot move forward toward peace until the trauma caused by war crimes is healed. For thousands of survivors, the dead and disappeared are the source of unresolved trauma. The absence of loved ones and the impunity that some perpetrators of injustice have enjoyed erode the social fabric, fueling mistrust and uncertainty. The war exacerbated the poverty of the rural areas, leading to the dispossession of family lands and the displacement of thousands. These deleterious effects have given rise to conflicts over land and water. The ripple effects of the wars in Central America—and the contribution of the United States to these problems, then and today—are undeniably at the root of the latest political and human crisis besetting Central America and North America: the so-called migration crisis.

As I write this essay, the government of Guatemala, with the support of the military and economic elites, has regressed from its anticorruption position. For example, the Congress has passed an amnesty act that will free the sentenced perpetrators of grave violations of human rights against the most vulnerable populations of Guatemala. To write about the war in this context, then, is to write about its long reach into the postwar. The war has not yet ended. Much work remains to be done.

The Search for National Identity: What the Discovery of the National Police Archive Reveals

The Peace Accords in Guatemala, signed in 1996 during the administration of then president Álvaro Arzú, included a set of provisions meant to repair the damage that the war had caused and to rebuild the country. The Peace Accords were extensive and brought great hope for national healing and growth. Activists and former guerrillas sat at the table with military officers and government representatives to envision what the new nation should be like. The process was celebrated worldwide as a model of civility and inclusiveness.

Nevertheless, in the first years after the Peace Accords, violence began to erupt as organized mafia groups gradually filled in the power gaps left by retrenching political factions. It is therefore pertinent to ask whether the Peace Accords have been a success. In the most immediate sense, they have been, since there has been no new outbreak of war. On the other hand, crime has risen to unprecedented levels, and most people have not seen any improvement in their living conditions. The Peace Accords have been implemented only partially, and there is widespread disillusionment with the process. Meanwhile, the national dialogue that was created to strengthen and build the project of peace and *resarcimiento* (reparations) has mostly given way to an oppressive obliviousness encouraged by groups in power, which promote a "forgive and forget" policy meant to silence the voices of those seeking answers and justice.

The Peace Accords stipulated the retreat of military troops from the areas most brutalized under their occupation during the years of the war and the need for oversight of the military by a civilian defense minister. These points were included in a referendum in May 1999, which would have added important stipulations into the Guatemalan constitution. However, the referendum's defeat allowed the military to remain in control of peace and security in the region, despite their past role in abuses.

In rural communities today, internal armed conflict victims must live side by side with their victimizers, and the wounds of war continue to fester. Mothers wait for disappeared children to return, and wives for husbands, often coming face-to-face with former members of paramilitary troops—recruited from local villages—known to have been involved in the atrocities of war. Peacekeeping duties in the areas most impacted by war remain in the hands of military authorities. One of the results of this situation is that, as groups of displaced Maya villagers return to their former lands, they find them occupied by landowners with government and military connections.

Denying the past has very real consequences in a community. After decades of war and more than two hundred thousand kidnapped and massacred, a scorched-earth military campaign, and whole villages razed, little is left to commemorate the dead or provide a space for inquiry and information. Under these circumstances, how can a national identity be forged?

In 2005, human rights activists in Guatemala discovered the National Police Archive, a warehouse holding a vast repository of deteriorating documents. The Archive houses more than a century of records, including those for the peak years of the civil war (1970s–1980s). This discovery has been the subject of international coverage in publications such as the *New York Times,* the *Smithsonian Magazine, Harper's,* and the *Harvard Review.* Now under United Nations and University of Texas stewardship, the National Police Archive has digitalized more than twenty-one million documents out of approximately eighty million.

When the discovery of the National Police Archive of Guatemala became public, survivors, victims' relatives, human rights organizations, and scholars felt hopeful that the trove held invaluable information that could help them investigate crimes committed during the internal armed conflict. The Archive provided huge amounts of information useful to transitional justice, such as chain of command, war plans, and practices used during the peak years of the war that led to forced disappearance, torture, and other forms of abuse. More than four hundred human rights' violations cases are currently under investigation at the Archive by Guatemalan district attorneys, local and international human rights organizations, victims' advocates, and Guatemalans who have traveled back from as far as Mexico and Costa Rica, hoping to find information on relatives. These efforts are already yielding important results at individual and national levels, as some highly publicized cases have been recently brought to court.

For example, almost thirty years after his forced disappearance at the hands of security forces, the family of labor activist Fernando García has found justice. A groundbreaking trial—based on information found in the Archive—convicted two former police officers to forty years in prison for his murder. The press followed the case avidly, possibly because it was the first such case to reach sentencing, and because Nineth Montenegro,

García's wife and a congresswoman, has waged a very public campaign for justice for decades.

La Isla, a documentary based on the discovery of the National Police Archive, has reached a wide audience in Guatemala, despite blatant and clumsy efforts by authorities to prevent its being shown. At several screenings that I attended, some viewers openly cried, and many expressed gratitude. Numerous sectors of the population, especially young adults, show a strong interest in opening windows to the past that have been closed to them until now. Events such as these screenings foster historical memory, empathy, and cohesion among participants, which is perhaps a first step toward forging a national identity.

In the absence of memorials that bear witness to the violence done to tens of thousands of Guatemalans during the war, the Archive provides opportunities for public memory. It brings Guatemalans together over a shared history of pain that extends across communities and encourages dialogue, which is the cornerstone of citizenship-creation and identity-shaping.

The records of Guatemala's dark and violent past actually hold the seeds of a hopeful future. The closure and healing the Police Archive have already brought to many Guatemalans, the light they shed on decades of darkness, and the roads they open toward legal justice make it possible to build bridges. National identity is not monolithic and monochromatic. National identity satisfies the need for belonging and bestows a sense of self-worth and dignity. For too long, large segments of the Guatemalan population have been prevented from sharing in these feelings of belonging and worth. Many have been denied access to basic goods essential to survival, making it impossible for them to live in dignity. However, there is now wider acknowledgment among Guatemalans that the marginalizing practices of the past are no longer acceptable.

An example of this is the formation of women's groups comprised of victims of wartime sexual violence, who advocate for legal and policy changes in government and for an end to patriarchal ideology in society. From reparations funds, one group of women coordinated the creation of an educational and health center for their community, which led to greater community cohesiveness and prosperity. Other groups representing diverse ethnic groups have undertaken similar projects.

However, to achieve their goals, these groups will need outside aid. Already the Archive, which is supported by a coalition of international organizations, has been seriously threatened by the Morales administration. From almost five hundred employees, the Archive staff has been reduced to fewer than fifty. The government refuses to provide the necessary resources and support or to continue receiving the aid international sources have offered. This stance puts the project of nation building and creating national identity at risk. Yet, as long as communities continue to foster historical memory, it is not dead.

Carmen Duarte

CARMEN DUARTE (Cuba) is a playwright and the author of several works of fiction. Her novels include *Hasta la vuelta* (Until I return), *La danza de los abanicos* (Fan dance), *Donde empieza y acaba el mundo* (Where the world begins and ends), and *El inevitable rumbo de la brújula* (The inevitable rhythm of the compass). She is author of the radio play *Ausencia quiere decir olvido* (Absence means forgetting), later adapted for the stage, and also the dramatic monologue *El adiós de Alejandra Sol* (Alejandra Sol's goodbye). Several of her plays are included in her collection *¿Cuánto me das marinero?* (How much will you give me, sailor?). She currently resides in Miami, where she teaches Spanish. The selection below is taken from her novel in progress "The Ship That Took Us to War."

Why I Write about War

When I was very young and studying dramaturgy in Havana, I took my inspiration from historical events. As I was eighteen and had limited life experience, I decided to take those passages from books about the Cuban wars of independence that seemed most dramatic to me and write plays based on them, experimenting and creating until I mastered the techniques of drama. Now, my theater and narrative sometimes rely on historical themes and sometimes not, but Cuban political reality continues to fascinate me.

Now that I am older, my focus is the senselessness of war. Soldiers kill each other in an instant and later do not remember why they fought. In the nineteenth century, Cubans battled Spain for independence in a war that lasted more than ten years. A few decades later, Cuba allowed hundreds and hundreds of immigrants from Spain seeking economic stability. By then, nobody in Cuba considered Spaniards to be enemies. Today, some politicians and leaders of fundamentalist organizations insist that war is the way to solve conflicts, gain land, or impose their beliefs on non-believers. For me, writing about war is an attempt to express my concern about the suffering of soldiers who are sent by powerful people to fight wars they did not cause, desire, or believe in, and about civilians who are the victims of war. I write about war to show that the soldiers on the front line always lose, no matter what side they are fighting for.

"The Ship That Took Us to War" is a novel in progress inspired by historical events that I observed firsthand. In 1988, the Cuban government sent the theater group in which I worked to accompany our troops headed for Angola—a journey that lasted forty days. We traveled on a cruise ship that left the port of Odessa and in Havana picked up around a thousand Cuban soldiers who sailed in civilian clothes and without weapons, to the south of Africa. Our mission was to perform for the ship's soldiers. After the troops disembarked in Luanda, we returned to Cuba on the cruise ship with soldiers who had completed service in Angola.

For thirteen years, Cuba, the former Soviet Union, and the United States intervened in the war that began after Angola won its independence from Portugal. From 1975 to 2002, a civil war raged. The Marxist Agostino Neto, leader of the Popular Movement for the Liberation of Angola, became the first president of the country, thanks to the support of Cuba and the Soviet Union. At the same time, the anticommunist Jonas Savimbi, creator of the National Union for the Total Independence of Angola, won the support of the United States. In July 1988, with the Cuito Cuanavale battle, the Cuban army managed to rout the South African troops who had staged an offensive in southern Angola, strengthening Agostino Neto's power. Although this action ended the conflict, the Cuban government continued to send soldiers to Angola until 1991.

Despite my personal connection to this novel, the narrated events, characters, and intrigues are fictional. I know that other participants will have different points of view based on their own experiences. After thirteen years of Cuban participation in the war in Angola, the soldiers' circumstances—the ways in which they traveled and fought, the different places in the country to which they were assigned, their ranks and tasks, and their individual states of mind—generated a multiplicity of notions about what happened.

As a woman and a civilian who traveled with the troops, I have my particular perspective on the situation, which is different than that of the male soldiers. The female battalion that went in Angola never participated in a battle. My experience was unlike that of both the male and female soldiers. I did not spend years in Angola, as they did, but I observed how civilian women were treated by military men. It made me realize that men who are going to war can be as brutal with their own women as with the enemy.

From The Ship That Took Us to War

I

From the boat, Santa Cruz de Tenerife seemed close. The fog of winter blurred its streets. I didn't have time to think. I placed my feet on the ship's rail and looked down from almost fifteen meters above the ocean. Everything was spinning. I held my breath. They shot to kill, but the bullet only grazed my arm. I lost my balance and fell sideways into the sea. The impact hurt as much as the bleeding wound. The water was icy, nothing like the warm waters of Cuba. Yemayá, the Yoruba goddess of the sea, hugged me tight as if she wanted to protect me. She squeezed me so hard that I felt awful pressure in my head. I was drowning. I saw seaweed, rocks. They say it's impossible that I sank deep enough to see the ocean's floor because if I had, I would have died. But I think it was a miracle because I saw the bottom as clearly as I'm seeing you now. Before, I was never a believer. I mocked the saints of all religions, but after that, I had to believe. I don't know how I reached the surface, but at first contact with the air, I cried out. I gulped air until I could fill my lungs completely and control my breathing.

Someone came to my rescue. Well, I was told that the harbor pilot threw a lifeline, which I held onto until I was close enough for someone to jump into the water to pull me out. But I don't remember clearly. Somehow, I was given a second chance at life. I had no strength to swim or speak. I arrived at the hospital with two fractured ribs and a displaced clavicle. Later, I was diagnosed with pneumonia. The wound on my arm was more bearable. It was superficial and gave me no trouble after it was sutured. My pneumonia improved within two weeks, but my bones took longer to heal, maybe because they're the hardest organs in the body. I don't know. Those days in the hospital were bitter. I didn't know anyone, and the authorities hung around me, trying to find out my identity. We were traveling without passports on the ship, and I couldn't prove who I was. They wanted to know everything. Why did I throw myself off the deck of a cruiser from such a height? Why did I risk my life? It was too complicated to explain.

II

Captain Aracelio Carmona of the Intelligence Division had suffered from severe acne in adolescence, evident from the holes in his face. He had an oily appearance that made him seem unpleasant at first. The day after we sailed from Havana, he summoned me to his cabin. I wasn't thrilled at all that someone from the military would want to talk to me, but I had to go. I was accompanying the army, and I had no choice but to obey. I'd always dreamed of knowing more than just Cuba. My parents were terrified that I was being sent to Angola, but I felt joy in leaving the country. I didn't care about the danger as long as I saw a little bit of the world. I never imagined what military life would be like. We were on a cruise ship on our way to war, not a vacation. I could never have imagined just how dicey the trip would turn out to be.

When I entered the cabin, I noticed a bottle of rum and some apples the Intelligence Officer Carmona had set out. The combination seemed strange to me. He said that the Russians drink vodka with sliced apples, and since we were on a Russian ship with a Russian crew, it only seemed appropriate. I didn't believe him. More likely than not, he didn't have anything better to offer. The ship had a Soviet military command and a Cuban military command onboard. It was a luxury cruiser bound for Angola that had departed from the port of Odessa, making a stop in Havana, where a thousand Cuban soldiers boarded. It was an undercover operation. The soldiers wore civilian clothes to appear like tourists.

I sat in the cabin's sole chair and accepted a drink. Instead of tasting it, I put it on the nightstand. I intended to sip it slowly to avoid getting tipsy. The conversation began with the army's mission and moved on to the group of artists traveling onboard to entertain the soldiers.

"You're the orchestra's singer, right?"

"I was the singer. I'm no longer with them."

"Why not?"

"We got into a bad argument two months ago."

"Now listen here, you guys can't be bickering. What was the problem?"

I can only imagine the look of disgust I gave him. He'd hit a sensitive nerve. I felt sick to my stomach. It was like reliving the fight with Gerardo and Alcides all over again. I was fed up with their abuse, their mockery. Carmona waited with amused eyes for an answer as if he knew beforehand what I was going to say. I looked up defiantly.

"I don't mind criticism, but to call my songs crap is disrespectful. Now, only my guitar accompanies me. I'm better as a solo. I don't have to have anyone's approval to sing whatever I want and however I want.

"You don't even talk to each other?"

"We greet one another, but that's all."

Carmona took a sip of his drink. He narrowed his eyes, perhaps searching his memory for a phrase or remembering an interrogation technique he'd learned in military training. It reminded me of those bad crime movies where the interrogation scenes are all the same. His expression was a mixture of drama and comedy. But then the look on his face changed. It took on a suspicious expression that would later result in devastating consequences for me.

"At the slightest fracas, I'll throw you all in the dungeon where you won't see the light of day until we're back in Cuba."

"We're not going to fight. We just can't work together."

He stood over me with a menacing stare, his nose almost touching mine. I leaned back, repulsed by the smell of rum on his breath, the grease on his face.

"Look, a fight on a boat is solved with more than just fists. In the middle of the sea, problems seem bigger . . . Imagine a fight where someone throws someone else overboard or hurls things that can cause a fire."

"I already said we're not going to fight!"

I stood up and turned around, annoyed. I feigned interest in the monotonous nocturnal scene visible from the hatch, a waning moon over a dark sea. Although I had my back to him, I could sense all his movements. I could hear his measured sips, interrupted at times by a hoarse cough from cigars and alcohol.

"Tomorrow we arrive in Santa Cruz de Tenerife," he said. The ship had to make two stops in the Canary Islands to restock the food and water cellars. We were scheduled to stay one day in the port of Santa Cruz in route to Angola and another day on our journey back to Havana.

I secretly smiled. My grandparents were born in the Canary Islands. I knew the islands without ever having seen them. I knew about the vineyards where my grandmother, as a girl, would hide from her mother in order to avoid house chores. I knew that my grandfather and grandmother lived in adjoining lands and that they'd known each other since they were little. The thought of finally seeing the islands filled me with emotion.

"I have family there," I said with all the naivety in the world.

He approached me like a snake, and I felt his hands firmly grab my arms. He turned me gently toward him. With measured breath, he said:

"If you jump ship, I'll shoot to kill."

I froze. How could I have been so reckless as to mention my family? I held his gaze and swallowed hard.

"You're crazy! I'm not jumping off any ship. I don't even know that family! They're my grandparents' relatives. I don't even know their names or where they live. Besides, my grandparents died years ago."

"If you jump, I'll kill you."

I freed myself from his hold, went to the table where I'd left my drink, and took a swig. I recovered a bit from my clumsiness and looked him in the eye. I realized that he enjoyed seeing me nervous. I felt tremendous rage at the thought of appearing frightened so I grabbed a piece of apple and began to eat it slowly to try to calm my nerves. His demeanor changed. His gaze turned lascivious. The last thing I wanted was to seduce him, and much less with an apple in my hand, as if I were Eve in the Garden of Eden. I stopped eating, thinking that might stem his desire, but no. He moved toward me. I held my breath. Did this man really think he could conquer women with the cat-and-mouse game? How could he possibly come on to me after threatening to kill me? Did he really believe I was capable of defecting, or did he just want to impress me?

He tried to kiss me, very delicately, but I turned away. He gently turned my face toward him and moved closer.

"No! You misunderstood! Get out of the way!"

He stood aside to give me room to pass, but when I reached the door, he pulled me back. I had the impression that he wanted to make things right. Maybe he was afraid that I would talk to the general, or make a fuss. I freed myself and opened the door. He stood in front of me, blocking my way.

"If you don't let me out, I'll scream so loud every single person on the whole damn ship will hear it!"

He moved out of my way, and I left. The trek back to my cabin seemed to take forever. Once I got there, I entered, closed the door, and fell into bed exhausted.

I told my roommate Yamile everything, without mincing words. When she saw how upset I was, she questioned me, and I had to let it all out.

"Ay Alicia," Yamile said." "Don't be so naïve. These officers have been stuck in the ship carrying troops for two years. It's not like in Havana, where real men who have sex with women want to ensure they both enjoy it. There's mutual pleasure."

"I know," I said. Yamile made perfect sense.

"But what you're telling me about Carmona is priceless," continued Yamile. "To threaten a girl with death and then ask for sex, it's like 'begging with a shotgun in your hand.' He'd better not mess with me."

We both laughed. I felt better after talking with her.

Days later, Carmona was going around with Julia on his arm. She was the head of the brigade of artists.

General Rosales was different. He didn't seem desperate for sex. He would invite us, Yamile and me, to his cabin to drink and talk. He never invited her or me alone and never made advances to us. The conversations flowed naturally and he was not bothered by any of the questions we asked him.

At our first performance on the ship, I was moved to see so many young soldiers. By the age of fifteen, Cuban males are eligible for compulsory military service, and some of those sitting in the audience were barely twenty. I found myself wondering: "Of all those who are going over there, which ones will return and which will not? Are they afraid?" They looked so calm, so innocent. When I had the chance, I asked General Rosales.

"Why do they send these children to war?"

"When did you ever see an army of old men? Those boys are ready. They're not children," replied the general.

"This war makes no sense," Yamile said. "They've been sending Cubans to Angola for ten years now. How many have died? What for? What does Cuba get from all of this?"

Her boldness surprised the general as much as it did me.

"Well, the ship returns to Cuba laden with precious woods, ivory, and other things. Something is gained from all this," argued the general.

Rosales's response was ridiculous. A haul of wood and ivory hardly justified the dead and mutilated Cubans, not to mention the suffering of their relatives and their friends. We were going to a foreign war that no one understood.

III

Onboard Diary
November 20, 1988

If it weren't because Yamile is six feet tall, I wouldn't have been considered for the position of magician's assistant. I get it. The magician is very short, and the job is not really a fit for Yamile, but I feel so ridiculous. She had no interest in being his assistant either, but if I had given her a nudge, she might have done it for fun. In fact, there isn't anything she wouldn't do for fun.

When he knocked on our door, he made it clear that the others had rejected him, and we were his last option. I couldn't bear the sad look on his face after he had to rule out Yamile because of her height, so I ended up saying yes. Now I'm the laughing stock of the whole brigade.

He's not to blame, but there's no place for a magician here. I don't know whose idea it was to bring him. Magicians are fine for children's parties, for the circus, but not for a show with an orchestra, singers, actors—a spectacle for soldiers. What's more, the poor man's haircut, sideburns, and mustache are from the 1970s. It's as if he was stuck in a time warp. It's true that he lives in a province where the styles never quite catch up to Havana. But, honestly, it's as though he were living in the past decade. He looks ridiculous.

The truth is, it's hard for me to identify with the image of "magician assistant." All of them seem to have idiotic faces. Without making a peep, they allow their bodies to be manipulated like mannequins to show off the magician's skills. I mean, why don't magicians just saw their own bodies in half? I feel no pride in being treated like a doll.

Gerardo and Alcides, who wanted me in the orchestra only for my voice and not for my lyrics or music, must be having a good laugh. They can't stand a woman who thinks for herself. To see me as the assistant of a fourth-rate magician must make them happy. Well, this is a temporary gig, and anyway, I play my guitar and sing my own songs at the top of every show.

If only Captain Carmona knew that the reason Gerardo and Alcides want any part in this mission is to network with the Russians in hope of getting invited to work in the Soviet Union. Truth is, I see a problem with their plan because the Russians want nothing to do with us. I didn't see any of them at the show the other day. They say they have their own separate theater, but I've never met any of their performers. It's as if the two countries cohabitate the same ship, separated by an invisible wall. Only the superiors associate with each other.

I get annoyed every time I bump into someone from the orchestra. They seem so mediocre, those artists who spend all their time groveling to secure a trip to other countries and, when they finally do, get cold feet and never stay for long. Of course, no one wants to stay precisely in the Soviet

Union, in Angola either, obviously. I don't know why Gerardo and Alcides want to go to the Soviet Union, where it's so cold. Angola is not very attractive because of the war, but I find it more interesting than the hammer and sickle and the *urraaaaahhhh* sounds you hear in Russian films.

I would love to travel as a normal citizen with a passport and to have money to pay for the visa paperwork and a ticket. But I live in a poor country run by a paranoid government that controls its people. To travel, you have to beg for an invitation from a foreign institution that can pay for your ticket because we don't have a cent, and then we have to plead with the Cuban authorities for a permit to leave. Our desire to travel is so great we'd risk everything.

The early days with the orchestra were good. I was excited. They were popular, frequently being invited to appear on television. I always thought that I'd have to sing from their repertoire at first, but that later, when I'd gained their confidence, I'd have the opportunity to sing my own songs. Why the hell would Gerardo, who was born in El Salvador and can travel without permission from Cuba, want to sing in the Soviet Union, where they don't even speak Spanish? Of course, as the son of Salvadoran guerrillas, he doesn't have a penny to his name and is looking for the right opportunity, but why not in Latin America? Perhaps his family is disgraced in Latin America and so he wants to go to another Communist country. Now, with Perestroika, everyone says things are better there. He's always rubbing it in everyone's face that he's from El Salvador and how the world outside the island is very different from what we're accustomed to. Perhaps he thought that I joined the orchestra just to travel. Well, I did want to travel, but I also wanted to sing my songs, to become known. The Ministry of Culture didn't want to certify me despite my studies in the art school. It was a miracle they allowed me to travel. Alcides protested. He even requested that the Communist Youth cancel my travel permit because my songs were, he said, antirevolutionary. They're not. They're in favor of transparency, in favor of Perestroika.

Is Alcides as intransigent as he seems? Has he been put here to befriend Gerardo, the son of guerrillas, in order to spy on him? Or is Gerardo spying on Alcides? How is it possible for anyone to trust anyone else? The only sure thing is that Alcides put me at odds with the Communist Youth by talking nonsense about my songs. What does he possibly think he'll gain from these lies? How does he sleep at night?

I have to go rehearse with the magician. I also have to remember to maintain my sense of humor. Otherwise, I'll go mad.

IV

Somehow, the other officers on the ship caught wind of my clash with
Carmona. Well, I can't be sure they knew for sure, but there were signs . . .
One night, we went to Captain Guzmán's cabin—Yamile, the singer from
Manzanillo, and I—and in came Carmona with Julia. As soon as they en-
tered, everyone tensed up, including the captain. No one really cared for
Carmona. He was annoying; he enjoyed offending people. We were just
talking nonsense. The captain noticed that I went silent when Carmona
spoke. He said to him:

"You think you're the one from intelligence. But I think the one from
intelligence is that one," pointing toward me, "the one who shuts up during
a conversation."

Carmona blanched. Why did the captain point me out when I wasn't
the only one not talking? It seemed to me that he wanted to make a point,
make Carmona feel small in front of the others, draw a parallel between
Carmona and me to embarrass him. He had to know something. Did
Carmona himself tell him? Why? I wondered if Carmona was spreading
a rumor that I didn't have sex with him because I was a lesbian. I'm not,
but I wouldn't put it past him to say that.

When we boarded the ship, Gerardo appeared with a sailor's cap he
had picked up. It's not easy getting things in Cuba, even a sailor's cap.
Well, at an artistic brigade meeting, Carmona asked Gerardo:

"And that fag hat?" insinuating that Gerardo was a homosexual.

Gerardo went pale. Being labeled a homosexual in Cuba was trouble.
You can get thrown out of school . . . put in prison . . . Gerardo had long
hair, a handsome face, and many girlfriends. I never knew him as gay.

"Sailor cap," he clarified without raising his voice, without appearing
offended.

What else could he do? That kind of talk between Cuban males usually
ends up in a fistfight, but he wasn't about to punch an army officer during
a military mission. Even I felt sorry for Gerardo.

It occurred to me that, as revenge, Carmona could very well have told
the other officers that he suspected I was a lesbian, especially since no one
ever saw me alone without Yamile. We stuck together to keep the "creeps"
at bay. The worst thing about dealing with Cuban intelligence is the haze
that they create around everything, the doubt that sticks in your mind, the
doubt about whether you can actually defend yourself in an unforeseen
situation. The scary truth is that anyone with the tiniest bit of power can
put an end to your life. We're always afraid, but even so, we sometimes do

things that are banned without thinking of the consequences because if we don't, we'll lose the will to live.

In spite of everything, there were things I enjoyed during the voyage. When I wasn't rehearsing or performing, I liked to watch the dolphins play together by the ship. The seascape interested me. It was the first time I'd ever been in the middle of the ocean, with no land in sight. The ocean looked as though it were a huge semicircle. It was like being inside a dish. No wonder some ancient civilizations imagined the world as a bowl of water pulled by elephants.

I didn't enjoy the food. The restaurant was beautiful, but the food was terrible. One day they served boiled cow's tongue. When I saw the complete tongue of the animal on the plate, with skin and thorns intact, I almost threw up. We had no choice but to cut into the tongue and eat it. Yamile said she found it delicious. I don't know if she was joking or if she really liked it. There was only one meal worthy of a luxury cruise, the farewell dinner the day before the troops landed in Luanda. It was a spectacle that ended with flamed baked Alaska. Even the servers were in a better mood that day. They wanted to please the tourists. It's just that we weren't tourists and didn't give tips because we had no cash. Anyway, Cuban currency was worthless.

Once a day, we could go to the designated bar to have a cup of Cuban coffee. One time I ran into Captain Guzmán, who recommended I try Malakoff coffee, an espresso with a little cream. I didn't like it. I'm used to strong coffee. He liked it because he was about sixty and suffered from heartburn. The captain ordered the waitress to serve me the same coffee as his, which was in a different container. That's the moment I realized that the coffee they served the officers was of better quality than the one they served us.

V

Onboard Diary
November 24, 1988

The magician looks like a boy, now that I've trimmed off his sideburns and had him shave his mustache. He's dying of embarrassment because he's not accustomed to a clean-shaven face, even though everyone compliments him on it. He spends most of his time in our cabin. I know people say there's something going on between us. Actually, I'm glad about that because it keeps officers and other creeps away. The magician is a sweet man who always smiles. He and I work well together. He's totally harmless, and I trust him. I even decided to tell him about my incident with the Intelligence Officer. He was outraged. He says he's going to protect me. It's funny! The poor guy is so small and skinny. But we have fun playing cards and talking. Now we're inseparable, Yamile, the magician, and I.

I'm learning how to do magic. I'm practicing making Ping-Pong balls appear between my fingers, which is extremely difficult for me because I have small hands. A few days ago, the magician said something amazing:

"The trick is to get people to focus on what you want them to look at. If you raise the hand that's rolling the Ping-Pong balls for everyone to see, and with the other hand you casually take the other balls out of your pants pocket, no one will realize it. The audience will see what you want them to see."

"Are you sure?"

"That's how it works, believe me."

I like the challenge of learning new things and watching the magician prepare for his show. He's a professional. He carefully sews a bouquet of flowers into the seam of a bag, and then pulls it out in front of everyone, as if from thin air. I know the guys in the orchestra want to find a way to humiliate him. Some have made snide remarks to me about him, but I've stopped them in their tracks: "Why does the magician annoy you so much?" I ask them. "Is it because he's my friend? The fact is, he's here because they sent him, like everyone else."

What I do is no big deal. I'm only part of the performance because magicians think women make shows more appealing. I just hand him some object and that's it. Yes, I smile and smile, like an idiot, playing the assistant the best I can. What I feel, though, is total indifference.

VI

Once ashore, we were forbidden to disembark in Angola. We were tempted, though, despite the horrendous smell. In Havana, we'd been vaccinated against malaria and given pills to take during the trip, so we were prepared for Africa. The officers were busy docking the ship.

Two Cuban soldiers arrived in a Volga to pick up Russian officers who might want to disembark, but none did. Yamile and I were standing there, hoping to step on land and feel stable after so many days of sailing. When we heard that no Russians were disembarking, we asked the soldiers to give us a tour of the city. They accepted and introduced themselves as Roberto and Amado.

There were Angolan and Cuban soldiers with rifles in every corner, a constant reminder that we were in a country at war. We wanted to go to the ghetto. We knew from hearsay that the poor Angolans lived there, and we were curious. Roberto and Amado took us along paths of ochre-colored earth that looked like sand. They said that people planted potatoes there for the troops and that the crop was good. They also harvested tapioca, maize, and plantain. In the ghetto, children and women waited in long lines to buy water, colorful plastic bowls on their heads to hold it. The huts were unfurnished and made of mud. People stared passed us, indifferent. They pretended not to see us because soldiers with machine guns accompanied us.

Later, we wanted to visit the barter market called *candongas*, which Cuban soldiers sometimes mentioned when they returned from Angola. They said they bought gifts there for their families. People exchanged animals, crops, ivory objects, clay utensils for other goods, as in ancient times, before currency existed. Cuban officers find better food for their soldiers in the *candongas*.

The soldiers were thirsty so we went to a bar in Luanda. The place was empty. The soldiers pointed to a table attached to a brick partition and told us to sit with our backs to the wall. They put the guns on the table and looked around nervously.

"In Luanda, you have to be very careful. It wouldn't be the first time we were attacked," said Amado.

"Why?" I asked. It seemed more logical to me that the attacks occurred in rural areas. We were in the city, in the daylight.

"Cubans aren't welcome here," replied Roberto.

The waiter came to our table and the soldiers ordered sodas for everyone. Yamile gave me a nervous look. Despite the medicines we were taking, it was a bad idea to drink anything in Luanda. The last thing we needed was to return to the ship with some type of tropical disease and have to spend the rest of the journey stuck in the infirmary. The heat was stifling, and the sodas were warm. I didn't feel like drinking, but I didn't want to be rude to the soldiers who had paid for the sodas, so I forced mine down. I flinched at the thought of putting my lips on the can, without even a straw, but I drank it. Yamile refused. The soldiers drank theirs.

"Why do you say they don't want Cubans here?" Yamile asked.

"There are all types of people in the army," said Amado. "Some of them have raped women and killed civilians, giving us a bad name."

"I thought that Cuba sent the best of the best, and that the people welcomed us," I noted.

"No, they're not always the best. Besides, we're human and we make mistakes. You should see how many children the Cubans have left scattered around here," answered Roberto. "It's doubtful that all Angolans believe we're saving them, especially when we've got Cubans here who make things worse."

An Angolan dressed in a white, short-sleeved *guayabera* and dressy, gray trousers came up to the table. I was struck by his appearance: he looked clean yet had no teeth. He spoke in Portuguese with the soldiers. They seemed worried. One pointed at me and the other pointed at Yamile. The man moved away from us but continued to stare.

"What did he want?" Yamile asked.

"To know if you were our wives." Said Roberto.

"And what did you tell him?" I asked.

"That you," he said pointing at Yamile, "are my wife and you," he pointed at me, "are Amado's wife."

"Why?" Yamile and I asked in unison.

"He wanted to buy you."

"Buy us?" I wasn't sure what he meant.

"Here, men purchase wives. The more money they have, the more wives they get. The women work in the field, and the men sell what the women cultivate."

The man continued hovering, so the soldiers decided it was time to return to the ship. He followed us out of the bar. We jumped into the Volga, he climbed into a Mercedes Benz.

"And that man can afford a luxury car?" Yamile asked.

"Yes. He may not have teeth, but he has money," Amado explained.

"And still lives in a mud house in the ghetto. They never leave, even if they have a million bucks. It's part of their tradition," said Roberto.

Knowing that someone saw me as a piece of property made me feel strange. It was 1988, and although I was aware that trafficking of women existed in the world, to experience a stranger looking at me as a commodity and not as a human being shook me to the core. Commander Carmona was a romantic compared to this man who tried to buy me. Now I understood why my father wanted sons instead of daughters. Even my grandmother retained those distorted views. "If that's how our loved ones see us, how must others?" I thought.

VII

Onboard Diary
November 30, 1988

I feel bad for the magician. They say he was looking for us when we went down to Luanda. He was afraid that something bad had happened. We should have warned him we were leaving. Maybe he would have joined us and not alerted the officers. Carmona threatened to throw me into the brig for disobeying orders. The insolent bastard didn't meddle with Yamile, but instead came straight after me. No other officer, not even Rosales, said anything. I know that Carmona is responsible for the safety of everyone on the ship, but we went into Luanda with soldiers familiar with the city and the country's situation. It's not as if we acted foolishly.

It amuses me to think that the Russians invited the magician to perform in their theater. His show was the only one from the artistic brigade that interested them. Alcides and Gerardo remained behind with no hope of getting an invitation to Odessa. I was pleased. They made fun of me for being the magician's "lackey," but I'm the one who's performing in the Russians' theater, not them. For the first time, I thought, I'm going to relish being the assistant. If only it weren't for Carmona's constant harassment.

The really perverse ones from the artistic brigade asked the magician for a special performance at the coffee bar, which is a small place. The magician naively said yes. I heard they plan to humiliate him by jumping all over him, examining his bag and looking up his sleeves to figure out how he does his tricks. I told him to perform the card tricks wearing a short-sleeved shirt and not to bring the magic bag. He hesitated at first, but I convinced him. The poor guy doesn't deserve to be hassled.

I'm alone in my cabin. Yamile went to the café, but I didn't want to go. No matter how much I try, I can't seem to get this song to gel. I'm nervous. The show went well, but I have a little bit of laryngitis. I feel like I'm coming down with something, maybe the flu. I hope it's not any sort of tropical disease . . . I'm sure it's fatigue. There comes a point in one's life when people are just exhausting. They drain you of all creativity. And the way Carmona pesters me . . . He just never lets up. I have to get away from him, I keep telling myself, but how?

That's when I started to think about jumping ship.

Translated from the Spanish by Elizabeth Cruz Petersen

Betty Milan

BETTY MILAN (Brazil) has written novels, *crônicas*, essays, plays, and blogs. Her articles have appeared in major Brazilian publications such as *Folha de São Paulo* and *Veja*. Her works have been published in France, Argentina, and China, as well as Brazil. Before becoming a writer, she received a medical degree and studied psychoanalysis in France with Jacques Lacan. Her novel, *O papagaio e o doutor* (Lacan's parrot) recounts the story of Lebanese immigration to Brazil and the author's encounter with a psychoanalyst, a character inspired by Lacan. The novel has been published in Brazil, in French and Spanish. It has been translated into English, and Milan adapted it for the theater. The stage version has played in New York and other major cities, and the rights for the movie have been sold to Good Soup Media, LLC. It has already been filmed by the director Richard Ledes, with David Patrick Kelly in the role of Lacan. Milan's most recent book is *Baal,* also a novel about Lebanese immigration. It was first presented in Beirut, where the author received a homage "for her contribution to the land of her ancestors."

Why I Write about War

War is a subject I've thought about quite a bit. I think there are two reasons for this. First, I descend from Lebanese immigrants who left the Middle East and settled in Brazil to escape war. Second, because war strikes me as an absurdity, and I've always striven to understand why it occurs. I even interviewed a general who was a pilot during World War II and served as an adviser to Charles de Gaulle. This general told me that there would always be wars because "men are fools."

His response didn't surprise me because I had read a text that Freud wrote in 1915, according to which wars will occur as long as living conditions and the value given to human life are so different from one nation to the other. Freud, whose modernity cannot be questioned, says that one need not be a sentimentalist to feel disillusioned by the fact that great nations, which have so much in common with each other in terms of lifestyle and ethical values, have not found a peaceful way to settle conflicts, especially when one considers that they are the masters of the technological progress necessary to control the forces of nature and prolong life. That is to say, in addition to opposing each other, they are contradicting their own stated moral principles.

There is no way to reconcile in our minds technological progress with the atavism that war implies. Reconcile, no, but understand this paradox, yes. No one believes in his or her own end. Unconsciously, we believe ourselves to be immortal, and that's why we repeatedly risk our lives. On the one hand, we don't believe in our own deaths, but on the other, the unconscious only knows how to punish another's crime by death—as we can see in the expressions, "The devil take you!" or "Go to hell!" We succumb to hatred without considering the devastating consequences.

Freud concludes that we should just adapt to war. We have only to think of the importance we give to the commandment "Thou shalt not kill" to deduce that we are the product of an infinite number of generations of assassins. We carry a lust for crime in our veins. The founder of psychoanalysis knew that ethical advances are achieved over many years. Many generations are necessary to accomplish a change.

Translated from the Portuguese by Bárbara Mujica

War in the City

"Living is dangerous," wrote João Guimarães Rosa, author of *Grande Sertão: Veredas* (English version: *The Devil to Pay in the Backlands*). This comment is valid anywhere in the world. However, the ways in which danger surrounds us aren't the same everywhere. In Europe or the United States, a person can be the victim of a terrorist attack at any moment. When you go into the Metro in Paris or New York, you have to be careful that there are no suspicious packages or abandoned suitcases lying around. The loudspeakers subtly bid you to engage in the struggle against terrorism.

In Brazil, there is no terrorism, but the risk of falling victim to an armed assailant is constant—because an assault can occur at home as easily as in the street. And since the possibility of being murdered is huge, people go around terrified. During the year when the terrorist attack on the World Trade Center paralyzed the world, there were twice as many victims in the city of São Paulo.

To live there, you have to be aware of the risk and trained to resist. Women must be especially alert, as assailants often target women walking alone, especially in isolated areas. However, anyone can be the victim of an attack. For that reason, you have to realize that you might be accosted at any moment, and you have to react intelligently, controlling your movements. That is, you have to accept the possibility that you might be surprised and not let yourself be immobilized by shock.

That's why a new delegation has been formed here in Brazil, the Antikidnapping Delegation, which has put out the following advisory:

Don't write down your residential phone number on the back of your check, especially in gas stations. In the case of a holdup, your telephone number could be used to make a threat, especially if you're a woman.

Don't display a decal of your college or university, the condominium where you reside, or your gym. An extortionist can use this information to threaten you.

Don't make purchases by phone or on the Internet by furnishing the number of your credit card.

When you're driving, maintain a safe distance from the car in front of you. If it's necessary to get out of the car, do so in just one maneuver, without slamming. At night, calculate the time and speed so you don't have to stop at a red light, because the risk of dying in a robbery at a stoplight is greater than in a kidnapping.

If you're assaulted, keep your hands on the steering wheel and try to communicate clearly what you're going to do. If you want to release the seatbelt, for example, say: "I'm going to release the seatbelt with this hand." If the assailant asks for your wallet say, "My wallet is in my back pocket. Will you allow me to get it?"

This text shows that survival requires obedience to the following rules: don't give out information about yourself—your residence, place of business, bank; don't respect traffic laws when they interfere with the assault; and don't do anything without the consent of the assailant.

This text counsels the citizen to practice dissimulation, civil disobedience, and negotiation with the thief, thereby legitimizing his actions. In other words, it teaches people to reject civic education and to legitimize crime to save their skins. Education is for peacetime, but Brazil is at war.

In large cities, we live in fear of thieves and muggers, and even worse, the stray bullet. The ones who suffer most are the women and children. A week doesn't go by when we don't hear something on the news about a mother burying her dead son, who was caught in the crossfire between drug dealers and police. According to a report by the United Nations, Brazil is the third-worst country in Latin America for deaths by a stray bullet. This obviously means that in addition to the war on drugs, we need a war on guns.

As if it weren't enough that we're terrified of muggers and stray bullets, our women are subject to a culture of rape. Last year (2018), 135 rapes and 12 murders of women per day were recorded in São Paulo.* Because the state is not adequately equipped to deal with all the cases, it cannot protect the women who appeal for help, and so the great majority of aggressors are never punished.

In Brazil today, there are more than sixty thousand homicides per year, and the police inform us that we must not obey the law.

Translated from the Portuguese by Bárbara Mujica

* Forum Brasileiro de Segurança Pública.

9 780813 945736